American Cinema of the 1940s

SCREEN
DECADES

AMERICAN CULTURE / AMERICAN CINEMA

Each volume in the Screen Decades: American Culture/American Cinema series presents a group of original essays analyzing the impact of cultural issues on the cinema and the impact of the cinema on American society. Because every chapter explores a spectrum of particularly significant motion pictures and the broad range of historical events in one year, readers will gain a continuing sense of the decade as it came to be depicted on movie screens across the continent. The integration of historical and cultural events with the sprawling progression of American cinema illuminates the pervasive themes and the essential movies that define an era. Our series represents one among many possible ways of confronting the past; we hope that these books will offer a better understanding of the connections between American culture and film history.

LESTER D. FRIEDMAN AND MURRAY POMERANCE
SERIES EDITORS

Wheeler Winston Dixon, editor, *American Cinema of the 1940s: Themes and Variations*

Murray Pomerance, editor, *American Cinema of the 1950s: Themes and Variations*

American Cinema of the

1940s

Themes and Variations

EDITED BY

WHEELER WINSTON DIXON

RUTGERS UNIVERSITY PRESS

NEW BRUNSWICK, NEW JERSEY, AND LONDON

LIBRARY OF CONGRESS CATALOGING-IN-PUBLICATION DATA

American cinema of the 1940s : themes and variations /
edited by Wheeler Winston Dixon.
   p.   cm. — (Screen decades)
Includes bibliographical references and index.
ISBN-13: 978-0-8135-3699-6 (hardcover : alk. paper)
ISBN-13: 978-0-8135-3700-9 (pbk. : alk. paper)
   1. Motion pictures—United States—History.   2. Motion pictures—Social aspects—
United States.   I. Dixon, Wheeler W., 1950-   II. Series.
   PN1993.5.U6A8574 2005
   791.43'0973'09044—dc22

2005004836

A British Cataloging-in-Publication record for this book is available
from the British Library.

Manufactured in the United States of America

For Gwendolyn

CONTENTS

ACKNOWLEDGMENTS

The editor wishes to thank Leslie Mitchner of Rutgers University Press, Lester Friedman and Murray Pomerance, the series editors, and the contributors to this volume who have given so generously of their time and talents in making it a reality. Dana Miller provided superb assistance with the typing; Jerry Ohlinger, as usual, came up with a collection of remarkable photos to illustrate this volume. Arne Kislenko and Dan Cazzola gave invaluable help with some matters of history and film narrative, and Alan E. Peterson, Esq., helped to clarify the issues surrounding the De Havilland decision. As with all my books, I want to thank Gwendolyn Audrey Foster, my kindest mentor and most perceptive critic, for helping me to shape these essays into their final form, during the long work of editing. To my contributors, then, and to my colleagues, my sincerest thanks.

T I M E L I N E

The 1940s

■ 1940

7 FEBRUARY Disney's *Pinocchio*, the first animated film with three-dimensional camera movement, premieres.

29 FEBRUARY Hattie McDaniel becomes the first African American to win an Oscar, for her role in *Gone With the Wind*.

3 APRIL Max Factor debuts Pan-Cake Makeup (which will be used in Technicolor production).

15 MAY Nylon stockings go on sale for the first time.

27 JULY Bugs Bunny makes his screen debut, in *A Wild Hare*.

1 NOVEMBER The studios put their facilities at the disposal of the government for making military training films.

5 NOVEMBER FDR is reelected to an unprecedented third term as U.S. president.

■ 1941

1 MAY *Citizen Kane* premieres at the RKO Palace.

1 JULY NBC and CBS start commercial television transmission on an experimental basis.

9 SEPTEMBER Senate hearings open on the subject of Hollywood as perpetrator of war propaganda.

31 OCTOBER Mount Rushmore Memorial is completed.

7 DECEMBER The Japanese bomb Pearl Harbor. President Roosevelt declares war the following day.

■ 1942

1 JANUARY The United States and twenty-five other Allied nations together sign the Declaration of the United Nations, which states that each government, "being convinced that complete victory over their enemies is essential to defend life, liberty, independence and religious freedom, . . . [is] now engaged in a common struggle against savage and brutal forces seeking to subjugate the world."

16 JANUARY Carole Lombard is killed in a plane crash.

10 FEBRUARY	The first gold record is awarded to Glenn Miller, for "The Chattanooga Choo Choo."
13 JULY	Frank Sinatra makes his singing debut in New York City.
26 NOVEMBER	*Casablanca* premieres.
8 AUGUST	Frank Capra declares, "Hollywood is a war plant!"

■ 1943

15 JANUARY	The Pentagon is completed.
15 JANUARY	Charlie Parker and Dizzy Gillespie join Earl Hines's band this week, launching the era of be-bop.
11 FEBRUARY	Dwight D. Eisenhower is chosen to command the Allied forces in Europe.
20 FEBRUARY	Studio heads agree that the Office of War Information may informally censor films.
20 JUNE	Race riots erupt in Detroit. Riots also break out in Harlem on 1 August.
10 AUGUST	Bob Hope goes on his first tour of war zones.

■ 1944

6 JUNE	D-Day: the Allies invade Normandy.
31 JULY	As of this date, all musicals at Twentieth Century Fox are to be made in Technicolor.
4 AUGUST	The Nazis discover Anne Frank and her family in hiding.
7 NOVEMBER	FDR is reelected for an unprecedented fourth term.
8 DECEMBER	The De Havilland decision forces studios to limit actor contracts to seven years maximum, including suspensions.

■ 1945

12 APRIL	FDR dies and is succeeded as president by Harry S. Truman.
24 APRIL	The Dachau concentration camp is liberated.
8 MAY	Germany surrenders.
21 MAY	Lauren Bacall marries Humphrey Bogart.
26 JUNE	The United Nations charter is enacted in San Francisco.
28 JULY	A U.S. bomber accidentally crashes into the Empire State Building.
6 AUGUST	The United States drops the first atomic bomb, nicknamed "Little Boy," on Hiroshima. "Big Boy" falls on Nagasaki three days later, followed the next day by Japan's surrender.

◼ 1946

22 MAY	Dr. Benjamin Spock publishes *Common Sense Book of Baby and Child Care*.
1 JULY	Atomic bomb tests at the Bikini atoll begin with a device decorated with Rita Hayworth's picture.
8 SEPTEMBER	Howard Hughes loses the Motion Picture Association of America (MPAA) Seal for *The Outlaw* because he refuses to submit ads for approval.
20 SEPTEMBER	The first Cannes Film Festival opens.
5 DECEMBER	Lew Wasserman becomes president of the Music Corporation of America (MCA).

◼ 1947

10 MARCH	Ronald Reagan becomes president of the Screen Actors Guild (SAG); one month later he becomes an FBI informant.
10 APRIL	Jackie Robinson of the Brooklyn Dodgers becomes the first African American to play major league baseball.
26 JULY	The Central Intelligence Agency is established.
7 OCTOBER	The Actors Studio opens in New York.
20 OCTOBER	The House Un-American Activities Committee (HUAC) begins to investigate Communist influence in Hollywood.
30 OCTOBER	The Hollywood Ten—Ring Lardner Jr., Lester Cole, John Howard Lawson, Alvah Bessie, Dalton Trumbo, Albert Maltz, Samuel Ornitz, Herbert Biberman, Edward Dmytryk, and Adrian Scott—are charged with contempt of Congress for refusing to testify.
25 NOVEMBER	The Blacklist begins after studio moguls meet at New York's Waldorf-Astoria.

◼ 1948

20 JUNE	"The Ed Sullivan Show" debuts.
23 JULY	D. W. Griffith dies.
30 OCTOBER	RKO becomes the first major studio to divest itself of wholly owned theaters, as mandated by the Paramount Consent Decree.
12 DECEMBER	The first McDonald's opens.

◼ 1949

18 JANUARY	Hollywood announces the switch to safety film, after years of using highly inflammable cellulose nitrate film.

10 MARCH   Apartheid begins in South Africa.

28 APRIL   *On the Town* begins shooting at the Brooklyn Navy Yard, the first location shoot for musicals.

28 DECEMBER   Twentieth Century Fox announces it will make programs for television.

American Cinema of the 1940s

INTRODUCTION

Movies and the 1940s

WHEELER WINSTON DIXON

◼◼◼◼◼◼ The War-Torn Forties

The 1940s was a watershed decade for American cinema, which found itself altered by developments both internal and external. Freed of the clumsy technical constraints of the early 1930s, Hollywood launched a massive wave of production, not only from the major studios (Paramount, Universal, MGM, Columbia, Twentieth Century Fox, Warner Bros., and RKO) but also from the minors (especially Monogram, Republic, and Producers Releasing Corporation [PRC]). As the decade began, Adolf Hitler was on the march in Europe, while isolationism was still the rule at home. Indeed, when in 1939 Warner's had had the audacity to produce Anatole Litvak's *Confessions of a Nazi Spy*, the other major studios tried to halt production, claiming that it would put a damper on the export of Hollywood films to an increasingly Nazified Europe (Griffith and Mayer 345). For nearly the first two years of the 1940s, this attitude prevailed in Hollywood and in an America still in the throes of the Great Depression. But then things changed, seemingly overnight.

On 7 December 1941, the Empire of Japan launched a sneak attack on Pearl Harbor, with horrific results. In less than thirty minutes the U.S. naval base on the island of Oahu in Hawaii was decimated, with much of the Pacific Fleet destroyed and nearly 3,500 military and civilian personnel killed. The Japanese used multiple aircraft carriers, battleships, cruisers, and destroyers from which they launched an assault force of 360 airplanes (Burrows 172). Retaliation was swift. On 8 December the United States declared war on Japan; on 11 December, the other Axis Powers, Germany and Italy, declared war on the United States, which the Congress quickly reciprocated. And so the battle was joined, and the isolationist ramblings of such holdouts as Charles A. Lindbergh, whose transatlantic flight had captured the public imagination in 1927, were all but forgotten. Signing the official declaration of war against Japan, President Roosevelt famously declared that the attack had occurred on "a date which will live in infamy," but little did he and the rest of the nation know the days of agony that lay ahead. Indeed, until late 1943, it seemed quite conceivable that the Allies might lose the war (Holmes 295–97). This was a do-or-die effort.

In many ways, the United States had been in a state of denial about the coming conflict for a number of years. The Spanish Civil War of 1936, which pitted workers and intellectuals on the Republican side against "the army, landowners, and businessmen" on the Nationalist side (Burrows 144), was the first indication that political trouble was soon to erupt on a global scale. The lawfully elected Republican government found itself challenged by the forces of wealth and power, and partisans on both sides around the world were drawn to the conflict. By 1938, Franco had seized power in Spain, Hitler had annexed Austria and Czechoslovakia, Mussolini had fully consolidated his power in Italy, and the exodus of Jews from Europe (many of whom wound up in Hollywood in the 1940s) had begun in earnest. World War II began in Europe on 3 September 1939, as Britain and France declared war on Germany, following the Nazi invasion of Poland a day earlier; now, in rapid succession, the dominoes began to fall. In 1940, the Soviet army invaded Finland. The Nazis invaded Denmark and Norway. Winston Churchill assumed the reins of the British government in 1940 after the appeasement policies of his predecessor, Neville Chamberlain, had been thoroughly discredited.

The Nazis pushed on through Europe, invading and conquering Holland and Belgium, and then, in the summer of 1940, Paris. Simultaneously, Hitler launched a nightly wave of terror on London with "buzz bomb" aerial bombardments, which became known as the Blitz. Beginning on 7 September 1940, the Nazis bombed the British capital for "57 consecutive nights . . . [as well as] industrially significant regions, such as Coventry and the port [city] of Liverpool" (Burrows 161). Yet Britain refused to buckle under the Nazi assault, meeting the attacking waves of Nazi aircraft with their own Spitfire bombers, aided considerably by their superiority in the new technology of radar (Burrows 161). On 10 June 1940, Italy declared war westward on Britain, and marched successfully southward into Libya, attempting to press their luck with a further attack on Egypt, which was ultimately repulsed by the British (Burrows 162).

All these events paved the way for the Battle of Britain, the Nazis' full-scale assault on the British Isles. Beginning on 8 August 1940, the Nazis, under the command of Reich Marshall Hermann Goering, launched a series of aerial assaults with as much as 1,500 aircraft at a time, but to no avail. Though severely outnumbered, the British military forces, especially the pilots of the Royal Air Force, effectively beat back the Nazi assault, leading Churchill to make his memorable statement that "never in the field of human conflict was so much owed by so many to so few" (Burrows 165).

As Hitler realized that this planned invasion of England (code-named Operation Sea Lion) was proving unsuccessful, he turned his sights toward Russia in a mad dash for world conquest, despite the fact that the two nations had previously signed a non-aggression pact. Hitler's invasion of Russia began on 22 June 1941, and involved no fewer than 190 divisions of infantry, the largest ground force ever assembled in any war. It began in typical Blitzkrieg (literally, "lightning war") style, but despite the use of 3.6 million troops, 3,600 tanks and 2,700 aircraft, Russia refused to capitulate to the invading hordes (Burrows 168). Like many a military commander before him, including Napoleon, Hitler underestimated the sheer size of Russia, the tenacity of its people once aroused, and the brutal rigors of its winter. In the Far East, Japan sought to increase its sphere of influence in China and the Pacific through military means, despite trade sanctions from the United States. And yet many in America somehow remained dimly convinced that the nation could avoid taking part in this massive global conflict, that the battles in Europe and Asia would pass them by. In late 1941, however, the attack on Pearl Harbor ended that illusion.

What sorts of films were produced as a response to the war? One need only survey films made in 1940 and early 1941, as opposed to films made after the United States entered the war, to see the stark contrast. The forties began with films like the escapist musical *The Boys from Syracuse,* directed by A. Edward Sutherland, W. C. Fields in Edward Cline's *The Bank Dick,* Albert S. Rogell's *Argentine Nights,* aimed at promoting the U.S. "Good Neighbor" policy toward South America, and the first Abbott and Costello comedy, *One Night in the Tropics.* All these films were produced by Universal, the most frankly commercial of the major Hollywood studios (arguably, a distinction it holds to this day).

In 1941, just before America's entry into World War II, Hollywood produced some of its most memorable classics, but nevertheless remained oddly insular in a world that was tottering on the brink of destruction (Higham and Greenberg 8). It was, of course, that year that Orson Welles, working for RKO, directed his first film, *Citizen Kane*, to near universal critical acclaim (except from the Hearst newspapers) and box office indifference. John Ford directed his epic tale of the hard lives of coal miners, *How Green Was My Valley*, for Twentieth Century Fox, which was both a critical and commercial success. Preston Sturges, Hollywood's foremost satirist, directed his deliciously cynical comedy *The Lady Eve,* with Barbara Stanwyck and

Henry Fonda, for Paramount, while Howard Hawks, the film capital's most reliable genre craftsman, produced and directed *Sergeant York*, a paean to Alvin York, pacifist turned exemplary soldier in World War I, expertly played by Gary Cooper. Of all these films, it is only *Sergeant York* that seems to hint at the coming conflict. We may have to put away our personal differences and peacetime pursuits in the defense of a common goal, *Sergeant York* argues, by "rendering unto Caesar that which is Caesar's, and unto God that which is God's." York's personal odyssey from passive noninvolvement and isolationism to full wartime engagement is an apt metaphor for the United States as a whole in 1941—a nation at the crossroads between global civic duty and self-interest.

By 1942, the die had been irrevocably cast, and Hollywood joined the war effort with a vengeance. In Michael Curtiz's *Casablanca*, Humphrey Bogart abandons his pacifism to join the fight against the forces of Nazism in Vichy-controlled France. William Wyler's *Mrs. Miniver* depicted the life of a supposedly typical middle-class English family surviving the war on the home front, hiding in bomb shelters during the Blitz, and even facing an invading Nazi paratrooper in the kitchen of their family home. RKO, quick to jump on the sensationalist bandwagon, and eager to recoup their losses after the financial disasters of *Citizen Kane* and Welles's follow-up film, the studio-butchered masterpiece *The Magnificent Ambersons* (1942), cashed in with the micro-budgeted *Hitler's Children* (1943), directed by Edward Dmytryk. *Hitler's Children*, with its lurid scenario of whippings, forced sterilizations, and schoolroom indoctrination, was made for a pittance, but became one of the biggest hits of the year for RKO, and for the industry as a whole. Lloyd Bacon's *Action in the North Atlantic* (1943), a rousing tale of the Merchant Marine during the war, was a propaganda and box office success for Warner Bros., convincingly casting the hard-boiled Humphrey Bogart as a courageous mariner under constant enemy fire. *Action in the North Atlantic* boasted superb special effects, and featured one of the first submarine chase sequences in which the enemy is actually allowed to speak German, rather than a heavily accented guttural English dialect (Griffith and Mayer 373).

At the same time, in the absence of television, which was still in its experimental stages, a flood of wartime documentaries were shown in theaters, most notably John Huston's *The Battle of San Pietro* (1945), Louis Hayward's *With the Marines at Tarawa* (1944), and John Ford's *The Battle of Midway* (1942), all of which vividly depicted the horrors of war for the average civilian (Griffith and Mayer 374–75). Indeed, many of these films would later be attacked for their unflinching and brutally accurate portrayal

Ingrid Bergman and Humphrey Bogart in a publicity shot for *Casablanca* (Michael Curtiz, Warner Bros., 1942). Courtesy Jerry Ohlinger Archives.

of life and death on the front lines, in sharp contrast to the images of warfare we often see today. But these films did their part; they inflamed the public to a fever pitch, and the country united to combat the Axis Powers. These documentaries were accompanied by Frank Capra's famous *Why We Fight* series, a group of six one-hour documentaries produced at the behest of President Roosevelt, designed to explain to the man and woman in the street precisely what the war was about. Starting with *Prelude to War* (1943) and continuing through *The Nazis Strike* (1943, co-directed with Anatole

Litvak), as well as *Divide and Conquer* (1943), *The Battle of Russia* (1943), *The Battle of China* (1944), (all co-directed with Litvak), and *The Battle of Britain* (1943, co-directed with Anthony Veiller), Capra and his team of editors and cameramen skillfully juxtaposed captured German newsreel film with animation, special effects, and staged recreations to produce a compelling argument for America's role in the war.

And yet the need for escapism was as strong as ever. When Charles Chaplin produced his superb satire on Hitler's regime, *The Great Dictator* (1940), it was seen as trivializing a monster whom the public would rather see destroyed than caricatured (Griffith and Mayer 376). Ernst Lubitsch suffered the same fate with his lightning-fast comedy of the Nazi invasion of Poland, *To Be or Not to Be* (1942), starring Jack Benny and Carole Lombard as two members of a Warsaw theater troupe successfully outwitting Hitler himself. Both were commercial failures in their time; both are now regarded as cinema classics, and regularly revived on television and in movie houses. More popular with wartime audiences were the antics of Bob Hope and Bing Crosby in their many *Road* pictures, especially David Butler's *The Road to Morocco* (1942); and the comedy team of Abbott and Costello, who hit their stride with the enormously successful war-themed comedy *Buck Privates* (1941), directed by Arthur Lubin, who helmed many of the duo's most successful comedies for Universal. Preston Sturges weighed in with the sly social satire of *The Miracle of Morgan's Creek* (1944), while David Butler's *Caught in the Draft* (1941), starring Bob Hope and Eddie Bracken, was a predictable service comedy (Griffith and Mayer 376–77).

As popular as comedies, however, were musicals, and the more patriotic they were, the better. Perhaps the most famous film in this genre of wartime musicals is Michael Curtiz's *Yankee Doodle Dandy* (1942), a sanitized life of ultrapatriotic song-and-dance man George M. Cohan. Veteran movie gangster James Cagney played the leading role of Cohan, and later commented that it was his favorite film; for once, he got to display his skill as a tap dancer rather than shoot people. Frank Borzage's *Stage Door Canteen* (1943) was an all-star variety show aimed directly at servicemen and women, as was Delmer Daves's *Hollywood Canteen* (1944), which celebrated the activities of the Hollywood USO, entertaining soldiers on leave with a moment's respite from the realities of war. If movies such as these proved anything, it was that Americans were, at last, united in their belief that the Axis Powers had to be utterly destroyed, no matter the cost (Griffith and Mayer 378–79).

And, as always, politics during wartime made strange bedfellows. With Stalin's Soviet Union as our uneasy ally in the war against Germany, Japan, and Italy, Michael Curtiz directed *Mission to Moscow* (1943), the story of U.S.

Ambassador Joseph E. Davies (played by Walter Huston) and his friendship with Stalin (here portrayed by character actor Manart Kippen). This film, along with Lewis Milestone's *North Star* (1943) and Gregory Ratoff's *Song of Russia* (1944), was part of Hollywood's attempt to fraternize with our new comrades in arms against the Nazis. With the conclusion of the war, and Stalin's gradual subjugation of most of Eastern Europe behind what Winston Churchill famously dubbed the "Iron Curtain," the writers, directors, and actors in these films would later come under scrutiny by the House Un-American Activities Committee (HUAC), and many would become victims of the infamous "Red Scare" Blacklist (Sklar, *Movie* 276–77). At the time of their production, of course, these films were not only officially sanctioned but also enthusiastically endorsed by the White House and the Pentagon as useful tools in the all-out war effort. But as the glow of mutual cooperation faded, and Stalin was revealed for the ruthless dictator he had always been, these once-popular films, and others like them, became a naive embarrassment to both the government and the film industry (Griffith and Mayer 370).

The Bleak Horizon

As America moved ahead in the war, and gradually, with the help of her allies, turned the tide of battle against the Axis Powers, a shift in attitude became readily apparent. One can look at the films from early 1942 to 1945 as a sort of frenzied and successful effort to keep the country's eye on victory, while simultaneously distracting it with light, escapist entertainment. But no one outside official government circles was counting on the creation of one of the most awesome weapons in any nation's arsenal: the atomic bomb. The bomb was first proposed by a group of scientists, including the German émigré Albert Einstein, who wrote President Roosevelt in 1939 urging that the United States undertake the creation of such a weapon to beat the Nazis to the punch (Burrows 198). Indeed, the Nazis were working along the same lines, and there can be little doubt that if Hitler had possessed such a weapon, he would have used it with impunity.

Under the direction of J. Robert Oppenheimer, a group of technicians and scientists labored from 1943 to 1945 in Los Alamos, New Mexico, to create a practical nuclear weapon in what was code-named the Manhattan Project. At 5:30 A.M. on 16 July 1945, they succeeded in exploding a test prototype of the bomb; the world and conventional warfare were thus changed forever (Burrows 198). By this time Harry S. Truman had succeeded to the presidency upon the death of Roosevelt in April, and Germany, having suffered continual losses since the D-Day invasion of the previous June, had formally capitulated in May 1945. It was Truman who decided that risking more American casualties in the prolonged conflict against the stubborn Japanese forces would be intolerable. It appeared that conventional weaponry could secure their surrender only through a protracted and bloody invasion that would cost tens of thousands of American lives.

Accordingly, on 6 August 1945, the first military use of the atomic bomb took place at Hiroshima, destroying the center of the city and approximately 130,000 people in a matter of seconds. Still the Japanese would not capitulate, and so President Truman ordered a second bomb dropped on Nagasaki on 9 August, with a loss of 75,000 lives (Holmes 342–43). Japan surrendered at last on 15 August. The long and brutal war, in which nearly 50,000,000 civilians and combatants lost their lives, was finally over (Holmes 396–97).

But at what cost? The American imagination had gone through a series of intense psychic shocks, from the vise of Hitler and the Axis Powers in Europe to the violent and protracted struggle for victory. But for many, the victory rang hollow. First, the atomic bomb unleashed a new horror on the world, which already had its surfeit of violence and depravity. Then, the true depth of the Nazis' evil became apparent only at the end of the war, when the concentration camps became public knowledge for the first time. Images of dead bodies heaped in piles and starving, beaten, and tortured prisoners stumbling from the camps became indelibly marked on the American consciousness. Amazingly, the Nazis themselves had thoroughly documented the depths of their own atrocities. German documentary footage of the camps soon became a matter of public record, incorporated into countless American newsreels shortly after the war.

On the home front, America was going through a period of massive inflation. Wholesale and retail prices jumped steeply in 1946, as Americans adjusted to life after the war. Women, who had been urged to work in defense plants in World War II, were now expected to give up their jobs and return to the kitchen. Many refused, having tasted for the first time the freedom of a paycheck, and the satisfaction of achievement in the workplace (see Costello 257–74). Marriages crumbled, and seeds of feminist discourse were sown. More people went to the movies each week than ever before or since (Sklar, *Movie* 278; Higham and Greenberg 15), but the beginning of the collapse of the studio system was also in the cards. In 1945, there were 20,457 cinemas in the United States; by 1947 the number of cinemas had dropped nearly 10 percent, to just 18,395 theaters (Robertson 219).

At the same time, Stalin was busily enslaving some of the very same nations that Hitler had once occupied, bringing them under the reign of the Soviet Union. Exchanging one dictator for another seemed no improvement at all, and in the United States Stalin's actions were understandably considered an act of outright betrayal. This, in turn, fueled the infamous HUAC hearings of 1947, in which a group of writers, actors, and directors was brought before Congress to testify as to whether or not they were part of a communist infiltration of Hollywood. The 1947 investigation of communism in the motion picture industry was only the curtain raiser for a full-scale blacklist, aimed for the most part at leftist Democrats, which consumed the public's attention through the end of the decade and beyond.

Before the Blacklist ended, hundreds of actors, directors, technicians, producers, and screenwriters had been forced out of the industry, to its eternal detriment. A few lucky exiles, such as director Joseph Losey, found new careers in England. Others, such as the screenwriter Dalton Trumbo, worked under a variety of pseudonyms. Yet the scars of the Blacklist remain. Elia Kazan, who would much later be honored by the Academy of Motion Picture Arts and Sciences and receive an Honorary Award, was one of the key "friendly witnesses" for HUAC, naming J. Edward Bromberg, Paula Strasberg (née Miller), Clifford Odets, Art Smith, and Morris Carnovsky as "fellow travelers." Other friendly witnesses included writer Martin Berkeley, who named Gale Sondergaard, Dorothy Parker, Howard Da Silva, Carl Foreman, Dashiell Hammett, Lillian Hellman, Robert Rossen, Lionel Stander, Budd Schulberg, and more than a hundred others as communists. Berkeley was followed in the witness chair by Lloyd Bridges, Lee J. Cobb, Edward Dmytryk (who first refused to testify on 29 October 1947, but recanted on 25 April 1951, naming twenty-five associates as Communist Party members, including director Jules Dassin), Roy Huggins, Frank Tuttle, and many others (see Vaughn 275–92). In addition, celebrities such as actor Robert Taylor and producer Jack L. Warner appeared before HUAC to commend its investigation of the motion picture industry.

In this climate of hyper-surveillant paranoia, Hollywood responded with a wave of films that reflected the new public mood. Film noir was not only a reaction to the paranoia of the postwar Stalinist world landscape; it was also a reflection of how America had changed as a society. Gone, if they ever really existed, were the small town values celebrated in, for example, the Andy Hardy films, to be replaced by a spiritual terrain of bleak and unrelenting despair. Whom could you trust? No one. The world was a new place, with families split apart, children in open rebellion against their parents, and mom-and-pop businesses metamorphosing into huge conglomerates.

Honor, truth, the values of hard work and discipline: these were for suckers. Film noir depicted an entirely amoral, cynical world in which there were really only two classes: winners and losers. As the decade progressed, noir became the defining genre of the late 1940s, accurately reflecting what most Americans now realized, albeit belatedly. The atomic bomb (and soon, the hydrogen bomb) had changed everything. Now, the world could be destroyed in an instant, by the merest flick of a switch, or even by accident. Noir took this rootless hopelessness and gave it a name. Noir depicted the Pyrrhic victory of World War II for what it really was: a passport to a new and dangerous era bereft of hope, decency, and fair play, a world in which only the strong survive, and the weak are destined to be nothing more than victims.

Many historians trace the advent of noir to Boris Ingster's curious, anti-Hollywood film *Stranger on the Third Floor* (1940), in which perennial fall guy Elisha Cook Jr. (an iconic fixture in such forties classics as John Huston's *The Maltese Falcon* [1941], Howard Hawks's *The Big Sleep* [1946], and numerous others) is framed for a brutal murder he did not commit, through damning but entirely circumstantial evidence. At the film's end, the real killer suddenly emerges—Peter Lorre. As Lorre tries to dispatch a final victim, he is killed in a hit-and-run accident, and Cook is exonerated. But the artificial happy ending tacked on to *Stranger on the Third Floor* is both arbitrary and unconvincing. In real life, audiences knew what would have happened to the man wrongly convicted. He would have gone to the electric chair.

Noir, as a film style, was essentially an essay on bleakness, despair, and darkness. Typically, a hard-boiled detective or private eye, clothed shabbily and working in the shadows, confronted duplicitous and manipulative women and unprincipled evil in a screen territory covered with rain-soaked streets at night, slimy alleyways, and brooding dead ends photographed in high contrast with very intense chiaroscuro.

From this bleak start, noir blossomed into its poisonous universe of femmes fatales, crooked lawyers, corrupt politicians, and psychopathic criminals. Certain studios—such as Columbia, Universal, and RKO—specialized in noir, but perhaps the genre's true essence can be found in the films of the minor studios, Monogram, Republic, and especially Producers Releasing Corporation. These studios operated on the most perilous of profit margins. Their films were made on the lowest possible budgets and rented on a straight fee basis to theaters rather than commanding a percentage of the box office gross. One or two commercial failures could put a studio like PRC out of existence. PRC was the home of the five-day picture, and perhaps the most infamous noir film of all time, Edgar G. Ulmer's *Detour* (1945), was shot there with a budget of less than $20,000.

In *Detour*, a doomed pianist, Al Roberts (Tom Neal), hitchhikes from New York across the United States to reunite with his girlfriend, Sue (Claudia Drake), in Hollywood. Along the way, he accepts a ride from a fast-talking hymnal salesman, Charles Haskell Jr. (Edmund MacDonald), who dies of a heart attack while Roberts drives the car. In a panic, Roberts assumes Haskell's identity, but is tripped up when he offers a ride to Vera (the appropriately named Ann Savage), who had previously been given a lift from the real Haskell. Vera threatens to turn Roberts over to the authorities, but then decides better of it, and instead spins a web of blackmail around Roberts that leads to a truly shocking conclusion. Once seen, never forgotten, *Detour* offers an unremittingly grim picture of the plight of the average citizen in postwar American society; rootless, drifting, predestined to fail.

Other classic noirs, such as H. Bruce Humberstone's *I Wake Up Screaming* (1941), Sam Newfield's *Apology for Murder* (1945), Gustav Machaty's *Jealousy* (1945), John M. Stahl's *Leave Her to Heaven* (1945), Henry Hathaway's *Kiss of Death* (1947), Jacques Tourneur's *Out of the Past* (1947), Abraham Polonsky's *Force of Evil* (1948), Max Ophüls's *Caught* (1949), and Alfred Werker's *He Walked by Night* (1948), to name just a few of the literally hundreds that were produced in the years after World War II, left an indelible impression on their viewers, in stark contrast to the forced optimism of mainstream Hollywood products in the early 1940s. Far from offering happy endings, noirs delighted in telling their audiences that hope itself was an illusion. There is, of course, a certain comfort in this; if life is hopeless, what's the point in planning for tomorrow? Classic noir remains a popular genre in today's uncertain political and economic climate, and has given rise to the neo-noir films of Quentin Tarantino, Martin Scorsese, and other directors.

New Threats

At the same time, Hollywood's most prestigious producers strove to project an image of an America faced with difficulties, but difficulties that could be overcome through concerted effort and responsible action. William Wyler's *The Best Years of Our Lives* (1946) deals with the plight of three returning veterans who must come to terms with postwar society. For all three, the war meant danger, but also adventure and excitement. Civilian life is dull and drab by comparison. *The Best Years of Our Lives* suggests that the transition from wartime to peacetime will never be easy, and the very title itself is highly ironic. These men's best years may be behind them; they must now join the rest of society as it attempts to rebuild the world (see Herman 278–93).

Other "social problem" films were also popular during the postwar era, addressing everything from racism to juvenile delinquency, but always with a positive ending that offered the hope of some sort of tentative solution. Billy Wilder's *The Lost Weekend* (1945) starred Ray Milland as Don Birnam, an alcoholic writer trying to break free of his addiction. In the end, Birnam seems to be able to kick the habit, but only after a harrowing bender (his "lost weekend") and a nightmarish trip to Bellevue. In Anatole Litvak's *The Snake Pit* (1948), Olivia de Havilland plunges into madness and is committed to a public mental hospital with horrific results. All the public agencies that are supposed to assist her fail, and de Havilland is left to cope as best she can, having lost the capability to care for herself. Elia Kazan's *Boomerang* (1947) deals with the murder of a priest, and the subsequent community outrage, suggesting that unreasoning violence could happen anywhere, anytime, to anyone. Henry Hathaway's espionage thriller *The House on 92nd Street* (1945) was shot largely on location in New York City, echoing the neorealist style of unadorned filmmaking first popularized by the Italian director Roberto Rossellini in his classic resistance film *Open City* (1945), and played to postwar fears of communist infiltration of the United States government. On all sides, new threats were springing up, and the existing prewar mechanisms seemed unable to cope.

Indeed, Rossellini's impact on postwar Hollywood cinema is considerable. Using non-actors, actual locations, and only the barest technical facilities, Rossellini eschewed conventional star-driven narratives to create realistic films about the difficulties of life in postwar Europe. The results made Hollywood films look glossy, artificial, and fake. At the same time, Neorealist plots were relentlessly downbeat; the wicked and well-connected triumphed, while solid citizens were ground into the dust. Hollywood filmmakers, impressed by the international acclaim given to *Open City,* soon began emulating Rossellini's methods, with interesting results. In Mark Robson's *Home of the Brave* (1949), an African American soldier suffering from shellshock is cured of his trauma by a sympathetic army psychiatrist, who nevertheless sees this one cure as an isolated incident in a sea of postwar mental illness. Kazan's *Gentleman's Agreement* (1947) deals with ingrained antisemitism in postwar American society, but suggests that there is no long-term answer to the problem. His 1949 film *Pinky* examines the problem of racial "passing" in American society, which in the late 1940s was still acutely color-conscious; again, the ending is left largely unresolved. These were all problems that were here to stay, the filmmakers suggested, problems that could not be solved by the artificial narrative closure of a happy ending.

Jean Negulesco's *Johnny Belinda* (1948) is the story of a young deaf-mute woman (Jane Wyman) who is brought back into society through the efforts of a kindly doctor (Lew Ayres). The film is unusually restrained and lacks the customary Hollywood gloss of an early 1940s production. Robert Rossen's drama *All the King's Men* (1949) starred Broderick Crawford as Willie Stark, a thinly disguised version of Louisiana governor and senator Huey P. Long, who became a virtual dictator in his own state and then started a campaign for the White House before he was assassinated by one of his constituents. Rossen's film was perhaps the most daring of all the films mentioned above because, unlike *Pinky, Home of the Brave*, and *Gentleman's Agreement, All the King's Men* suggested that only murder could prevent Willie Stark from extending his corrupt regime across the nation. As with many of the films in the post–World War II era, *All the King's Men* benefited greatly from location shooting, and used natural sound and lighting whenever possible for a documentary feel. Hollywood was experiencing a true artistic renaissance.

But just as this new wave of realistic, challenging social criticism began, it was all but snuffed out by the effects of the Blacklist, which would soon reach a peak of hysteria. A group of prominent Hollywood actors, led by Humphrey Bogart, chartered a plane belonging to Howard Hughes and went to Washington to protest the HUAC hearings, but soon folded their tents when they realized that the government was serious in its intent to prosecute all who questioned its authority. The key "problem films" of the 1940s were now seen as communist propaganda. Bogart was chafing at the bit at Warner Bros., and would soon leave to form his own production company, Santana, which would finance more off-beat vehicles for the actor, such as the bitterly cynical Hollywood noir *In a Lonely Place* (Nicholas Ray, 1950). Yet the enduring image of the 1940s, despite the social, political, and economic turbulence that surrounded it and the experimentation with the basic studio formula at the end of the decade, is one of aggressive entertainment in which Hollywood sought to divert audiences from the cares of their daily existence during the war.

The Screen Habit

Movie theaters regularly featured double bills, in which an "A," or big-budget film, would be accompanied by a "B," or lower-budget film, in addition to a cartoon, a newsreel, a travelogue, some previews of coming attractions, and perhaps a serial chapter or two. Serials, which were invented in the 1910s and remained highly popular until television wiped them out in the mid-1950s, were weekly chapter plays, usually running across twelve to fifteen episodes. They were typically screened at Saturday morning matinees for children, along with some westerns, science fiction or horror films, and cartoons. Each episode of a serial was twenty minutes in length, except for the first episode, which set up the framing story and usually clocked in at half an hour. Each episode ended with a spectacular cliffhanger in which the hero or heroine faced certain death. Audiences would have to return the following week to see how Captain Marvel, Flash Gordon, or Nyoka the Jungle Girl escaped from their impending doom. These serials, with superb special effects, non-stop action, and spectacularly choreographed fight sequences, represent the apex of American action filmmaking in the 1940s, and continue to influence cinema today.

Republic Pictures, the greatest of the western and serial studios, dominated both genres through the directorial talents of William Witney, arguably the most accomplished action director of the era. In addition to a string of serials such as *The Adventures of Captain Marvel* (1941), *Jungle Girl* (1941), *Dick Tracy vs. Crime Incorporated* (1941), *The Perils of Nyoka* (1942), and *The Crimson Ghost* (1946), in which he handled the action sequences while either John English or Fred C. Brannon directed the dialogue scenes (most serials employed two directors in this fashion), Witney also directed an enormous number of westerns with Roy Rogers, making Republic's films a staple of movie houses throughout the nation (see Witney). Universal and Columbia also made numerous serials, but most observers agree that their work was mediocre, with the exception of Spencer Gordon Bennet and Thomas Carr's *Superman* serial from 1948 and Lambert Hillyer's *Batman* serial from 1943, both produced by Columbia. Republic's serials and westerns in the 1940s had the production gloss of a major studio, and Republic had what was widely considered the best special effects department of any studio, under the supervision of brothers Howard and Theodore Lydecker, who set the standard for visual pyrotechnics in the 1940s.

At Monogram Pictures, producers Sam Katzman and Jack Dietz ground out a seemingly endless series of Bowery Boys films and Bela Lugosi horror programmers, such as *Let's Get Tough* (1942) and *Bowery at Midnight* (1942), both directed by Wallace Fox. These films were made simply to fill up the bottom half of the double bill, and were technically shoddy and aesthetically indifferent. Producers Releasing Corporation had at least one dubious claim to fame. Its major house director, Sam Newfield, holds the distinction of being the most prolific feature film director of all time, with an astound-

Frances Gifford as Nyoka in *Jungle Girl* (John English and William Witney, Republic, 1941).
Courtesy Jerry Ohlinger Archives.

ing 267 feature films to his credit. Indeed, PRC forced Newfield to adopt
two aliases (Sherman Scott and Peter Stewart) to cover his tracks, as he
hastily directed such films as *Border Badmen, The Lady Confesses, His Brother's
Ghost, The Kid Sister, White Pongo, Shadows of Death* (all 1945) and numerous
other productions in every imaginable genre. This alone should give the
reader some indication of the hunger for product in theaters of the 1940s;

moviegoing was a weekly habit, not just for the youngsters, but for the entire family.

While the minors attended to the lower half of the double bill, the major studios saw the 1940s as a chance to consolidate their hold on the "A" feature, and also, eventually, to squeeze out their low-rent competition. The 1940s saw each studio emphasizing its identification with a specific genre, or type, of film, with MGM leading the way as a multi-genre studio, boasting a roster of stars that was the envy of all the other majors, including Clark Gable, Spencer Tracy, Myrna Loy, Lionel Barrymore, William Powell, Judy Garland, Mickey Rooney, and many others. Universal, which had pioneered the horror genre a decade before, capitalized on early successes in the 1940s by reprising established characters in a string of sequels, including Roy William Neill's *Frankenstein Meets the Wolfman* (1943) and Erle C. Kenton's *House of Frankenstein* (1944) and *House of Dracula* (1945), before combining their stable of monsters with the studio's top comedy team in Charles T. Barton's *Abbott and Costello Meet Frankenstein* (1948).

At MGM, legendary producer Arthur Freed created a stylish series of splashy, Technicolor musicals and romances such as *Good News* (1947), a college musical with June Allyson and Peter Lawford; *Till the Clouds Roll By,* the story of Jerome Kern, with Robert Walker in the leading role; *Ziegfeld Follies* (1946), a lavish tribute to the great showman, who from his heavenly bower views a spectacle featuring the talents of Lucille Ball, Fanny Brice, Judy Garland, Lena Horne, and Gene Kelly; *The Harvey Girls* (1946) and *Meet Me in St. Louis* (1944), two of Judy Garland's very greatest musicals, and many other lavish productions. In addition, with Charles Walters's *The Barkleys of Broadway* (1949), Freed brought dance legends Fred Astaire and Ginger Rogers firmly into the Technicolor era.

In the earlier years of the decade, traditional "let's put on a show" musicals such as Busby Berkeley's *Strike Up the Band* (1940), with Mickey Rooney and Judy Garland, Norman Taurog's *Girl Crazy* (1943), again with Rooney and Garland, and Robert Z. Leonard's *Ziegfeld Girl* (1941), all from MGM, dominated studio product. Twentieth Century Fox offered Betty Grable in a series of lavish Technicolor musicals starting with Irving Cummings's *Down Argentine Way* (1940), while Paramount presented Victor Schertzinger's brassy wartime effort *The Fleet's In* (1942). Columbia teamed Fred Astaire and Rita Hayworth in Sidney Lanfield's *You'll Never Get Rich* (1941), and MGM presented the spectacle of Gene Kelly dancing with cartoon characters Tom and Jerry in George Sidney's glossy fantasy *Anchors Aweigh* (1945). By the end of the decade, however, musicals were adapting the location shooting techniques of noirs and conventional dramas, as evidenced in Stanley Donen and Gene Kelly's groundbreaking musical *On the Town* (1949), which was largely filmed on the streets of New York (see Sennett 160–233).

The western entered a new phase of maturity with Howard Hawks's *Red River* (1948), in which John Wayne starred as Tom Dunson, an autocratic rancher on an epic cattle drive, opposite a young Montgomery Clift as Matthew Garth, Wayne's "surrogate son" (Sklar, *Movie* 285). The film's depth and detail brought new dimensions to the western, allowing Wayne to play a surprisingly unsympathetic character with skill and assurance, and producing an interesting tension between the Old Hollywood acting style of Wayne and Clift's New York Method acting approach. John Ford continued on his long journey through his signature location, Monument Valley, in such films as *Fort Apache* (1948) and *She Wore a Yellow Ribbon* (1949), in which duty, honor, and country were always foregrounded, in contrast to Hawks's focus on professionalism and the knowledge of one's own limitations.

Hawks, too, acknowledged the changing role of women in American society in *His Girl Friday* (1940), *To Have and Have Not* (1944), and *The Big Sleep* (1946) by creating the "Hawksian woman," a figure of feminist pride and self-determination, unwilling to defer to men, capable of acting decisively on her own. Hawks's most important postwar discovery, Lauren Bacall, represented a new type of heroine on the screen: tough, insolent, and self-reliant, while still exuding an unmistakable sexual impulse. At the same time, in guiding the postwar career of Humphrey Bogart, Hawks created a new kind of postwar male star, suspicious of authority and very much his own free agent. Indeed, Bogart was one of the first stars to split with his home studio, Warner Bros., and set up his own production company, Santana Productions, so that he could have more control over the roles he played on the screen.

With loved ones far away during the war, the romance film flourished in the early part of the decade, with a heavy emphasis on the maternal melodrama. Sam Wood's *Kitty Foyle* (1940) starred Ginger Rogers as a working girl entangled in an affair of the heart; John Cromwell's *Since You Went Away* (1944) stars Claudette Colbert, Jennifer Jones, Joseph Cotten, and Shirley Temple in the story of a family coping with the hardships of World War II. In Edmund Goulding's *Claudia* (1943), young Dorothy McGuire impulsively marries Robert Young and learns the realities of married life; the film was so popular that it spawned a sequel, Walter Lang's *Claudia and David* (1946). By the end of the decade, one senses nostalgia for a past that has now irrevocably vanished, whether in William Dieterle's fantasy romance *Portrait of Jennie,* or in George Stevens's *I Remember Mama* (both 1948). In *Jennie,* artist Joseph Cotten is entranced by a phantasmal, ageless figure of desire played by Jennifer Jones; *I Remember Mama* dwells in the serene American past, free from the cares of postwar life. Other genres went through a similar adaptive process as the decade progressed.

Paramount became home to Cecil B. DeMille's epic productions, such as *North West Mounted Police* (1940), *Reap the Wild Wind* (1942), and *Unconquered* (1947). All of DeMille's lavish costume melodramas made a profit, but they centered on spectacle rather than substance, and seemed oddly out of place in the midst of World War II and its immediate aftermath. Fox, which had survived the Depression Era almost entirely through the efforts of child actress Shirley Temple, and then dropped her unceremoniously after the failure of Walter Lang's Technicolor extravaganza *The Blue Bird* (1940), now relied on the dashing charm of Tyrone Power and the lush beauty of Linda Darnell and Gene Tierney in such films as Rouben Mamoulian's swashbuckling *The Mark of Zorro* (1940), John Cromwell's epic romance/adventure film *Son of Fury* (1942), and John M. Stahl's Technicolor saga of psychotic possessiveness, *Leave Her to Heaven* (1945).

At Columbia, studio boss Harry Cohn was molding the tragic sex symbol Rita Hayworth into a major star with Charles Vidor's *Gilda* (1946), while RKO floundered in the new postwar economy and was eventually purchased by the elusive tool and die manufacturer Howard Hughes. Independent production flourished, as proven by Max Ophüls's exquisite romance *Letter from an Unknown Woman,* produced by William Dozier's Rampart Productions. David O. Selznick produced Alfred Hitchcock's *Rebecca* (1940) the director's first American picture, and Frank Capra's Liberty Films produced the famous Christmas classic *It's A Wonderful Life* (1946); his earlier film *Meet John Doe* (1941) was also an independent film, although it was released through Warner Bros. John Ford, Fritz Lang, and Howard Hawks all set up their own independent units (Sklar, *Movie* 282). At all the majors, the minors, and the independents, production in the early to mid-1940s proceeded at a rapid pace.

▪ Running Scared

But as the 1940s came to a close, it was evident that the winds of change were blowing. The De Havilland Decision of December 1944 (upheld in February 1945), which limited the term of an actor's contract to seven years, including suspensions (rather than excluding them and thus lengthening the term of the contract, as had been standard studio prac-

Donna Reed and James Stewart (center) are surrounded by love in *It's a Wonderful Life* (Frank Capra, Liberty Films/RKO, 1946). Courtesy Jerry Ohlinger Archives.

tice up to that time), rocked the studio system; actors were, at last, becoming more than mere employees of the studio bosses (Behlmer, *Inside* 234–35). The Paramount Decision of 1948, which had been pending since the case landed in the courts in 1938, forced the studios to divest themselves of their theaters, which until that point had been allowed to screen only the films of the studio that owned them. Paramount became the primary target of the Justice Department's action, but the suit had been filed against MGM/Loew's, Warner Bros., RKO, and Twentieth Century Fox as well (Sklar, *Movie* 274), forcing all the majors to comply.

Universal Pictures, which never owned any theaters, was unaffected by the decision, and rapidly realized that the future of the studio depended on its success in a new medium: television. Television was introduced on a mass scale in the late 1940s, and theater audience attendance began to drop precipitously as families stayed home to watch the magic box that offered free entertainment (Robertson 219). Columbia also made an early entry into the new medium, releasing their old Three Stooges shorts and other "B" products under the Screen Gems subsidiary, and producing thirty- and sixty-minute shows exclusively for television. MGM, in contrast, held back on their vast film library, producing instead "The MGM Parade," a television show that showcased clips from classic MGM films, and urged audiences to see revivals of these films "at your local theater." The other major studios followed suit, believing that television would merely be a short-lived fad. No one, they reasoned, would want to sit at home and watch a small, flickering black-and-white image when they could go out to the movies and be really entertained. But increasingly, audiences did stay home. By the late 1940s, the studios were running scared.

At the same time, the actors and technical unions took center stage in Hollywood business. The major studio chiefs, such as Jack L. Warner, Harry Cohn, Darryl F. Zanuck, Samuel Goldwyn, and Louis B. Mayer, had operated as the unchallenged rulers of their various studios, and deeply resented being told what to do by their employees. The lighting, sound, camera, and costume department workers, at the same time, rightly felt that they were being exploited by a system that gave huge salary bonuses to their bosses, but forced them to survive on a relative pittance. The studio chiefs now had to deal with the International Alliance of Theatrical Stage Employees and Moving Picture Machine Operators, informally known as IATSE, and Actors' Equity, the Screen Actors Guild (SAG), the Screen Extras Guild (SEG), the American Society of Cinematographers (ASC), the Screen Cartoonists Guild, the Screen Directors Guild, and numerous other labor organizations, all of which were firmly entrenched as powers within the industry.

Actors began dropping their studio contracts and operating as free agents on a per-picture basis, an act that would have been unheard of for major stars at the beginning of the decade. Color was rapidly replacing black and white as the preferred production medium; three-strip Technicolor, which had an exclusive lock on Hollywood filmmaking in the early 1940s, was being challenged by a variety of "monopack" color processes, using only one strip of film, which would shortly facilitate the mass move to color production. The studios also began to sell off their back lots as location shooting increased, and they also cut back on their roster of stars and character actors.

Thus, the 1940s, which had begun so robustly for the major and minor studios, and which had been given an additional boost by the exigencies of World War II, ended in a mass exodus from the theaters to the new home entertainment center, the television. Radio had never really been any competition for the film studios; if anything, it served as an ideal advertising medium to bolster the box office receipts of films and showcase the major stars. Television played by a different set of rules, and soon a whole new breed of personalities, such as Lucille Ball, Milton Berle, Desi Arnaz, Jack Webb, and others, rushed in to create programming specifically designed for the new medium.

Hollywood, typically, watched and waited. The major studios had been suspicious of sound when Warner Bros. first introduced it on a large commercial scale. Color, too, was seen as a fad, designed only for "special" productions. Television changed all that, and no better example can be given than the fact that when Howard Hughes finally ran RKO Studios into the ground through financial mismanagement, Desi Arnaz snapped it up and transformed it into Desilu, his new production company (see Dixon 66). The 1940s was a decade of enormous political, technological, social, and economic changes in Hollywood, and it would take many years—more than a decade—before the studios found their footing again, in an entirely transformed landscape.

1940

Movies and the Reassessment of America

MATTHEW BERNSTEIN

It was a time of marked transition for American film, just as it was a time of reassessment for America itself. Hollywood films responded to several trends in American politics and culture, such as the nation's slow recovery from the Great Depression and the devastatingly destructive aggression of the Nazi empire in Europe. These two major phenomena affected Hollywood via shifts in the industry itself. Hollywood studios agreed by year's end to make fewer films of higher quality in response to the government's anti-monopoly efforts at making the film industry more competitive. Combined with the greater creative freedom the studios granted to certain above-the-line talents (directors, screenwriters, actors), the year witnessed new directions in topical subjects and film style and also a number of major stage and novel adaptations that affirmed or bid farewell to popular genre formulas (romantic comedies and the woman's picture).

The transitional nature of this year is apparent in many kinds of cultural expression. The New York theater world saw more musicals produced, such as *Cabin in the Sky*, enjoyed the eighth season of Erskine Caldwell's *Tobacco Road*, and witnessed William Saroyan win the Pulitzer Prize for his portrait of ordinary moral dilemmas in *The Time of Your Life*—all three of which would soon be adapted into folksy Hollywood films. The posthumous publication of Thomas Wolfe's *You Can't Go Home Again* dramatized similar themes of nostalgia and regret in depicting a small-town writer whose autobiographical novel alienates friends and family and who returns home after a restless tour of Europe. These works express sentiments that explain in part the ranking of Mickey Rooney, the movies' Andy Hardy and Judy Garland's co-star in several low-budget musicals about kids putting on a show, as the number-one box office star. Indeed, not a single top box office star this year (Spencer Tracy, Clark Gable, Gene Autry, Tyrone Power, James Cagney, Bing Crosby, Wallace Beery, and Bette Davis) appeared in a film that explicitly depicted the current European conflict, though Gable's *Com-*

rade X and Cagney's *The Fighting 69th* did so implicitly and allusively. Yet this same year also marked the publication of Richard Wright's *Native Son,* a devastating portrait of African American life and consciousness, and Carson McCullers's astonishing first novel of southern small town unhappiness, *The Heart Is a Lonely Hunter,* which counted Wright himself among its admirers. These were depictions of the repressive and melancholy aspects of American life that waited decades for film adaptation.

The film industry was en route to only a modest recovery from the difficult years of the thirties with a relatively steady stock market. The nation elected Franklin D. Roosevelt to an unprecedented third term in November, yet his New Deal was far from an overwhelming success. Many sectors of the American economy continued to struggle. Unemployment (especially for African Americans) remained uncomfortably high. An estimated nine to ten million Americans, or up to 16 percent of the workforce, remained without a job. Not surprisingly, labor unions remained strong. Like so many developments in American politics, this had ramifications for Hollywood. In January, Martin Dies, a Texas congressman and chair of the House Un-American Activities Committee (HUAC), accused Hollywood of harboring communists in powerful places; the following month he would publish his claims in *Liberty* magazine. Dies had in mind both the industry labor unions and talent guilds, particularly after the recent formation of the Screen Writers Guild (which subsequently signed its first contract with producers in September), and various popular front groups in Hollywood that had taken a stand against the Loyalists in the Spanish Civil War. Although Dies's accusations came to naught (he proceeded with limited hearings that summer), his assertions and Walt Disney's agreement in November to spy on communists for the FBI were a preview of coming postwar attractions (Schatz, *Boom* 13; Brown 154–56). In the short term, Pearl Harbor was soon enough to make all these accusations irrelevant.

If labor relations and foreign policy were controversial territory for filmmakers, the industry also faced government regulation that boded ill for its long-term business health. In 1938, Roosevelt's Department of Justice had brought suit against the major studios (Columbia, MGM, Paramount, RKO, Twentieth Century Fox, Universal, Warner Bros., and United Artists) for monopolistic practices. Just weeks after Roosevelt's reelection, the studios signed a consent decree with the government. The terms of the decree would not take effect until the following year, but the studios were compelled to begin to produce "fewer and better" films. And of course the film industry would be buoyed by the unprecedented movie attendance initiated with World War II (Schatz, *Boom* 19–21). Hollywood, then, was little more than a year away from the dramatic benefits that Pearl Harbor and America's full commitment to war unfortunately brought to American industry in general.

But early in the year, and well before Pearl Harbor, Hitler's continuing conquest of Western Europe met with strong isolationist sentiment, and this was the most popular subject for Hollywood's government critics. In January, Senator Burton K. Wheeler, an isolationist from Montana, accused the studios of encouraging America's entry into the war (Schatz, *Boom* 13). Ernest Hemingway could publish a strident anti-fascist novel like *For Whom the Bell Tolls* without much rancor; but movies could broach such topics and positions only at the risk of outraging politicians and citizens, a difference in reception that reflected both the movies' more extensive audience reach and the constant threat of federal censorship the movies faced. Enduring the barking of isolationist congressmen at home, the studios also aimed to make films set in contemporary Europe which would not offend the Axis powers, so that the industry could collect ticket sales even from occupied territories; for example, Paramount director Mitchell Leisen was asked to shoot two versions of the Spanish Civil War drama *Arise My Love*, one of which less forcefully condemned the Nazis (Brown 156).

But in the course of the year, Hollywood studios recognized that they would inevitably lose German-occupied markets, and this development would embolden screenwriters, directors, and producers to make more topical films on the European conflict since they had to write off foreign box office in those territories. Germany had already banned selected American films. The Nazi invasion of Denmark and Norway in April further curtailed foreign distribution of Hollywood product. By the end of May, producers could also write off the Netherlands, Belgium, and Luxembourg. By 22 June, France had surrendered as well. As summer progressed, England remained the studios' only major foreign market, but then the Nazi blitzkrieg began (Schatz, *Boom* 22–27), curtailing show times for American movies. One response in Hollywood was to increase its production of films with South American themes, such as *Down Argentine Way*, reflecting the industry's awareness that following a Good Neighbor policy toward the South American market could compensate, if only partially, for the loss of European film rentals. Such films appeared during a year in which the rumba dance from Cuba joined the jitterbug and lindy hop as some of the most popular social dances in the country. Still, the industry remained focused on Europe and Germany's distressing expansion. Finally, in August, Germany banned MGM and Twentieth Century Fox films outright, accusing the studios of producing films with anti-German sentiments; they likely had Frank Borzage's *The Mor-*

tal Storm (MGM) and Archie Mayo's *Four Sons* (Fox) in mind. Finally, film-makers so inclined could take off their gloves and openly portray the cruelty and ruthlessness of the fascist threat (Brown 156).

As the Third Reich expanded, American isolationists themselves became increasingly marginalized. America's woeful lack of military pre-paredness was dramatically apparent to Roosevelt and other government leaders when Hitler had invaded the Low Countries that spring with a dev-astating combination of air bombings and ground troop advances; on 16 May, President Roosevelt called for the unprecedented manufacture of 50,000 planes for air defenses. His stance on America's urgent need for mil-itary preparedness met broad support, even from his eventual challenger Wendell Willkie and with the approval of the Selective Service Act that reinstated the draft. Yet isolationists still spoke out, if in fewer numbers, and they cheered when soon after Charles Lindbergh infamously accused Roo-sevelt and a minority of Americans of shaping propaganda to drag America into war, rather than preparing America against military attacks.

Faced with the shocking aggressiveness and success of the Nazi military machine, which bombed civilians as well as military targets, it was now clear to most Americans that nothing could or would stop the Nazi ambi-tion to dominate the world. With nothing to lose by making films that con-demned Nazi barbarity, by mid-year the industry was releasing family melodramas, romantic melodramas, and action films that focused on the Nazi menace, such as Mervyn LeRoy's *Escape* and Irving Pichel's *The Man I Married*, constituting a trend, along with Hitchcock's *Foreign Correspondent*, that culminated in Chaplin's watershed comedy/melodrama/message movie, *The Great Dictator*. Pichel's film may well have been the first in Hollywood to use the word "Jew" in reference to Nazi victims (Schatz, *Boom* 119).

Meanwhile, commercially successful filmmakers such as Walt Disney (*Pinocchio* and *Fantasia*) and John Ford and cinematographer Gregg Toland (*The Long Voyage Home*) ventured to experiment with the parameters of clas-sical Hollywood form and style. Such topical and creative license for Holly-wood filmmakers was rooted in part in the recent (March 1939) agreement between the film studios and the Screen Directors Guild, which gave direc-tors more latitude to participate in the scripting, casting, and editing of their films. Studio executives recognized that director-dominated projects could help them produce higher quality films more frequently for what appeared to be a more selective American audience. This would also constitute coop-eration with the consent decree's terms, even when the films in question were adaptations of popular novels and plays (Schatz, *Boom* 80–82), that is, "safe" or at least pre-sold subjects. Hollywood filmmakers took advantage of their newly acquired clout in the industry to pursue projects and techniques that would not have been tolerated even a year earlier. In other words, thanks to world developments, America's economic status, and industry negotiations, many of Hollywood's most memorable films from the year represented topical innovations that would flourish in war time, amplified by the increase in semi-independent production that allowed creative personnel to take home greater income (Bernstein 93–113, 197–216).

Hence, the year witnessed not only the continued roadshowing of David O. Selznick's 1939 blockbuster *Gone With the Wind*, but also of innovative films and several highly regarded works in well-established genres. Howard Hawks's *His Girl Friday*, Ernst Lubitsch's *Shop Around the Corner*, John Ford's *The Grapes of Wrath*, and Walt Disney's *Pinocchio* all appeared in January alone. Such films, and many that appeared later in the year (such as George Cukor's *The Philadelphia Story*), effectively assessed the nature of American identity in terms of its past and recent history, and its cultural norms (gender relations in the battles between the sexes in romantic comedies, for example), affirming in various ways that women of whatever class should choose marriage when the opportunity arises.

Seven films were emblematic of the industry's refined artistry and prophetic of future trends: the romantic comedies *His Girl Friday* and *The Philadelphia Story*, the romantic melodramas *Kitty Foyle, Dance, Girl, Dance,* and *Rebecca,* the social consciousness film *The Grapes of Wrath,* and finally the international message movie *The Great Dictator*. These films demonstrate consolidation and innovation in a transitional year for the industry and the nation. They either took stock of genre conventions with vitality and finesse or explored broader possibilities for creating screen realism. The result was a year that simultaneously reflected the usual diversity of genres and tones in Hollywood's annual output and also featured extraordinary works that typified and extended Hollywood's style and substance.

Romantic Comedies

His Girl Friday and *The Philadelphia Story* bookended the year as commentaries on the possibilities of romance when charismatic and morally ambiguous men are faced with the challenge of capable, independent-minded women. *His Girl Friday* was an adaptation of Ben Hecht and Charles MacArthur's irresistibly cynical stage exposé of corrupt journalism, *The Front Page* (previously adapted in 1931 by Lewis Milestone), and preserved its fast-talking and fast-thinking reporters in the best Hollywood tradition. In this film, no one talks or thinks faster than editor Walter Burns

(Cary Grant) and his former star reporter, Hildy Johnson (a man in the play, but Rosalind Russell here), who contemplates leaving journalism for marriage and quiet domestic bliss. Walter goes through various contortions to persuade Hildy to return to the paper, and together they struggle to scoop the competing papers with a story on Earl Williams, a pathetic, out-of-work loser who has impulsively shot a black police officer and been cynically sentenced to hang by a corrupt city hall out to gain reelection. Though Walter appears to be willing to let Hildy go as soon as the Williams story is published, a final tag line indicates that he will continue to thwart Hildy's departure from the newspaper business.

Director Howard Hawks brilliantly perceived that Hecht and MacArthur's star reporter Hildy could be Walter's ex-wife—and Hawks enjoyed a creative autonomy at Columbia Pictures (from studio boss Harry Cohn's rigid rule) that enabled him to revamp the play to his specifications. In this new incarnation, the cynical, pathologically lying editor Walter has to detain Hildy as she plans to marry—within twenty-four hours, to keep the narrative pressure up—Bruce Baldwin (Ralph Bellamy), a staid, decent insurance salesman from boring Albany, New York. Appealing to Hildy's pride as an ex-reporter and to her pocketbook as a near-newlywed, Walter persuades the couple to postpone their trip for a few hours and assigns Hildy to the Earl Williams case. To sweeten the deal, he arranges to purchase a life insurance policy from Bruce. Working on the Williams story and witnessing Bruce's endless series of mishaps as arranged by Walter, Hildy inevitably recognizes that she belongs with her ex-husband at the paper.

The enduring appeal and charm of Hawks's film (diminished, it should be acknowledged, by brief racist references to "pickaninnies" by reporters at City Hall) came from its pervasive intelligence, embodied most of all in Grant and Russell's working glamour and hectic verbal byplay, which (as in many romantic comedies of the period) substitute for sexual tensions and desires that could not be explicitly portrayed under Hollywood's Production Code. Hildy taunts Walter about her impending marriage and unconsciously indicates that she really wants to get back in the reporting game and with him. Walter's machinations are positively Machiavellian: he lies outrageously to Hildy about the unavailability of his top reporter, and he uses and abuses the newspaper staff to reinforce his fictions. He is irresistible not only because he is portrayed by Cary Grant; Walter's moral ambiguity pales in comparison to the absurdly corrupt and self-serving city officials who seek Williams's execution at all costs.

Hawks's low-key style—the entire film, in fact—is in utter sympathy with Walter's aims and methods. The gritty press room sets—appropriately enough, the creation of low-budget Columbia Pictures—visually reek of cigar and cigarette smoke, and Hawks stages virtually every scene so that we can watch Walter assert his prerogatives from wherever he stands. When Walter is in the background, he dominates. Even the sound-image relations in this film convey Walter's overarching power over every other character. Late in *His Girl Friday*, Bruce comes to the City Hall pressroom to plead with Hildy to leave with him on the next train to Albany, only to find her too wrapped up in writing her Earl Williams exclusive. Hawks frequently films Bruce's appeals over shots of Walter jabbering at Hildy to keep writing and making nonstop calls to the office, reducing Bruce's reasonable pleas to faint, offscreen plaints.

Bruce should know he has no chance against Walter when he acquiesces to the threesome lunch in the film's second scene. Walter here uses a seemingly innocent occasion to stall the engaged couple's departure and to propose new business deals, in a bewildering barrage of nonstop conversational assault. The viewer, like Hildy herself, can only admire Walter's incredible energy, ability, and intelligence. And viewers appreciated this scene even more by recognizing it as a rehash of a comparable scene in Leo McCarey's *The Awful Truth*, an outstanding 1937 comedy of remarriage which also pitted Cary Grant successfully against Ralph Bellamy for the hand of ex-wife Irene Dunne. Hawks and Lederer even include Grant's opening line from the earlier film's table scene between an awkward threesome of ex-husband, ex-wife, and new fiancé: "So you two are going to get married." In fact, *His Girl Friday*'s acknowledgment of its own place within the rich tradition of 1930s romantic and screwball comedies is another significant source of its pleasure. In a throwaway line at one point, Walter sends a lieutenant to find Bruce, describing him as looking like "that fellow in the movies, Ralph Bellamy."

But Walter's true winning hand in this contest, in a perfect blending of Hawks's own thematic preoccupations, resides in his recognition that Hildy cannot resist the obsessive, powerful nature of the reporting business. Hildy, like any other Hawksian protagonist, takes pride in doing her work professionally. Her climactic realization that she belongs in the newsroom is heightened all the more because earlier in the film Hildy delivers to her colleagues in the City Hall newsroom the definitive condemnation of journalism as voyeuristic, trivializing, and uncivilized, a profession she intends to leave to recover her femininity in the sanity of domestic life. After Bruce has beaten a hasty retreat, Walter fails to open the door for the suitcase-laden Hildy when they exit the press room in the film's final scene. Here, Hawks gives the climactic happy ending an ironic undertone: Hildy will remarry Walter with no illusions about his romantic character, but recognizes him nonetheless as her truest partner.

Hawks's decision to remake Hildy Johnson into a working woman was plausible because of the growing ranks of women in the American work force in the earliest decades of the twentieth century, which had reached 25 percent of all workers and 28 percent of all American women by this year (Ware 22, 23). More specifically, women represented 25.3 percent of all American editors and reporters, according to the census. Yet Hildy's desire to be married is never challenged in the course of the film—the only question is to whom. What marks the film as progressive on this score is that Hildy will keep working for Walter, thus avoiding the highly consequential choice most women were unhappily given in films of the era to sacrifice love for a career or a career for love. Hildy Johnson, it seems, has both, and *His Girl Friday* likewise has it both ways, looking to past romantic comedies nostalgically and demonstrating that the often idle rich who populated them could be happily placed within the working world.

Tracy Lord (Katharine Hepburn) of George Cukor's *The Philadelphia Story* avoids this tortured dilemma of work or marriage because, unlike Hildy, she is so wealthy she has never had to work. She is therefore more typical of the rich heiress who populated the most successful romantic comedies. Indeed, the setting of *The Philadelphia Story*'s glossy, polished MGM production could not look more different from *His Girl Friday*'s pressrooms. Yet *The Philadelphia Story*, like so many romantic comedies before it, ponders the same question—whom will the heroine marry?—without questioning the rightness of marriage itself. Like the Hawks film, Cukor's focuses on an independently minded heroine who has to be taught by the man in her life what she truly desires—himself. Haughty, intolerant heiress Tracy is critical of both her philandering father, Seth Lord (John Halliday), and her alcoholic ex-husband, C. K. Dexter Haven (Cary Grant), and she is determined to marry the social climbing, stiff, self-made man George Kittredge (John Howard), who, like Tracy herself, is abstemious and judgmental. Yet by the end of the film, she is made humble not by the discomforting lectures from her father (that his infidelities are none of her concern) and ex-husband, but by her impulsive dalliance with another cynical reporter, Macaulay Connor (James Stewart), after an inappropriate drunken night alone that included some undignified (offscreen) skinny dipping. Kittredge's narrow-minded embarrassment fares poorly next to Connor's poetic exuberance (he is an aspiring writer slumming at a gossip magazine), and *The Philadelphia Story* seems headed for an interclass marriage. But at the very last minute Tracy realizes it is truly Dexter who is her soulmate. They agree to give marriage another try.

The Philadelphia Story endorses the man's greater wisdom, teaching his ex-wife where her true desires lie. And just as viewers might take pleasure in seeing Cary Grant in *His Girl Friday* replay the awkward meal scene from an earlier film, fans of *The Philadelphia Story* could enjoy the way that Tracy Lord's humbling could be read as an allegory of the allegedly haughty Hepburn's own Hollywood demise in the late 1930s. An extra-textual reading of the film as Hepburn's punishment could thrive in spite of the fact that *The Philadelphia Story* was as much her pet project—adapted from Philip Barry's stage triumph written expressly for Hepburn and sold to MGM on the condition that she retain control over major decisions such as casting and direction—as *His Girl Friday*'s was Hawks's. In both these romantic comedies, creative talents with unusual autonomy could craft major contributions to a popular genre that would undergo baroque transformations in subsequent years (as in the films of Preston Sturges).

In its impromptu resolution, *The Philadelphia Story* not only provides a twist (courtesy of screenwriter Donald Ogden Stewart) whereby the upper-class characters are morally preferable to their parvenu or lower-class counterparts, but betrays an underlying romanticism that is nowhere to be found in the profoundly cynical *His Girl Friday*. Tracy's acceptance of Dexter, flaws and all, expresses a need for genuine forgiveness and reconciliation in romantic relationships (Cavell 19) that Hildy can only grudgingly consider offering to the clearly undeserving Walter Burns.

▮▮▮▮▮▮ Romantic Melodramas and the Woman's Film

By contrast with the romantic comedies, the notable romantic melodramas of the year focused, in a generically appropriate manner, on the frustration of the working girl heroine's struggle to achieve personal happiness. Ginger Rogers, Fred Astaire's former dancing partner, pointedly made the shift from romantic comedy to melodrama in her first dramatic role, *Kitty Foyle*. It is interesting to compare Hepburn's character in *The Philadelphia Story* to Kitty Foyle because, as Jeanine Basinger has suggested, the two actresses constitute "the upper- and lower-class versions of the feisty American woman" (*Woman's View* 184). As Basinger notes, "Hepburn seems above it all, keeping herself separate from the ordinary, while Rogers proudly defines herself as one of the crowd, typical. . . . They represent courage and independence; they represent women who wanted to do it their own way. . . . Their independence finally separates both of them from the pack" (184–85). In each of their films of the year, Hepburn and Rogers's characters enjoy an independence that allows them to choose a husband.

But in the romantic melodrama, even that choice—a climactic moment in *Kitty Foyle* as it is in *The Philadelphia Story*—is highly circumscribed.

As an adaptation of a popular Christopher Morley novel, *Kitty Foyle: The Natural History of a Woman* is yet another major Hollywood production based on a pre-sold property. Yet this ostensibly conservative production policy resulted in a surprisingly emphatic depiction of class stratification in American society, as Philadelphia high society is taken as the epitome of upper-class America and its snobbery. Kitty is an Irish American stenographer and then cosmetic saleswoman who has an affair and unsuccessful marriage with the wealthy scion of a Philadelphia family, publisher Wyn Stafford (Dennis Morgan), her former boss. After her divorce, Kitty conceals her pregnancy from Wyn, for she learns that Wyn is engaged to someone of his social class. In a poignant scene, she finds herself waiting on Wyn's wife when she sells cosmetics for a New York company and learns that they have had a child. Subsequently, Wyn comes to Kitty unhappily married and invites her to travel as his mistress to South America; but his offer immediately follows Kitty's acceptance of a marriage proposal from the less exciting, impoverished New York doctor Mark (James Craig), whose idea of a first date is to play cards and drink coffee all night as a test of a woman's moral character. Kitty ultimately decides to marry him.

Kitty Foyle's choice highlights the 1940 heroine's typical dilemma of whom to marry, without, again, questioning the desirability of marriage for American women. As film historian Lea Jacobs has shown, the Production Code Administration worked to ensure that Kitty's past decisions to be with the alluring Wyn before and during their marriage would be repudiated in the course of the film, since their relationship began as an affair. Kitty's love of Wyn is genuine (she suffers the anguish of a stillborn child by him) but the solitude that follows her no-fault divorce from Wyn (recognizing that he cannot break free of his judgmental family) and her general, personal unhappiness make Kitty's ultimate decision to marry the unexciting Mark more plausible. Wyn may ultimately be the wrong partner for Kitty, yet his sudden appearances, lavish spending, and romantic allure make him irresistible. Thus the film's narrative of class stasis and moral conduct is undercut by the visual glamour associated with Wyn, suggesting contradictory meanings (Kitty should not marry out of her class or resume an illicit affair with Wyn, yet he is so appealing!) that it attempts to resolve by casting the relationship with Wyn as a fairy tale or a dream (Jacobs 138–47).

Yet, in adapting Morley's novel, screenwriters Donald Ogden Stewart and Dalton Trumbo restructure *Kitty Foyle* as a series of flashbacks, which ultimately suggests Kitty's choices are preordained. *The Philadelphia Story*

Choosing a romantic partner: Kitty (Ginger Rogers) debates her mirror image over whether to run off unmarried with the dashing, wealthy Wyn or marry the staid, impoverished doctor, Mark, in *Kitty Foyle: The Natural History of a Woman* (Sam Wood, RKO). Courtesy Jerry Ohlinger Archives.

makes Tracy's choice of Dexter a hectic (because the guests are waiting inside for the procession and ceremony) but serendipitous decision, a modified version of the runaway bride who in this case runs back to her first husband. *Kitty Foyle,* by contrast, begins with Kitty's momentous crisis of choice. As the film progresses, she reviews her recent personal history, standing completely alone in front of a mirror in her cramped New York apartment and arguing with her mirror image about her options. (The mirror, functioning as what PCA chief Joseph Breen would call the voice of morality, argues for Mark.) The film concludes in the present with her decision to do the decent thing and marry Mark rather than succumb to the seductive, immoral affair and travel to South America with Wyn, whom she truly loves.

Perhaps *Kitty Foyle*'s flashback structure can be seen as another of the year's films taking stock of the American experience of the recent past. Flashbacks appear with increasing regularity during the decade, but what is less noticed is that, as Jeanine Basinger points out, they appear with great regularity in women's films of the decade. As Basinger notes,

> The flashback is a perfect cinematic form for a story about a woman being in and of itself a rigid, entrapping format that says clearly that there are no choices but the one already made. When a woman faces her final dramatic crisis, she begins to relive her life. This becomes a review of how she made the choice that got her where she is, and in true woman's film attitude, this choice is always, but always, the wrong one. A flashback is a passive form of storytelling, in that it visualizes events that are allegedly past, inactive and over with, done.   (*Woman's View* 197–98)

Significantly, these connotations of passivity and helplessness would eventually extend to male heroes of films noir as well.

Dance, Girl, Dance, one of the few classical Hollywood films directed by a woman (Dorothy Arzner), dispensed with the flashback structure so crucial to *Kitty Foyle* in its portrayal of working women's struggles for economic independence, personal autonomy and creativity, and romantic happiness. In this genre mélange of backstage musical, romantic comedy, and woman's picture, both the sexually provocative, self-assured Bubbles (Lucille Ball) and the innocent, introverted, ballet-trained dancer Judy O'Brien (Maureen O'Hara) dance as part of an all-female troupe under the direction of a former Russian ballet dancer, Madame Balisova (Maria Ouspenskaya). They face major setbacks—unemployment, Madame's untimely death, and Judy's rebuffing of a major dance troupe leader, Steven Adams (Ralph Bellamy)—yet Bubbles becomes a sensation dancing burlesque. She hires Judy to act as her stooge by performing a ballet dance between Bubbles's more popular, sexually teasing numbers. The film's climactic scene occurs during a performance in which Judy harangues the burlesque audience, which boos her and cheers Bubbles. The two fight onstage, and everyone winds up in court. Afterward Judy meets Steven, who tells her she will dance with his group. The film ends as she cries on his shoulder and he tells her she will follow his instructions henceforth. Where Kitty Foyle made her own choices, in *Dance, Girl, Dance*, the man knows best.

Arzner's film is that rare instance of feminist filmmaking in male-dominated Hollywood, and it has been appropriately celebrated for Judy's speech to the burlesque show audience near the end of the film. Here, for once, the female object of the audience's gaze returns that look and makes the audience in the burlesque house, and by implication the one in the movie theater, uncomfortable (Johnston; Cook; Mayne 140). The audience's taunts grow so raucous that the music stops and Judy, on the verge of exiting, instead advances to the catwalk at the front of the stage. The camera remains behind her and shoots from a high angle as she stops and folds her arms, then cuts to a medium shot of her from a slightly low angle as she speaks to the audience:

> Go ahead and stare. I'm not ashamed. Go on. Laugh! Get your money's worth. Nobody's going to hurt you. I know you want me to tear my clothes so's you can look your fifty cents' worth. [*Medium long shot of audience reaction. Cut back to medium close up of Judy.*] Fifty cents for the privilege of staring at a girl the way your wives won't let you. What do you suppose we think of you up here—with your silly smirks your mothers would be ashamed of? [*Reverse angle, medium shot of a row of uncomfortable spectators, men and women.*] And we know it's the thing of the moment for the dress suits to come and laugh at us too. We'd laugh right back at the lot of you, only we're paid to let you sit there and roll your eyes and make your screamingly clever remarks. [*Close up of Judy.*] What's it for? So's you can go home when the show's over and strut before your wives and sweethearts and play at being the stronger sex for a minute? [*Static long shot of the audience. Cut back to close up of Judy.*] I'm sure they see through you just like we do.

Dance, Girl, Dance had personalized the leering male gaze earlier in the film via the New Jersey club manager who widens his eyes and rolls his cigar in his mouth lasciviously as he watches Bubbles's audition for hula dancing; he was impassive as Judy danced (Mayne 151). Judy's challenge is all the more admirable for addressing an entire audience. And as Mayne points out, Judy's speech does not condemn only male viewers: the audience at this show is mixed, and the women look as uncomfortable as the men while Judy delivers her speech.

Yet *Dance, Girl, Dance* also affirms female solidarity in ways not possible in *His Girl Friday* or *The Philadelphia Story* and only briefly glimpsed in *Kitty Foyle* (as Kitty's roommates wait out her first date with Mark in their shared

Bubbles (Lucille Ball, center l.) and Judy (Maureen O'Hara, center r.) represent opposing dance styles (burlesque versus modern classical) and cultures in the self-reflexive musical, *Dance, Girl, Dance* (Dorothy Arzner, RKO). In spite of being romantic rivals as well, they ultimately support each other when hauled into court. Courtesy Jerry Ohlinger Archives.

apartment bathroom). Choreographer Steven Adams's intelligent secretary, Sally (Mary Carlisle), stands and gives Judy a standing ovation when her lecture to the burlesque house ends, and the rest of the audience, as well as the band-leading violinist, joins in (Mayne 145–46). The onstage cat fight between Judy and Bubbles that ensues appears to modify the disruptive nature of Judy's speech, making both just one more kind of visual entertainment worthy of applause (Johnston 6)—but the secretary's applause is a spontaneous gesture of support that echoes Madame's devotion to her protégées and the dancers' to each other (Mayne 144–46). Even in the courtroom scene, Judy offers the judge a sympathetic explanation for the selfish, gold-digging Bubbles's childish behavior, a gesture that wins her Bubbles's admiration and astonishment, all the more so because they have been romantic rivals for the affections of an Akron heir they met in the film's opening scene. Mayne insightfully suggests that "relations between and among women are every bit—if not more—important than the entry of the female characters into the world of 'coupledom' and heterosexual romance" (143) in the film. As Lucy Fischer notes, "Although Arzner positions Bubbles and Judy dialectically, she makes them both rather sympathetic. Though we are urged to reject Bubbles's values, we nonetheless like her spunk, and, in the final courtroom scene, Judy realizes that her enemy's behavior is symptomatic of a broader patriarchal system" (151).

Any film about stage performers will be reflexive. As Mayne points out, in *Dance, Girl, Dance* "two radically different modes of performance—burlesque and ballet—and two radically different approaches to one's career—exploitation versus artistic self-expression—are juxtaposed." Moreover, Mayne notes, "One of the achievements of the film is the fact that while Bubbles and Judy embody different poles of the opposition, neither woman is villainized in the process, surprising in terms of Bubbles" (140–41). Bubbles is so practiced in the art of persuading men of her charms with her body that as she pulls off clothes in court to show the judge where Judy attacked her, he has to remind her that she's in court, not in burlesque. Moreover, one of Bubbles's numbers—"Mother, What Do I Do?"—satirizes the kind of romantic innocence that Judy fully embodies (not drinking, not smoking, never kissing a man), and assigns it to an upper-class, restrained sense of propriety that Bubbles herself (in Lucille Ball's performance) mimics perfectly and then undermines as she takes off more and more clothes. As the cigar-chomping Hoboken bar owner tells Judy after the dancers perform a hula number, "Classy. Too classy." Bubbles, lacking "an ounce of class," gets that job. And Judy's speech onstage acknowledges that burlesque has cross-class appeal with her reference to the "dress suits," the upper-class patrons, who come to ogle the women (Mayne 145). This RKO film in effect distances itself from the Astaire-Rogers films that were the studio's mainstay in the 1930s, as if struggling to imagine how to narrate a romantic musical comedy devoid of charismatic, deserving equal partners.

The gold digger Bubbles in *Dance, Girl, Dance* is another incarnation of the 1940 working heroine, who contrasts not only with the shy, unassertive Judy, but with Kitty Foyle, the resourceful, independent woman who refuses to indulge in self-pity. But where Judy's talents go unappreciated by an entire city except for choreographer Steve Adams, the heroine of Alfred Hitchcock's first American film, *Rebecca*, lacks Judy's talent and is even more helpless. Known only as the second Mrs. de Winter (Joan Fontaine), she is so dependent and ordinary that she is never named, even though the film, like *Kitty Foyle*, is narrated from her point of view as a flashback. And if *Kitty Foyle* dramatizes the dangers for American women of attempting a rise in class status through marriage (or implicitly, though sexual favors), *Rebecca* reinforces this idea by depicting the insecure heroine's rocky marriage to a moody, wealthy, British aristocrat, Maxim De Winter (Laurence Olivier), after living as an orphan and working as a paid companion to a wealthy, talkative American dowager (Florence Bates). The heroine is intimidated by her new husband and his housekeeper, Mrs. Danvers (Judith Anderson), a woman so obsessively devoted to keeping alive the memory of her first mistress—the elegant, beautiful, talented Rebecca—that she even tries to persuade the heroine to kill herself.

Rebecca famously benefited from the creative tension between semi-independent producer David O. Selznick and Hitchcock, then a newcomer to Hollywood who could, at this point, futilely hope for the creative autonomy of Howard Hawks at Columbia or Katharine Hepburn at MGM. Selznick insisted on the film remaining faithful to Daphne du Maurier's best-selling novel (though the Production Code Administration would not allow Maxim to be revealed as Rebecca's killer in the film, as he is in the novel); by contrast, Hitchcock was accustomed to jettisoning and reshaping source material. They found agreement in the film's depiction of the heroine's fragile subjectivity and awkward social predicament: Hitchcock emphasized character point of view more strongly than most Hollywood directors, and producer and director ensured that viewers would suffer and sympathize with the heroine's humiliations and embarrassments. She fails to cheer up her husband—most poignantly when she and Maxim watch home movies of their happy honeymoon, scenes that unfold in dramatic low-key side lighting from the projector and to which their present uncertain misery ("But we *are* happy, aren't we?" she pleads with him) make an awful comparison. Only the recovery, later in the film, of Rebecca's body compels Maxim to confess to the heroine that Rebecca was in fact a faithless, cynical, if beautiful woman who made him so unhappy that she incited him to try to kill her. Once this truth is revealed ("Then you don't love her!"), the heroine can finally be a capable helpmeet to Maxim, supporting him in his effort to face the inquiries about his role in Rebecca's death and face down the threatened blackmail of Rebecca's paramour and decadent cousin Jack Favell (George Sanders).

Rebecca set a template for the 1940s women's gothic film, which typically concerned the trials of a woman newly married to a barely known husband who brings her to a large dark house and whom the heroine suspects of being a murderer. Selznick made sure that the lavishly produced film included overwhelming sets not just in the opening scenes in Monte Carlo but especially at de Winter's family estate, Manderley, whose massive size and aristocratic luxuries dwarf the clumsy, incompetent heroine. Indeed, Hitchcock's atmospheric treatment of Manderley, as much as the assorted props (pillows, daybooks) that fill it, fully embodies the spirit of Rebecca in keeping with literary gothic romantic conventions. In addition, *Rebecca* demonstrated how thoroughly such films could be narrated from the point of view of the heroine (starting with the novel's first sentence in voiceover: "Last night I dreamt I went to Manderley again"). Viewers share her limited range of knowledge, learning only late in the film along with the heroine why Maxim is so moody on the subject of his first wife.

If the revelation to the heroine of Maxim's true feelings about Rebecca emboldens her to assert herself for the first time, his confession casts a less pleasant light on Maxim and his attraction to her. Rebecca is a character whose power is so great that she is associated with the crashing of the ocean waves on shore. She is never shown or contained by the film frame—even as the camera traces her movements described from offscreen by Maxim as he recounts her fatal last night. Unseen throughout the entire film (except in a portrait), Rebecca acts out a rebellion against traditional marriage, monogamy, and male privilege, a challenge that Mrs. Danvers vicariously (if unhealthily) enjoys and continues, but one which our other heroines—Hildy Johnson, Tracy Lord, and Kitty Foyle—could not success-fully attempt, even if they wanted to. Rebecca is duly punished for her unruliness by the cancer that will kill her, and by her accidental death that intervenes. Maxim's affection for the heroine, we come to understand by the end of the film, stems not from her positive qualities but from what she is not—Rebecca. She is childlike, unassertive, and susceptible to Maxim's control, as in his notorious comment to her, "Promise me you'll never wear black satin, pearls, or be 36 years old." This unsettling undercurrent remains in the film even during the "happy" ending: Manderley burns to the ground, we never do see Maxim and his second wife in a final embrace, nor do we hear a reassuring voiceover from the heroine that they lived happily ever after (Modleski 43–56). Manderley's destruction consti-tutes only an implicit basis for a renewed marriage between the heroine and Maxim, perhaps comparable in some respects to Hildy and Walter's or Tracy and Dexter's.

That class distinctions, as impediments or catalysts to romantic happi-ness, figure so prominently in the British-written and -set *Rebecca* or in the tony confines of the Lord family in *The Philadelphia Story* is not surprising; that they do so implicitly or half-heartedly in *His Girl Friday* and *Dance, Girl, Dance* seems equally typical for Hollywood filmmaking of this period. *Kitty Foyle*, by contrast, represented a new kind of directness on the topic, not because of Kitty's voluntary retreat from Wyn's family's upper-class snob-bery but largely because of the left- liberal Stewart and Trumbo's script.

Aside from placing Kitty as a member of the "white collar brigade" with a class consciousness that most Hollywood screenwriters would never dream of invoking, were they so inclined, the prologue they created exclusively for the film before Rogers first appears onscreen provides a synoptic history of the white-collar girl in New York City from the early 1900s to the 1930s. Vignettes take us through private front-porch courtships through marriages that place women on Victorian pedestals; in public life, other brief scenes show men courteously giving up their seats on streetcars for ladies and then refusing to do so after women have successfully lobbied for the right to vote. The prologue's bemused tone at this loss of civility belittles women's efforts at political equality and independence (Basinger, *Woman's View* 496–97). On a broader scale, it parallels the flashback structure of the film proper and makes *Kitty Foyle* yet another example of a film that at once looks backward and forward in delineating the limited choices that American women faced, here in their public as well as private lives.

The Apotheosis of the Social Consciousness Film

The Grapes of Wrath depicted the plight of Oklahoma tenant farmers living in dire poverty and being pushed off their land after devastating dust storms kill their crops. The film could not help but be as class conscious as *Kitty Foyle* while depicting a social stratum well below the urban "white collar girl" and far beneath the focus of the overwhelming majority of Hollywood films. And like *His Girl Friday* and *The Philadelphia Story, The Grapes of Wrath* constituted the culmination of a type of film genre that had long flourished: the "social consciousness" movie which Warner Bros. had crystallized for the early sound era under the leadership of production executive Darryl F. Zanuck. *Grapes* thus represented Zanuck's triumphant return to this genre from his perch as production chief at his own studio, Twentieth Century Fox. While the film was an adaptation of Steinbeck's epic 1939 novel, it also addressed the abiding problem of tenant farmers' and sharecroppers' meager existence. In this year, an estimated forty percent of farming families were still tenants in spite of the Farm Security Administration's efforts to finance their acquisition of farms.

As adapted by screenwriter Nunnally Johnson, directed by John Ford, and photographed by innovative cinematographer Gregg Toland, the film followed the Joad family's drive to California in search of work to survive. Arriving west, they find harsh, dispiriting work conditions. Brutal labor agents, backed by local police, hire desperate farmers like the Joads for meager pay to break strikes that their predecessors initiated. Farmers who understand and explain this exploitation to new arrivals are brutally murdered and labeled as "agitators."

Johnson's script aligns the audience's introduction and perception of these dire circumstances with that of Tom Joad (Henry Fonda), the plainspoken son who is returning home from several years in the penitentiary for killing a man in self-defense. In an extraordinarily dark scene inside the abandoned, lightless Joad home, we learn with Tom that his family has been dispossessed, an ordeal that his neighbor Muley (John Qualen), now hiding in the Joad house, helplessly describes. These interior nighttime scenes set a despairing mood in Expressionist style, and the daytime scenes of Muley's flashback in which the farm agent directs a tractor driver to demolish Muley's house—as in so many daylight scenes in the rest of the film—constitute an overwhelming studio realism (including the absence of make-up for the cast). These exterior daylight scenes were shot in a straightforward style inspired by the famous photographic studies of southern sharecroppers, most notably James Agee and Walker Evans's *Let Us Now Praise Famous Men* and Margaret Bourke-White's *You Have Seen Their Faces* (Campbell 107).

This studio realism drawn from documentary expression is most apparent during the Joads' arrival at the peach farm camp where, from the hood of their overloaded truck, we see the dregs of the dispossessed farming families, barely surviving and existing without hope. As Zanuck biographer George Custen has described it, the sequence constitutes "a tightly choreographed, carefully selected parade of dispirited, defeated grotesques. Their stooped shoulders, worn clothing, and suspicious glares into the camera are unnerving and accusatory. They are an index of the life in this and all Hoovervilles. It is one of the most shattering scenes in the film" (235). Indeed, it is one of the most shattering scenes of any Hollywood film of the previous ten years.

The Joads' arrival in California is especially dispiriting. When their one instance of work turns out to be strikebreaking, and when Tom instinctively kills a deputy who kills Casy (John Carradine)—a former preacher who had "lost the call" at the start of the film but recovers it in labor organizing—the family must move on. They happily settle into a Department of Agriculture campground whose operations are run by cooperative committees. Even local hooligans are subdued before they can disrupt a Saturday dance and provoke an invasion of sheriffs. Still, Tom decides to leave his family, vaguely suggesting to Ma Joad (Jane Darwell) that he will follow Casy's path and work in organized labor. The rest of the Joads leave the camp for an uncertain future.

Here, as always, Ford idealizes the family. The Joads are humble, folksy, spirited people, as embodied by Pa Joad's game comment, first heard as he wades into the Colorado River for a swim, "Let's give this thing a whirl." Ford elicited superlative performances from an outstanding cast of stock company regulars. Darwell and Simpson embody the virtues of steadfast decency through their plain-spoken wisdom and uneducated eloquence. An array of accomplished Hollywood character actors, such as Carradine, Qualen, and Grapewin, vivified character types with astonishingly effective economy. Most of all, the family's fortitude and heart are embodied in Ma Joad; Ford's staging of her small gestures, like her resigned burning of various souvenirs before they leave Oklahoma, accompanied by nondiegetic strains of "Red River Valley," a song of sad farewells, brings an understated, sympathetic eloquence to her solitary leave-taking scene.

As is typical of Hollywood filmmaking of this era, *The Grapes of Wrath* does not show the intangible forces that cause the suffering of disenfranchised Joads and the thousands like them. Instead, the film dramatizes the impact of these developments on one representative family, whose initial cohesiveness gradually frays, in spite of Ma Joad's stalwart efforts to hold it together. The devastating sight of Muley's cabin destroyed by tractor at the start of the film is only the beginning. A more subtle hint of what is to come occurs the following day, during Tom's happy reunion outside his uncle's house, in which all his family proudly assume he has "broke out" from jail rather than being paroled. Tom tells pregnant sister Rose of Sharon (Dorris Bowdon) that he sees he will be an uncle. As the family laughs at this uncomfortably direct reference to her pregnancy and gathers around Rose of Sharon, the camera slowly tracks back to take them in as a group (though Tom himself has stepped to the background alone). The scene is disrupted by Muley's nemesis, the same cigar-chomping land agent who arrives to remind the family they must be gone by morning. Their jovial mood is unalterably broken.

Economic and political considerations shaped the filmmakers' decision not to specify for whom the farm agents work, and which elements of American society, including the profit-oriented capitalist economy and the agriculture industry, are responsible for the Joads' predicament. The political implications of Steinbeck's novel—that under the circumstances the American capitalist system was inhumane and actually destructive—had to be toned down in Johnson's script. Additional incidents of sharecropper exploitation were eliminated; the sequence whereby the Joads find refuge in a government camp and then are exploited at the Keene peach farm was reversed to provide a more optimistic feeling that government could be helpful, but this switch also provided more motivation for Tom's decision to work at labor organizing (Stowell 65). The novel's conclusion, in which a flood destroys the family's efforts, while Rose of Sharon's child is stillborn and she breastfeeds a starving farmer, had to be eliminated entirely. As Russell Campbell put it, Johnson's adaptation functioned "to preserve Steinbeck's outrage at the miserable fate of the Okies while muting the book's radical implications" (110–12). Zanuck biographer Custen elaborates on Campbell's observation: "Where Steinbeck's novel clearly stood for organizing the oppressed against powerful institutions like banks and agribusiness, Zanuck (who opposed most Hollywood unionization of 'creative' personnel) was content to suggest something as vague as that the American spirit would overcome the Depression" (233). The film offered "two alternatives" to the Okies' plight, Ford critic Peter Stowell notes, "plodding survival for some, political action for others" (59); the film also, Stowell points out, managed to depict a positive shift from individual consciousness (Tom Joad alone in the film's very first shot) through family solidarity to social commitment (64).

A condemnation of the agriculture industry could inspire box office failure as well as boycotts of Fox films and other political reprisals. The vagueness about political remedies to which Custen refers appears in the film's prologue: "This is the story of one farmer's family, driven from their fields by natural disasters and economic changes beyond anyone's control and their great journey in search of peace, security, and another home." The notion that the story events were "beyond anyone's control" is echoed throughout the film: the land agent gives Muley a verbal, bureaucratic runaround when Muley asks whom he can shoot for taking away his land (the banks, the corporation—everyone's just doing their job); the film never identifies the source of the "jobs available" handbills that bring thousands of workers to a few hundred jobs in California; nor are we told who or what are the government or industry auspices of the labor agents whose game among the farm hands is to divide and conquer. Zanuck specifically demanded this kind of vagueness about government or industry malfeasance or indifference in his directives to screenwriter Johnson. Still, the film retains scenes of appalling brutality in the exploitation of the sharecroppers; one thinks, for example, of the sheriff who casually kills a bystander at the transient camp while trying to shoot a fleeing laborer who reasonably asked what his pay rate would be. Conversely, Zanuck insisted that the audience be told that the Department of Agriculture ran the clean, well-organized camp that is the Joad's last stop in the film (Custen 233–34).

After Tom witnesses and avenges Casy's brutal murder, he realizes he must leave his family to avoid arrest. His farewell speech to his mother—

among the most famous in all of Hollywood filmmaking—is heartbreaking and eloquent in its reframing of Casy's lost spirituality and Tom's incipient political consciousness:

> Well, maybe it's like Casy says. A fella ain't got a soul of his own, just a little piece of a big soul, the one big soul that belongs to everybody. Then . . . it don't matter. I'll be all around in the dark, I'll be everywhere, wherever you can look. Wherever there's a fight so hungry people can eat, I'll be there, wherever there's a copy beatin' up a guy, I'll be there. I'll be in the way guys yell when they're mad, in the way kids laugh when they're hungry and they know supper's ready. And when the people are eating the stuff they raise and living in the house they build, I'll be there too.

With this speech, and throughout the film, Henry Fonda consolidated his star image as the ordinary, flawed American of ambiguous but fundamentally decent morality and generous sensibility. As critic/historian Campbell noted, Fonda's "controlled belligerence" and "brash candor" constitute "an intensely felt moral anger that is perfect for the part" (116). Thus the Joads' and our geographical journey west is accompanied by Tom's growth from solitary ex-convict to labor organizer, following in Casy's footsteps.

The Grapes of Wrath affirmed, however tentatively, the possibilities for survival and a better future in America. If the American capitalist economy had wrought such havoc on ordinary people who could barely comprehend the larger forces informing their lives, the sturdy endurance of such people, the notion of the American character as an unmoveable bedrock of national life, prevailed. With a class consciousness that equaled or surpassed *Kitty Foyle*'s, even Hollywood's starkest depiction to date of economic deprivation in American life concluded with an affirmation of optimism for the future.

Addressing the Nazi Threat

The Grapes of Wrath was a milestone in Hollywood trends toward increased realism of style and subject matter. A comparable awareness of foreign conditions encouraged industry filmmakers to attempt to depict the horrific consequences of European fascism. Hitchcock's *Foreign Correspondent* depicted the picaresque adventures of an ignorant all-American reporter, Johnny Jones (Joel McCrea), investigating anti-peace espionage and torture in contemporary Europe. Forbidden by the Code to specify Nazis as the torturing villains, *Foreign Correspondent* got very specific with a brief epilogue shot in July at the insistence of producer Walter Wanger. Here, Jones broadcasts from London to America during an unspecified—but certainly Nazi—air attack, à la radio reporters Quentin Reynolds

Adenoid Hynkel (Charles Chaplin, r.), dictator of Tomania, refuses to be overly impressed with his ally and archrival Benzino Napaloni (Jack Oakie), dictator of Bacteria, in *The Great Dictator*, a bold satire of Hitler's Nazi empire and an unprecedented cinematic plea for world peace (Charles Chaplin, Charles Chaplin Productions). Courtesy Jerry Ohlinger Archives.

or Edward R. Murrow: "This is a big story and you're a part of it," he tells his radio audience as the station loses electricity but somehow manages to keep broadcasting. "Hang on to your lights, America! They're the only lights left in the world!" Such vague exhortations to military preparedness were certainly in line with Roosevelt's and other government leaders' priorities in speeches and policies, which were well established by the film's premiere in late August. Yet *Foreign Correspondent* and its filmmakers would be accused by isolationist senators of propagandistic warmongering.

Both *Foreign Correspondent* and Chaplin's *The Great Dictator* were semi-independently produced (Wanger and Chaplin had their own filmmaking companies but released their films through United Artists). This accounts in part for their comparative political boldness, which United Artists distribution executives actively condemned. The filmmakers' political convictions are noteworthy. Hitchcock was anxious while in Hollywood to produce a film to support England's battle against Germany, and Wanger, unlike Selznick, gave him a completely free hand to script and direct a pet project

(Bernstein 157–63). Chaplin was passionate about the anti-fascist struggle, having participated in a multifaceted alliance with liberals and radicals in Popular Front activities of the 1930s; one reason he was so passionate was that Hollywood, with its recently arrived influx of refugees, was second only to New York City as an "important center of international awareness and activism in the United States" (Maland 159–61). As American public concern about the European war increased in the early half of the year and especially after the fall of France, Chaplin's film could count on a more favorable reception than was conceivable even a year before.

The central conceit of *The Great Dictator*, in which Chaplin plays dual roles, grew from his Tramp's physical resemblance to Hitler (Brownlow and Kloft). The film followed the comic adventures of a Jewish barber from the battlefields of World War I, where his combat experience, specifically his aborted attempt to escape, ends in a plane crash and amnesia. Recovering his memory during the 1930s, he discovers that his country, Tomania, is now led by a narcissistic megalomaniac known as the Phooey, Adenoid Hynkel (Chaplin), assisted by Minister of the Interior Garbitsch (Henry Daniell) and Minister of War Herring (Billy Gilbert). The barber resumes his work in the Jewish ghetto and becomes friends with Hannah (Paulette Goddard), but his protests against the persecution of Jews result in his arrest and camp internment (here the camp is not devoted to killing undesirables; Hitler would embark on the Final Solution later, and no one in America believed reports of such camps when they first appeared). Meanwhile, Hynkel plans an invasion of nearby Oesterlich in alliance with Benzino Napoloni, dictator of Bacteria (Jackie Oakie). Because Hynkel and the barber are identical, it is the dictator who is arrested, and the latter arrives at a war rally where he instead calls for peace.

No film of this year more directly or undeniably referenced recent events in Europe than Chaplin's. As Maland has shown, Chaplin included scenes that referenced and satirized specific events in recent history: Hynkel's hilariously incomprehensible opening speech alludes to the Nuremberg Rallies of 1933 and 1938; his competitive meetings with fellow dictator Napaloni refers to Hitler's alliance with, and reception of, Mussolini in 1937; and their planned invasion of Oesterlich in the film references Hitler's annexation of Austria (171). Chaplin also inserted documentary footage of historical events, including the persecution of Jews.

The Great Dictator is undeniably bold in its depiction of controversial subject matter that other Hollywood filmmakers approached allusively, but Chaplin attempts to ease his audience into his new phase of filmmaking as the film progresses. The film's opening World War I sequence features hilarious physical comedy that is typical of Chaplin's earlier work (the poor barber struggling to evade a huge unexploded missile that rotates to follow his every move); the subsequent satirical scene of Hynkel's ballet "duet" with a balloon in the shape of the globe remains one of Chaplin's most celebrated sequences of physical comedy, one that deftly expresses Hynkel's arrogance, self-love, and desire for world domination. Such routines prepared the ground for later, more serious sequences. Since the early 1920s, Chaplin had worked to alternate physical comedy with scenes of heartbreaking sadness. Now, he focused much of the film's pathos not on the barber but on his neighbors in the Jewish ghetto, including Hannah, who suffer far worse persecution from the storm troopers who destroy their homes and their businesses.

Not only does Chaplin here break an aesthetic contract with his audience by making his first all-dialogue picture, but he takes a risk in the barber's final speech to the camera, in which he pleads with the Tomanian soldiers to abandon their dictator and join "the people" to live in a democracy rather than a dictatorship (Maland 170–78). Photographed with static long takes rather than continuity editing, Chaplin articulated a hopeful plea for peace that ends the film, one that does not tie up the loose ends of the preceding story: we do not know what will become of Hannah and the other neighbors, and what will even become of the barber once he steps down from the podium. To have taken the narrative further would have been to descend into a depressing ending or ascend to fantasy; in a sense, Chaplin's ending implies that it is up to moviegoers to write their own conclusion to the story. Nevertheless, *The Great Dictator* was, as Maland notes, "the beginning of the decline of [Chaplin's] enormous public popularity in America" (178). *The Great Dictator* would join Frank Borzage's *The Mortal Storm* and *Foreign Correspondent* on an inadvertent "honor roll" of Hollywood films denouncing Nazi aggression, a list of films which isolationist senators Burton Wheeler and Gerald Nye promised to soon investigate. For Chaplin, as for many others in the film industry, the accusations of warmongering would turn to Red-baiting in the postwar atmosphere of anti-communism, and Chaplin would be eventually hounded from America.

▨ ▨ ▨

These highly accomplished romantic comedies, romantic melodramas, and message movies reinvigorated their genres with both fond nostalgia and new variations on their conventions. They examined crucial aspects of American life—gender roles, class stratification, and unprecedented economic deprivation—as well as appalling atrocities abroad. Other Hollywood films anticipated film noir (Boris Ingster's *Stranger on the Third Floor*), or they returned to vaudevillian film comedy (Edward Sutherland's *One Night in the Tropics* with Abbott and Costello and Victor Schertzinger's *The Road to Singapore*, the first Bob Hope–Bing Crosby lark). One film even anticipated the alienation and helplessness of European art cinema (John Ford and Gregg Toland's *The Long Voyage Home*). The previous year had displayed a Hollywood cinema that perfected its alchemy of genre, star, and visual style. This year affirmed Hollywood films' classical qualities while beginning to explore more striking subject matter and cinematic techniques. Its most notable films responded to a dynamic and changing world with a vitality and ingenuity that subsequent years would extend and develop even further in a dynamic and profoundly changing world.

Thanks to David B. Pratt for research assistance.

1941

Movies on the Edge of War

SARAH KOZLOFF

The year began with Roosevelt's "Four Freedoms" speech to Congress on 6 January. Although fear of war and anti-interventionist sentiments still ran high, he defined the country's values and began to steel the public for what he knew was inevitable. The president was blunt:

> Every realist knows that the democratic way of life is at this moment being directly assailed in every part of the world—assailed: either by arms, or by secret spreading of poisonous propaganda by those who seek to destroy unity and promote discord in nations that are still at peace. During sixteen long months this assault has blotted out the whole pattern of democratic life in an appalling number of independent nations, great and small. Therefore, as your President, performing my constitutional duty to "give to the Congress information of the state of the Union," I find it, unhappily, necessary to report that the future and the safety of our country and of our democracy are overwhelmingly involved in events far beyond our borders. . . . I have called for personal sacrifice, and I am assured of the willingness of almost all Americans to respond to that call. (76–83)

As *Time* magazine commented, the country had thought that it had more time to dither and argue in determining its response to the gathering storm, and the rest of the world had been watching to see how the disparate public opinion would jell. "But when the President spoke, the U.S. began to realize that its mind was more made up than it had thought" ("War and Peace" 12).

The year ended with the attack on Pearl Harbor, and with Congress declaring war against Japan and Germany. In the intervening months, the military threat dominated the news: in April, the Nazis invaded Greece and Yugoslavia; in June, Hitler broke his pact with Stalin by marching into the Soviet Union; in July, Japan occupied the southern part of French Indochina. During the autumn, American ships clashed with U-boats and Japanese forces. The United States responded to the dire events by passing the Lend-Lease bill to give arms to countries fighting the Nazis; increasing industrial production; raising taxes; prolonging the term of service for draftees; declaring a state of national emergency; freezing Japanese assets;

and instituting an embargo on Japanese purchases of oil. The Manhattan Project—the secret national effort to build an atomic bomb—moved from preliminary research into an official government goal.

While waiting for the other shoe to drop, the public went about its business. Radio was central to people's lives: the president and first lady were broadcast frequently, Edward R. Murrow summarized the latest events from Europe for CBS, and Lowell Thomas was on NBC. Gene Autry ("the Singing Cowboy") had a popular show, and stations played the latest hits of the famous big bands. "Chattanooga Choo Choo," "Deep in the Heart of Texas," and "The Jersey Bounce" were among the most popular songs of the year. However, movies were the dominant communal entertainment—Americans spent $809 million dollars going to the movies this year, nineteen percent of all their recreational spending. Hollywood produced nearly 500 films, and imported about 100 from other countries (which, due to the war upsetting trade and production, was a marked decrease from the nearly 200 imported in 1940).

Hollywood's Response to Tense Times

The studios' relationship to these troubled times was contradictory. On the one hand, Leo Rosten in *The Movie Colony* ridiculed Hollywood's insularity and triviality. "The movie colony's intense engrossment in its work gives Hollywood a feverish, self-fascinated quality, and lends a despotic priority to its own values. . . . In the week in which Mussolini raped Albania, Louella Parsons . . . began one of her extraordinary columns: 'The deadly dullness of the past week was lifted today when Darryl Zanuck announced he had bought all rights to *The Bluebird* for Shirley Temple" (404–05).

However, in avoiding serious topics, Hollywood may have been capitulating to audience preferences. A poll conducted by George Gallup found that only New York City audiences had an interest in movies about the war ("Boy Meets Facts" 73). Some of the biggest moneymakers included escapist fare such as the Ginger Rogers vehicle *Tom, Dick, and Harry*, the Hope and Crosby spoof *The Road to Zanzibar*, and Clark Gable and Lana Turner lusting after one another in a gold-mining town in *Honky Tonk*.

Of the major studios, MGM had the greatest number of popular stars under contract and was the most devoted to making uncontroversial movies. As we shall see, when filmmakers did venture to make anti-Nazi or pro-interventionist films, they found themselves hauled before a congressional subcommittee top-heavy with isolationists and accused of warmongering. Until Roosevelt officially called upon Hollywood to contribute to the war effort—on 18 December—filmmakers were taking something of a risk if they addressed the war or political issues in general.

Nevertheless, address the conflict they did, sometimes comically, sometimes consciously, sometimes inadvertently, sometimes speaking in parables. Hollywood produced a series of "service comedies" featuring unlikely draftees: *Buck Privates* starred Bud Abbott and Lou Costello, while Bob Hope was *Caught in the Draft*. Howard Hawks's romantic comedy *Ball of Fire* tells the story of a sheltered professor (Gary Cooper) writing an encyclopedia who learns that he has to fight to protect his girl (Barbara Stanwyck) and his associates from evil; "rolling up one's sleeves and deciding to fight" had a special meaning that year.

As the year progressed, more filmmakers risked addressing the international conflict and such related issues as the role of democracy or religion more boldly. Actually, the cautious discipline of the factory system began to break down in the early part of the decade. To Tom Schatz, who has written the authoritative film history of the time: "The increasing clout of top filmmaking talent created unique opportunities for innovation and individual creativity in the production process—opportunities which a good many filmmakers actively pursued. This had a significant effect on the films of the period, and in fact the early 1940s saw changes in both film style and the filmmaking process, particularly with regard to directorial 'authorship,' that would have enormous impact throughout the decade" (*Boom* 79).

Six films of the year bear reevaluation in light of Schatz's insight and their relation to their historical moment: Preston Sturges's *The Lady Eve*, Frank Capra's *Meet John Doe*, Orson Welles's *Citizen Kane*, Howard Hawks's *Sergeant York*, Henry King's *A Yank in the R.A.F.*, and John Ford's *How Green Was My Valley*. Four of these—*The Lady Eve, Sergeant York, A Yank in the R.A.F.*, and *How Green Was My Valley*—were major successes at the box office. Five of the six (all except *Yank*) were recognized in the *New York Times* annual "Ten Best" list, and industry insiders saluted all of them.

Diversion: A Different Kind of Battle

The Lady Eve is the least overtly linked to its temporal moment. As Brian Henderson details, it was only very loosely based on a short story that Sturges had originally developed into a screenplay in 1938 (323–51). This project was set aside, however, while he was allowed to try his hand directing *The Great McGinty* and *Christmas in July* (both 1940). The success of these two films convinced Paramount to increase his budget for his newest venture and accede to his demands for Barbara Stanwyck and Henry Fonda as the leads. Sturges shot *The Lady Eve* from 21 October to 5 December 1940. It premiered in February.

Paramount promoted the film with a telling tag line: "Barbara Stanwyck has Henry Fonda Bewitched and Bewildered." ("Bewitched, Bothered and Bewildered," music by Richard Rodgers, lyrics by Lorenz Hart, was dazzling audiences in the play *Pal Joey*, then a hit on Broadway.) The movie tells the story of Charles Pike (Fonda), heir to the fortune his father makes as the brewer of Pike's Pale, "The Ale that won for Yale." Charles (nicknamed "Hopsy") leaves an Amazonian snake-hunting expedition to board an ocean liner, where he falls into the designs of Jean Harrington (Stanwyck), a professional card shark and con artist who works cruise ships along with her associate, Colonel Harrington (Charles Coburn), who poses as her father. Jean originally sets Charles up for the colonel's schemes, but falls in love with his innocence and adoration of her. Before she has a chance to convince him of the genuineness of her affection and her decision to go straight, however, Charles finds out about her past and cruelly rejects her.

In the second half of the film, Jean perpetrates an elaborate revenge upon Charles by visiting his hometown in Connecticut disguised as the Lady Eve Sidwich. Although Charles is suspicious, he falls in love with Eve and she marries him. On their wedding night Eve lets slip a story of her past amours, a story with so many tawdry chapters that Charles leaves his noble bride in disgust. Jean regrets her trick and wishes to see Charles, but learns he has fled the country on an ocean liner to South America. She races after him. On board, Charles sees Jean as Jean, and realizes that he loved her all along; he finally understands her earlier statement, "The best [girls] aren't as good as you probably think they are, and the bad ones aren't as bad, not nearly as bad."

The Lady Eve does contain a certain number of topical references. Muggsy (William Demarest), Charles's valet, holds a bristly black shoe brush under his nose and pretends to be Hitler; several comments allude to the cancellation of cruise ships across the Atlantic. However, Sturges's philosophy, which he was to discuss explicitly in his next film, *Sullivan's Travels*, is to exalt the moral utility of movies that provide distraction over those dealing with boring social issues. Sturges was in touch with his audience's preferences; Bosley Crowther, for one, adored *The Lady Eve* for its light touch in these "grim and mirthless times."

The battleground in *The Lady Eve* is not on land or sea, but between the sexes, and, secondarily, between appearance and reality. We learn that

Jean's worldliness and unscrupulousness actually overlay an acute moral compass. Her characterization is deepened by Barbara Stanwyck's performance, which shimmers with what one critic calls "the glint of steely intelligence" in her eyes (Weis 357). As for Charles Pike, who seems so guileless and so abused, Sturges gradually reveals him to be a hypocritical snob. Robin Wood recognizes that "Fonda's image, . . . compounded of innocence, naiveté and idealism, is here subjected to astringent revision. The 'innocence' prevents him from recognizing the sincerity of Jean's feelings, and is shown to be inseparable from an assumption of gender and class superiority, so that we register his chastisement at the hands of 'Eve' as at once a just revenge and the necessary prerequisite for his final acceptance of the 'real' Jean" ("Lady Eve" 488).

Although many of the romantic comedies of the thirties and forties present a variation of *The Taming of the Shrew*, with the unruly, upper-class, willful woman brought to heel by the moral superiority of her socially inferior, virile lover, in *The Lady Eve* the tables are gleefully turned. As James Harvey notes, "The special tone of *The Lady Eve* is a kind of energetic cruelty, a malicious exuberance, reflected chiefly in Stanwyck's treatment of Fonda. . . . Its final effect is not only exhilarating but positively good natured" (570).

The Lady Eve's sparkling style adds to the exhilaration. The major sets are ocean liners and Connecticut estates—locales of ease and luxury. Stanwyck changes her costume numerous times and Edith Head's outfits reinforce the character's emotional arc: as Jean-the-seductress she shows off her shapely legs; when cruelly rejected by Charles she is wearing a schoolgirl-like plaid skirt and vest; as the pretentious Eve she overdresses with feathers and jewels and keeps her hair tightly crimped. Fonda's Charles may be socially ill at ease, and often stumbles into couches and food trays, but he looks dashing in each change of smartly tailored evening wear. Victor Milner, the director of cinematography, captures the stars in shallow focus close-ups and mid-shots. Romantic background music—which was almost never used in previous screwball comedies—suffuses the scenes. Paramount dived into its treasure chest to pull out familiar Rodgers and Hart tunes such as "Isn't It Romantic."

Most exhilarating of all is Sturges's dialogue. Nobody writes like Sturges—his diction careens from educated usage to slang, his phrases take surprising turns and send the viewer spinning (Kozloff, *Overhearing* 170–200). Early on, Colonel Harrington rebukes his "daughter": "Let us be crooked but never common." Hopsy reveals more of his desire and befuddlement than he knows when he tells Jean, "Snakes are my life—in a way."

Jean purposely switches a drinking toast from famous military to romantic conquests.

Harrington (raising his glass): Washington and Valley Forge!
Charles (raising his): Dewey and Manila!
Jean (a tiny pause, then with delight): Napoleon and Josephine!

Throughout, Sturges shows a wry self-consciousness. In the middle of the film, Horace Pike, Charles's father, played with portly pomp and gravelly voiced deadpan by Eugene Pallette, walks down a formal staircase in his Connecticut mansion. He is singing to himself a vaguely Elizabethan drinking song. The last lines run:

For tonight, we'll merry, merry be.
To-mor-row we'll be so-ber.

For tonight, watching *The Lady Eve*, we'll indeed be merry. Tomorrow is soon enough to face the gathering gloom.

Capra Faces Fascism at Home

Like Preston Sturges, Frank Capra was in a position to exert even more creative control over his filmmaking than ever before. After a decade under contract at Columbia Pictures, where he had made such films as *Mr. Deeds Goes to Town* (1936) and *Mr. Smith Goes to Washington* (1939), he left to start his own production company with his long-time screenwriter, Robert Riskin. He financed his new film, *Meet John Doe*, by taking out a $750,000 mortgage on his own home. Although the script was loosely based on a short story published in 1922, Capra was determined that the film would be relentlessly topical: unlike Sturges, he believed that the cinema could and should be a tool for public enlightenment, not distraction. In his autobiography, Capra remarks:

> Hitler's strong-arm success against democracy was catching. Little "führers" were springing up in America, to proclaim that freedom was weak, sterile, passé. The "new wave" was Blood Power! Destroy the weak, the Jews, the blacks; destroy Christianity and its old-hat commandment "Love thy neighbor." . . . Riskin and I would astonish the critics with contemporary realities: the ugly face of hate; the power of uniformed bigots in red, white, and blue shirts; the agony of disillusionment, and wild dark passions of mobs. We would give them a brutal story. (297)

Although *Meet John Doe* was shot the previous summer, it did not premiere until 12 March, mostly because Capra and Riskin could not decide how to

John Doe (Gary Cooper) on the City Hall Roof in *Meet John Doe* (Frank Capra, Frank Capra Productions/Warner Bros.). Collection Sarah Kozloff.

end it. Even after the opening, Capra—still unsatisfied with the conclusion—withdrew the film and reshot the last scene one more time. As Charles Wolfe has uncovered through his archival research, each of the five different endings had a slightly different ideological shading.

Meet John Doe begins as the story of Ann Mitchell (Barbara Stanwyck), who is being fired from the *New Bulletin,* a newspaper newly acquired by the wealthy D. B. Norton (Edward Arnold). As a ploy to keep her job as a reporter, Ann forges a letter from a "John Doe," saying he is so disgusted with the whole world that he is going to commit suicide by jumping off the roof of City Hall at midnight on Christmas Eve. His purported reasons are rather vague: "It's on account of slimy politics we have all this unemployment [and] in looking around it seems the whole world's going to pot." When public interest in John Doe mounts, Ann and the editor of the *New Bulletin*, Henry Connell (James Gleason), hire Long John Willoughby (Gary Cooper), a down-and-out, former bush league baseball pitcher, to assume the role. Reflecting the importance of the baseball motif, the film's score relies heavily on "Take Me Out to the Ball Game." (The year was memorable for its happenings on the diamond: Joltin' Joe DiMaggio hit safely in fifty-six straight games, Ted Williams of Boston closed the season with a .406 batting average, and DiMaggio's Yankees bested the Brooklyn Dodgers in the World Series. On a darker note, the country also mourned the premature death of Lou Gehrig, at age thirty-seven, from a rare neurological disease.)

With Ann ghostwriting his radio speeches and with Norton's financial backing, John Doe becomes a national hero, inspiring a nationwide reform movement of John Doe Clubs, dedicated to neighborliness. Willoughby falls in love with Ann, but he is shocked to discover that Norton, a proto-fascist, is cynically manipulating the movement to propel himself into the White House. At the major John Doe convention—held in a baseball stadium— Willoughby tries to expose Norton, but finds himself denounced as a fraud, booed by the crowd, and silenced by a cut microphone wire. On Christmas Eve, distraught, Willoughby attempts to make amends by actually jumping off the City Hall roof. Ultimately Ann, who, repentant and ill, has anticipated his decision and climbed the fourteen flights of stairs, dissuades the anguished Willoughby. The two are supported by the loyalty of the Millville John Doe Club.

Frank Capra today has a controversial reputation. Pauline Kael expresses both admiration and loathing: "No one else can balance the ups and downs of wistful sentiment and corny humor the way Capra can—but if anyone else should learn to, kill him" (quoted in Harvey 139). Raymond Carney is convinced of Capra's utmost profundity, believing that *Meet John Doe*'s stress on Willoughby's fabrication by media handlers is a reflective work on the lack of identity in the postmodern world (347–64). James Harvey, on the other hand, focuses on what he perceives as Capra's condescension: "While you may feel there's a nice man trying to be helpful behind the film, you feel even more clearly that he's not trying hard enough. Just the opposite, in fact: the flow of rhetoric about goodness and kindness and caring about your neighbor seems so utterly remote from any real experience of doing good or attempting it that it becomes finally offensive" (141).

Critical reception was similarly split. In the *New York Times* Crowther wrote, "This is by far the hardest-hitting and most trenchant picture on the theme of democracy that the Messrs. Capra and Riskin have yet made." Meanwhile *Time* called the movie "super-schmaltz" and the *New Yorker* was completely dismissive: "Mr. Capra's love of the common man, the average man, the dope, the punk, passeth all understanding" (Mosher 80). While Gary Cooper's performance is subtle and generous, Willoughby is something of a cipher—Carney is right that he is a man without a center. The filmmakers also misuse Ann; although she starts as the film's protagonist, they chasten her and toss her aside. Thus, *Meet John Doe* is less satisfying as a whole than it is impressive in its ambition and its parts. Three sequences in particular stand out: the scene in the Millville mayor's office, the convention debacle, and the ending on the rooftop.

In Millville, Willoughby and his cynical friend the Colonel (Walter Brennan) are hoping to flee John Doe's notoriety when they are recognized and cornered. Ann and D. B. Norton arrive and strive to persuade "John" to return to his figurehead role; he resists until the appearance of a group of townspeople. These townspeople, headed by Bert Hansen (Regis Toomey), a soda jerk, and his wife, testify that John Doe's radio address has inspired them to create a John Doe Club. They have reached out to their hard-of-hearing neighbor, Sourpuss Smithers, and organized help for the impoverished Delaney family and the unemployed Mr. Grimes. One must admire filmmakers who dare to pause their story for this lesson on the importance of neighborliness, and the actors, helped by Capra's camera catching the sincerity in their faces, do such a tender job they almost pull it off. More worrisome than Capra and Riskin's outspoken advocacy of "Love Thy Neighbor" is their conception of whom the filmgoer should love. Ironically, despite Capra's personal background as an Italian immigrant, a modern-day viewer will notice that none of the Millville residents is African American or Asian American; none even has a Jewish or Eastern European or Italian surname. (In the film as a whole one sees two black extras, a cook and a janitor.)

The hardest-hitting scene in the film takes place at the ballpark convention. It is night, and raining. The camera captures both the magnitude of the crowd and hopeful expectancy on individual faces. Willoughby arrives, dying to reveal the truth about his own identity and Norton's shady dealings, but the suspense builds as one thing or another delays him. In the meantime, the camera cuts back and forth showing Norton gathering his counterattack by flooding the stadium with goons and newsboys carrying exposés of Willoughby. Norton gains the podium and turns the tables on Willoughby, discrediting him; the crowd that minutes before worshipped John Doe turns into a violent rabble.

As Donald Willis argues, this scene "constitutes the most brutal rejection of the possibility or practicability of mass idealism imaginable. In just several minutes it transforms that idealism into disillusionment and scorn and turns the John Does into a jeering mob. The tomato striking John's forehead just after, trying to make himself heard without the loudspeakers, he cries out the phrase, 'You're the hope of the world . . .!' will probably stand for a long time as the ultimate filmic image of crushed idealism" (42, 44).

Meet John Doe's conclusion was so troubled because it had the impossible task of reconciling Capra's contradictory views of "the people" as wonderful folk, just waiting to have their idealism and kindliness called forth, and as suckers easily swayed by the media and ambitious would-be dictators. To convey a typically "closed" Hollywood ending, the final scene also needs to redeem Willoughby and Ann from their early opportunistic acts and patch up their romance. None of the endings the filmmakers considered differ radically; the variants show indecision about which characters will be present during the final scene and how their closing lines can pull together the film's thematic conflicts. Ultimately, Capra and Riskin, who have seeded the ground with mentions of the Christmas spirit, Pontius Pilate, crucifixions, and the wisdom of absent Fathers, move their playing field from the worldly to the Christian.

The climax of *Meet John Doe* takes place on Christmas Eve, with snow softly falling and church bells sounding in the distance. Ann, a repentant Magdalene, persuades John that he does not have to jump, because Christ has already died for our sins (Harvey 163). Through His sacrifice, the characters and the American public will be redeemed. The film ends with the formerly cynical newspaper editor, Connell, turning to Norton and saying, "There you are, Norton. The people! Try and lick that!" Although the ending attempts to reconfirm viewers' faith in democracy, it would have been more logical for Connell to say, "There you are, Norton. Christ! Try and lick that!" What Capra and Riskin refuse to recognize is that fascists, too, believe they have divine approval.

Power Struggles within and around *Citizen Kane*

Set side by side, the parallels between *Meet John Doe* and *Citizen Kane* are striking. Both films foreground contemporaneous fears of being led astray by the media: throughout the prewar years, citizens and policy makers alike were extremely nervous about manipulation and outright propaganda. Orson Welles's own Mercury Theater broadcast of "War of the Worlds" in 1938 had proven a radio show could cause a public panic, and Leni Riefenstahl's documentaries, *Triumph of the Will* (1934) and *Olympia* (1938), provided chilling examples of the power of film. Thus, it is not really a coincidence that both *Meet John Doe* and *Citizen Kane* concentrate on rich, unscrupulous industrialists who will slant or fabricate the news to gain political power. Moreover, both films were made by directors operating outside of studio control.

Citizen Kane, of course, is the ultimate example of a director being given complete authority and using it for creative innovation. Orson Welles, youthful wunderkind of radio, the daring innovator on Federal Theater projects, who had never before made a movie, was given an unprecedented opportunity by RKO, a studio reorganizing from bankruptcy and thus willing to take a bold gamble. As Robert Carringer notes, "Welles was to be allowed to work without interference, developing the story as he saw fit, engaging his own talent—not just performers but creative and technical personnel as well—and, most significantly, editing the final product his own way" (1).

The story of the making of *Citizen Kane* has moved into movie lore. Screenwriter Herman Mankiewicz wrote the early versions, which Welles later revised. Welles hired a bold team of professionals to assist him in realizing his vision: Gregg Toland, the cinematographer, Perry Ferguson, the art director, Bernard Herrmann, the composer, and Robert Wise, the editor, all responded to the atmosphere of freedom with imaginative contributions. Filming progressed smoothly enough—notwithstanding Welles's broken leg—from late July to late October of 1940, with minor pickups scheduled thereafter. In January, *Citizen Kane* was nearly complete, but as with *Meet John Doe*, the release was postponed. The delay in this case had nothing to do with directorial indecision and everything to do with a power struggle between opposing forces in the movie colony and, by proxy, in the country at large.

The plot of *Citizen Kane* never ceases to be absorbing. A wealthy media tycoon, Charles Foster Kane (played by Welles), dies alone in his costly and exotic mansion, murmuring the word "Rosebud." *News on the March*, a newsreel firm, sends one of its reporters to investigate what this cryptic last word might mean. As *Citizen Kane* attests, newsreels were an important element of the film industry at the time. Regular theaters showed them before every feature film, and a few venues even converted to showing newsreels exclusively. The most famous series were *The March of Time*, produced by Louis de Rochemont, and *News of the Day*, produced by the Hearst Corporation and distributed by MGM.

The reporter, Thompson (William Alland), whose face the viewer never sees, visits several of Kane's associates: he reads the diary of his guardian, Mr. Thatcher (George Coulouris); he speaks with Kane's associates Bernstein (Everett Sloane) and Leland (Joseph Cotten); he interviews Kane's second wife (Dorothy Comingore) and his butler (Paul Stewart). While each informant speaks with Thompson, viewers see a flashback of a different portion of Kane's life. Piecing together information given out of chronological order, we learn that his mother inherited a fortune from a silver mine; that she sent young Charles away to Chicago to give him advantages unavailable in her Colorado boarding house; that after flunking out of colleges Kane thought it "would be fun to run a newspaper," the *Inquirer*.

With shady journalistic and business practices, Kane soon created an empire of newspaper and radio stations. His first marriage to a president's niece was unhappy, and Kane began an affair with a would-be singer, Susan Alexander. When his political opponent in a gubernatorial campaign, "Boss" Jim Gettys (Ray Collins), exposed the affair, Kane lost both the election and his marriage. Kane consoled himself by trying to make the marginally talented Susan, whom he subsequently married, into a major opera star, but when she refused to continue humiliating herself, he retired to his majestic palace, Xanadu. Eventually, Susan left him, and he died alone thinking of the sled, Rosebud, that he owned as a boy in Colorado. Thompson, however, never learns of Rosebud's identity and departs Xanadu believing that no one word could serve as the key to a man's life. Ironically, workmen are engaged in burning the sled as the reporter leaves. *Kane* thus presents viewers with a baffling mélange of psychological speculation, artistry, and social commentary.

One of the questions posed by *Citizen Kane* is: What leads a man of great intelligence and promise—aided by everything money can buy—to make a hash of his life? The question is posed in relation to Kane, but it becomes eerily prophetic in terms of Welles himself (who never again reached the level of accomplishment marked by this film, and became in his later years an embarrassingly obese has-been, hawking Paul Masson wine in television commercials). As Pauline Kael notes, *"Citizen Kane . . .* employs the simplification, so convenient to melodrama, that there is a unity between a man's private life and his public one" ("Raising Kane" 70). The film's detective story leads us to conclude that Kane's problems stem from being ripped from his family at a young age. As a young man (Welles's performance of this central role makes him magnetic), Kane seems poised for great accomplishments. Yet as he ages and faces setbacks in love, finance, and politics, all this promise turns to ashes. In the space of the film, the viewer is forced to compare the lumbering, enraged old man who physically destroys Susan's bedroom to the shirt-sleeved young iconoclast who hoped to use his privilege to protect the poor. The film charts Charlie's inability to love others on anything but "his own terms," and shows how ambition, lust for power, and a superabundance of material objects fail to fill his emotional void. Critics have accused the movie of a shallow Freudianism, but I think the loss-of-the-mother-and-home theme strikes a chord, as does the clichéd reiteration of the fact that money cannot buy happiness.

This tale of failure, loneliness, and lovelessness would seem to call for a bleak movie, but the seriousness with which the filmmakers offer these psychological themes is undercut by technical virtuosity and general gleefulness. As Kael argues, "Kane is closer to comedy than to tragedy, though so overwrought in style as to be almost a Gothic comedy" ("Raising Kane" 5). *Citizen Kane* is so crammed with formal innovations that it mounts a deliberate challenge to studio conventions.

First, Welles and Mankiewicz created an intricate, fractured time scheme that the viewer must work to unravel, and the filmmakers force us to question the reliability of each narrator, and ultimately the reliability of all storytelling. Second, Welles and cinematographer Gregg Toland used a visual style that had never been employed so dramatically before: the deep-focus, high-contrast cinematography allows them to stage many dramatic confrontations in shots where every actor's face is simultaneously in focus, forcing the viewer to notice and compare the characters' contrasting actions and attitudes. For example, during the scene in Susan's apartment, when Boss Jim Gettys summons Kane and his then-wife, Emily, to blackmail him into withdrawing his candidacy with the threat of publicizing his affair with Susan, Welles stages the confrontation with the characters arranged in a triangle formation. In the foreground, Gettys speaks reasonably to Emily, who reacts with icy calm; in the mid-ground, Susan looks scared and interrupts plaintively; at the triangle's apex Kane glowers with rage. Moreover, this camera is mobile, investigatory, almost a character in its own right, at times sneaking into Xanadu, climbing in through a skylight to find Susan in an old bar haunt, craning up to show the stagehands' dismissive reaction to her operatic performance at the opera house Kane builds just for her in Chicago, surveying the mass of objects in storage at Xanadu and pointing out the name of the sled as it burns.

In fact, all the elements of the film are equally highly wrought. Welles's background in radio is apparent in *Citizen Kane* through the film's innovative and attention-grabbing use of sound. The pretentious music of *News on the March* blares out at us; in the Colorado scene where Kane's mother is giving him up, Agnes Moorhead's voice is brittle with strain; Kane's and Susan's voices echo in the loneliness of Xanadu's great hall. Many of the sound effects are expressionistic; Susan's nervous breakdown is accompanied by the sound of a machine breaking down, and suddenly the viewer is startled with the shriek of a cockatoo. The actors do not hesitate to stress their characters' unlikeability, and the performances are vivid. The set design, the special effects, the lighting, the editing, the credit sequence— Welles and his collaborators set out to prove that they could do everything with more self-conscious panache than Hollywood usually allowed.

In its social implications, the film is equally daring and elusive. As is well known, *Citizen Kane* is an unauthorized—and somewhat unfair—biography of William Randolph Hearst (1863–1951), a major press magnate, a force in Hollywood, and a national political figure. Like Kane, Hearst originally harbored reform-minded populist ideals, but he ran his newspapers with utter cynicism and total disregard for the truth. (The film's anecdote about starting the war in Cuba to boost circulation is accurately based on Hearst's interventions in the Spanish-American War in 1898.) Like Kane, Hearst was defeated in his bid for governor. Like Kane, Hearst had a liaison with a woman not his wife—the actress Marion Davies—whose career he did his utmost to promote.

What is less clear in the film, though hinted at in the parody newsreel, and undoubtedly more obvious to audiences, was where Hearst stood politically. According to Louis Pizzitola, Hearst had been an admirer of Hitler; he was Hitler's guest in Nuremberg during the famous rally in 1934, lodging at a luxury hotel with the most prominent Nazis and SS leaders. Hearst and his wife were also on cordial terms with Mussolini, and as late as 1936 and 1937 Hearst discussed film deals with Mussolini's son, Vittorio. Hearst took anti–New Deal, anti–income tax, pro-isolationist positions, and advocated the buying of American products and "Americanism." Moreover, Pizzitola displays evidence that he was a shadowy but influential backer of the America First Committee, a group formed in 1940 to lobby against American involvement in World War II. This fervent strand of isolationist nationalism lies behind the quote in the parody newsreel: "I am, have been, and will be only one thing—an American."

Thus, on another level, *Citizen Kane* asks: What makes a man like Hearst—or D. B. Norton in *Meet John Doe*—become a proto-fascist? Welles once answered the question: "The protagonist of my 'failure story' must retreat from a democracy which his money fails to buy and his power fails to control" (AFI 433). But because Hearst had been very close to his own mother, Phoebe (who died in the flu epidemic of 1919), and because Welles himself was orphaned by the death of his parents at a young age, *Citizen Kane* appears even more brash and personal. Are Welles and Mankiewicz really suggesting that people become isolationists or fascists when they lose their mothers, or—more generally—suffer from an inability to love? Is this meant as serious social analysis or as some kind of joke?

The film's troubled release is intimately tied to its historical moment. Far from being secluded or ill in the early 1940s, Hearst was still a prominent figure in Hollywood. When Louella Parsons, the loyal Hearst columnist, saw a screening of *Citizen Kane* in January, she was enraged on her boss's behalf. Welles, studio head of production George Schaefer, and RKO soon came in for a barrage of threats and intimidation. These included not only legal action, but also a warning that Hearst papers would start a campaign against the number of "foreigners" (read Jews) in Hollywood taking jobs away from Americans, and hints that old personal scandals might be revived in print. Hearst instruments attacked Welles as a communist and Hearst's friend J. Edgar Hoover instructed the FBI to open a file investigating his loyalty. Radio City Music Hall was intimidated into breaking its plan to premiere the film in February (Higham, *Films* 167–69).

Eager to quiet the storm, Louis B. Mayer approached Schaefer on behalf of an obscure group with an offer to buy the negative of *Citizen Kane* for $800,000 so it could be destroyed. Schaefer turned him down. Meanwhile, Welles showed the film to RKO executives and the press in New York and made fervent pleas about freedom of speech (the first of the Four Freedoms so eloquently outlined by Roosevelt in his State of the Union address).

For all these reasons, it is not much of a stretch to see the battle over *Citizen Kane* as a struggle between FDR's detractors and New Deal Democrats, between isolationists and interventionists, between the old guard and the young Turks. To *Time*, the release of *Citizen Kane* would be a challenge "to the long, long reign of Louis B. Mayer and his court" ("Citizen Kane" 68). Retrospectively, film historians can see this as the beginning of the end of an era when studio conventions and moguls' conservatism constrained artistry. As Martin Scorsese would later comment, "The one key element we learned from Welles was the power of ambition" (qtd. in Leaming 200). Although Hearst newspapers refused to advertise *Citizen Kane* and other RKO releases, and although the studio had difficulty booking theaters to show it, the film opened on 1 May. Critics praised it lavishly, immoderately, but contemporary audiences seemed only mildly interested.

■ Sergeant York Enters the Fray

Sergeant York is another landmark film, but not because it had the formal innovation or the strength of *Citizen Kane*. Like *Kane,* however, *Sergeant York* was intimately entangled with historical forces.

As Michael Birdwell details in his study, *Celluloid Soldiers: Warner Bros.' Campaign Against Nazism*, producer Jesse Lasky, a powerhouse in the industry since the silent era, had cherished the hope of making a film about World War I hero Alvin York after witnessing the 1918 ticker-tape parade in the soldier's honor. In 1939, when his career and fortunes were at their nadir, Lasky revived the idea, and personally traveled to Tennessee four times to persuade the reluctant York. York was not favorably disposed toward movies, had never had much contact with Jews, and was loath to exploit his wartime fame. He finally granted his approval in 1940, with many provisos, including that Gary Cooper must play the lead, that the actress who played his wife, Gracie, "could not drink, smoke, or swear," and that York himself would have final say over the screenplay (108).

Lasky was able to secure backing from Warner and even—with much travail—to obtain Cooper on loan from Samuel Goldwyn. The first draft of the screenplay was relatively faithful to York's original wishes and treated the war experiences gingerly. However, when Howard Hawks came on to direct (he claims he took the assignment solely out of loyalty to Lasky, who in 1924 and 1925 had boosted Hawks's nascent career by hiring him as editor and production manager on a series of silent films), he started rewriting the screenplay with the help of John Huston and Howard Koch. Hawks shot the film in Burbank from February to May, with all the Tennessee scenes recreated in a studio and only the battle sequences staged out of doors. The budget exceeded $2 million, a record high for Warner Bros., so the film was given an enormous publicity buildup when it premiered on 2 July at Broadway's Astor Theater, "including a VFW parade down Fifth Avenue with hordes of veterans marching to the theater" (Birdwell 125).

Sergeant York loosely follows Alvin York's biography. It starts with his youth as an uneducated hell-raiser in the remote mountains of Tennessee. The story details his falling in love with Gracie (Joan Leslie); his failed attempts to earn enough money to buy a prized piece of bottomland; and his heartfelt conversion to a Christian fundamentalist sect.

When he is drafted, he files as a conscientious objector, but his petition is turned down because the authorities do not recognize the validity of his church. At basic training, he distinguishes himself as a marksman, and thus comes to the attention of his commanding officers, who seek to understand why he objects to fighting. Major Buxton (Stanley Ridges) sends him home to Tennessee on furlough to study a book of American history and reconcile his faith with his duty to his country.

During an agonized mountaintop vigil, York reads the passage in the Bible "Render unto Caesar the things which are Caesar's; and unto God the things that are God's" (Matt. 22:21, King James Version). He rejoins the army and when his unit is involved in combat in the Argonne he distinguishes himself by his courage and skill, leading a troop of seven Americans in capturing one hundred thirty-two German prisoners. Upon returning to the United States, he is feted and honored with a Congressional Medal of Honor, but he declines to profit from his celebrity, wanting only his simple life. He goes home to wed Gracie and to live on a farm on the land he has been hankering for.

Viewers familiar with Hawks's other films, such as *Only Angels Have Wings* (1939), *The Big Sleep* (1946), or *Red River* (1948), will hardly recognize this text as his. Common Hawksian themes—such as male camaraderie, single-minded devotion to duty, erotic sparring between lovers—are only vaguely discernable here, muffled under folksy cotton. The director, whose trademark is fast, overlapping dialogue, can't do much with characters who speak in a slow regional dialect, saying "obleeged" rather than "obliged," "kin" instead of "can," "thar" instead of "there." The film's strongest performance may be Margaret Wycherly's Mother York; her quiet demeanor and lined face speak of her noble endurance of poverty and hard labor.

The film's politics are clear from the moment the titles appear in American flag typeface. Max Steiner's score moves back and forth between religious and nationalistic tunes, from "My Country 'Tis of Thee" to "Give Me that Old Time Religion" to "Taps" and "Yankee Doodle Dandy," echoing the story's emphasis on both faith and nation. *Sergeant York* exemplifies Roosevelt's Second Freedom, Americans' choice in matters of conscience and religion; it argues that sometimes one's *country* calls for painful sacrifices; and it extols the frontiersman of legend (for example, Daniel Boone), implying that all it takes is the stoic masculinity of a Boone or a York (or a Cooper) to best the cowardly Germans.

And yet, the film's reputation as stirringly effective pro-war propaganda is a bit mystifying. Thomas Doherty argues, "The creation of a new mythos for the Second World War began with the de-mythologizing of the First

World War. Hollywood had to recast the Great War as a reasonable national enterprise, not as the crazy slaughterhouse depicted in literature and film for the previous twenty years. Despair, meaninglessness, pacifism—the dominant legacy of the suicide of Europe—had to be erased, rejected, or revamped" (100). But the one thing that all the filmmakers involved in *Sergeant York* pointedly do not do is excuse World War I. When York's sister asks what the war is about, Mother York responds, "I don't rightly know." Nothing in *Sergeant York* even vaguely points to the current threat: no specter of fascism, no persecution of Jews and others, no territorial aggression in Europe, no peril to the United States. As *Time* noticed, "*Sergeant York* does not glorify war, does not try to horn in on the U.S. and World War II. It stays scrupulously within the bounds of one man's part in another war" ("Sergeant York" 71).

Perhaps the film's reputation as propaganda stems not from the text but from subsequent public events and publicity. Although in 1939 Alvin York had been an avowed isolationist who had never known any Jews, the increasingly grim international news and his collaboration with his new friends led him to a major change of heart. When the national spotlight turned on him, York became one of the most important spokespersons advocating American entrance into the war. He gave a series of speeches strongly attacking the most vocal opponents of involvement, Charles Lindbergh and the America First Committee. Moreover, controversy over the film erupted onto the national stage. As Birdwell narrates,

> On August 1, 1941, Senators Gerald P. Nye of North Dakota and Bennett Champ Clark of Missouri introduced Senate Resolution 152, drafted largely by America First's true believer, John T. Flynn, calling for a thorough investigation of the film industry. . . . The subcommittee leveled several charges against Hollywood, saying that it was dedicated to warmongering, that it constituted a Jewish-controlled monopoly, and that it was engaged in covert dealings with the Roosevelt administration. In their isolationist—and some would argue anti-Semitic—opinion, Hollywood had willingly violated the official neutrality of the United States and spread war fever among a gullible public. (154)

One of the films the Senate most fervently objected to was *Sergeant York*. Although Harry Warner and others scored rhetorical points against senators who hadn't even seen the movie, and although the hearings were ultimately postponed and then made moot by Pearl Harbor, the fact that the hearings were convened at all further illustrates the constrictions on filmmakers. Ironically, the attacks on *Sergeant York* gave it a smashing promotional boost. It became the highest grossing film of the year.

■ *Yank* Drops Any Pretense of Neutrality

Sergeant York was Lasky's pet project, not really Howard Hawks's baby. Similarly, *A Yank in the R.A.F.* (also a major box office success) was driven by the passion of its producer, not its director. Darryl F. Zanuck dictated the original story, based loosely on the real life of William "Billy" M. L. Fiske II, an American athlete who had won medals on the bobsled at the 1928 Olympics. Fiske married a British countess, joined the Royal Air Force (R.A.F.) in September 1939, served with distinction, but died in August 1940 from combat injuries. Mel Gussow explains: "Almost a year before Pearl Harbor, Zanuck came down with a case of war fever. In January 1941 he was commissioned a reserve lieutenant colonel in the Signal Corps, and whenever possible he spoke in favor of America's joining Great Britain in fighting the war. He gave many speeches including one to the National Convention of the American Legion in September. 'If you charge us with being anti Nazi, you are right,' he told the Legionnaires, 'and if you accuse us of producing films in the interest of preparedness and national defense again you are right'" (104).

Zanuck entrusted this pro-war, pro-British film to one of his most reliable directors, Henry King. Not as famous as the major auteurs, King would later have many distinguished credits, including *12 O'Clock High* (1949) and *The Gunfighter* (1950). King and Zanuck cast Tyrone Power, who had been under contract with Fox since 1936, and Betty Grable, soon to become one of the biggest stars of the war era. Leon Shamroy—with eighteen Oscar nominations and four statues for cinematography—was signed on. *A Yank in the R.A.F.* was shot between late April and July. Once again, however, filmmakers jettisoned their original ending, necessitating reshoots in August.

Power plays Tim Baker, a brash American pilot who ferries bombers to England. While in London he accidentally encounters his old flame, Carol Brown (Grable), who is dancing at the Regency Club by night and serving as a member of the Women's Royal Navy Service, a "Wren," by day. Carol is reluctant to restart their relationship because Tim was so unreliable in the past, but she is persuaded partly by his joining the R.A.F. and partly by his overwhelming sex appeal. (Not surprisingly, the Hays censorship office found their liaison too suggestive, and asked for cuts.)

Carol and Tim's relationship runs aground because of his inveterate womanizing and undependability. In the meantime, another British flyer, John Morley (John Sutton), falls in love with Carol and proposes. Bombing sorties and the deaths of his British friends teach Tim the value of teamwork

The poster for *A Yank in the R.A.F.* (Henry King, Twentieth Century Fox) balances adventure and romance. Collection Sarah Kozloff.

and self-sacrifice, especially after he and John are shot down together in Holland and engage in heroics fighting German soldiers. Originally, Zanuck planned for Tim to be killed but pressures—variously described as coming from Tyrone Power or the British government—persuaded him otherwise. Thus, the film ends with an unsatisfactory conclusion (because Tim is such a cad, and Morley such a gentleman): when Tim is shot down at the Battle of Dunkirk, Carol's distress proves where her heart really lies. Carol and John are relieved to find Tim, injured but up to his old tricks, on the last ship of evacuees from the battle.

A Yank in the R.A.F. reflects the strong strain of support for the U.K. sweeping the nation in the years when the British Isles were holding out against the Nazis. For example, the British documentary-drama, *Target for Tonight*, which focuses on an R.A.F. plane on a bomber mission over Germany, was enormously popular in the United States. A hit song was "The White Cliffs of Dover," a lyrical ballad hoping for peace so British children can sleep in their own beds at night. Among the top five best-selling nonfiction books was a collection of Winston Churchill's speeches entitled *Blood, Sweat, and Tears*. A reader would find there Churchill's own remarks about Dunkirk, remarks addressed particularly to the American public:

> We shall go on to the end, we shall fight in France, we shall fight on the seas and oceans, we shall fight with growing confidence and growing strength in the air, we shall defend our Island, whatever the cost may be, we shall fight on the beaches, we shall fight on the landing grounds, we shall fight in the fields and in the streets, we shall fight in the hills; we shall never surrender, and even if, which I do not for a moment believe, this Island or a large part of it were subjugated and starving, then our Empire beyond the seas, armed and guarded by the British Fleet, would carry on the struggle, until, in God's good time, the New World, with all its power and might, steps forth to the rescue and liberation of the old. (297)

Stylistically and in storyline, *A Yank in the R.A.F.* displays several minds. Production strategy at that time called for each film to contain elements that would appeal to different segments of its audience, such as romance for the women, adventure for the men, and excitement for children. King's film offers a grab bag of attractions. We witness nightclub performance scenes: Grable is not much of a dancer or a singer, but she does indeed have lovely legs. With her bouncy blond curls, big eyes, and light voice, she's a softened Ginger Rogers, without the skepticism or steeliness. The romantic triangle is sometimes played for laughs, as if this were a screwball comedy, and sometimes—in highly charged confrontation scenes—as melodrama. (Shamroy lights these melodramatic scenes very effectively, using slashes of light over the actors' eyes, putting the rest of their faces in relative darkness.) Sequences centering on the romance, however, are interspersed with exciting scenes of nighttime air battles with German floodlights piercing the sky. King also includes surprisingly bleak moments, such as when Tim wakes up in a hospital disorientated after suffering exposure crossing the English Channel and for a long beat the camera focuses in extreme close-up on his fright and confusion.

Interesting enough, even the production numbers take place on a realistically small stage, in a nightclub surrounded by sandbags, with all the windows covered by blackout curtains. A strong documentary impulse co-exists alongside the fictional elements. Voiceover narration explains the historical setting during shots of London: "This is London in the early days of the war. A city of homes and churches, and shops and pubs, roast beef and old school ties and Big Ben in the fog. The very heart and core of England." More daring is the aerial footage included in the film, footage—the opening credits proudly trumpet—shot in England with the cooperation of the R.A.F. Thus, *A Yank in the R.A.F.* prefigures the documentaries that Hollywood filmmakers, including Capra, Zanuck, and John Ford, would soon be producing.

Gearing Up for Sacrifice

Twentieth Century Fox's *How Green Was My Valley* is an adaptation of a 1940 best-selling novel of the same name by Richard Llewellyn. When the film was released, publicity rode on the coattails of the author, not any of the filmmakers: the name above the title was Llewellyn's. Several screenwriters tried their hands at the adaptation, but finally the script was written primarily by Philip Dunne, with a great deal of input from William Wyler, who was originally slated to direct, and from Darryl F. Zanuck, who took a lively personal interest in the property, making such key decisions as to use voiceover narration and never to show Huw, the central figure, as a grown-up (Kozloff, *Invisible* 53–62).

When the filming was delayed, however, Wyler moved on to *The Little Foxes* and John Ford was brought in. The film was shot on an elaborate set at the San Fernando Valley Fox ranch, built to replicate the Welsh village of Cerrig Ceinnen. Dunne believes that had Wyler shot the film it would have been "more realistic" and "colder"; Ford is responsible for the film's emotional tenor (Daniell 159). Arthur Miller aided Ford in this quest with cinematography that captures the story's movement from light to dark, and conveys the characters as archetypal, timeless figures against the

The family in *How Green Was My Valley* (John Ford, Twentieth Century Fox). Collection Sarah Kozloff.

horizon. Alfred Newman's score ranges from orchestral music and "God Save the Queen" to traditional Welsh choir arrangements. The film opened in October.

How Green Was My Valley tells, in flashback, the story of the Morgan family's disintegration. Huw, the narrator (Roddy McDowall), is the youngest son of a Welsh coal-mining family. His father, Gwilym Morgan (Donald Crisp), and five older brothers work in the collieries; his mother, Bess Morgan (Sara Allgood), and sister Angharad (Maureen O'Hara) run the household. The episodic plot proceeds through the following events: Ivor, the eldest son (Patric Knowles), gets married to Bronwyn (Anna Lee); Angharad falls in love with the village's new preacher, Mr. Gruffydd (Walter Pidgeon); the colliery cuts wages, leading to a strike that divides the community and the Morgan family (the sons are pro-union, the father more ameliorative); Bess and Huw are injured in an accident in the snow; two of the brothers are fired from the mine and emigrate to America. Mr. Gruffydd rejects Angharad because of his poverty and devotion to duty, forcing her into an unhappy marriage with the mine owner's son; Ivor is killed in a mine accident; Huw attends a national school where he excels and discards his opportunities to work in the mine; Angharad returns to the valley, without her husband, causing the family to be the focus of scandal; Gwilym Morgan is killed in another mine accident.

The film mirrors then-current labor unrest in the United States. In 1940 the country had been rocked by a series of mining accidents that claimed many lives: ninety-one persons died in West Virginia; seventy-three perished in Ohio; and sixty-three died in Pennsylvania. The American mining industry was infamous for strikes and brutal working conditions, but additional labor problems beset the country at both Ford Motor Company and Walt Disney Studios.

Unlike the films previously discussed, *How Green Was My Valley* is not a star vehicle. Walter Pidgeon, a Canadian actor, was the only moderately famous name at the time. A wide variety of characters populate this valley, and the crisscrossing relationships are finely etched: viewers are given insights into Bess and Gwilym's marriage, into how the mine owner, Mr. Evans (Lionel Pape), uses his servants to intimidate Angharad, and into Mr. Gruffydd's attachment to Huw. The film differs from most American movies in privileging neither a single, goal-driven protagonist nor a matched romantic couple, but in concentrating on a family and a community. This diffusion is inherent in the novel, but also central to John Ford's vision. Many of Ford's films—think of *The Grapes of Wrath* (1940), *My Darling Clementine* (1946), or *The Man Who Shot Liberty Valance* (1962)—share these concerns with familial and communal bonds.

Although *How Green Was My Valley* has a reputation as being overly saccharine (the scene where Huw walks among the daffodils is indeed cloying), Tag Gallagher maintains that "the movie is actually a succession of frightening tragedies, failures, oppressions. It is arguably Ford's most cynical and pessimistic film" (188). The large, happy family of Huw's boyhood, which gathered around the big table for meals, and the town where people sang, drank, worshipped, and celebrated together, have suffered such reversals that hearth and street are desolate when the film begins.

The film does not assign responsibility for this decay in a simple-minded way. The exploitative, local mine owners are themselves responding to larger, national economic forces. Moreover, the family members are not merely victims, but individuals who have made choices about how to react to the changing conditions. Gallagher argues that Gwilym Morgan's authoritarianism drives his older sons away; that Bess's anti-intellectualism and conservatism keep Huw from fulfilling his potential; that Huw himself becomes overly invested in being his parents' most faithful, reverential son, and in idealizing the past.

In particular, one can agree with J. A. Place that the minister of Cerrig Ceinnen makes a fatal error, dooming himself and Angharad. "Mr. Gruffydd failed in his personal life in the village by refusing Angharad. His failure in his professional life is demonstrated by his leaving the church. There is a causal relationship which is more than suggested: he leaves because the community is going to censure Angharad, whereas the only crime has been his, and it was against their love. His inability to bring his kind of religion to the community is irrevocably tied to the deterioration of the town" (187–88, 191). *How Green Was My Valley*'s treatment of the church is thus much more nuanced than that of either *Meet John Doe* or *Sergeant York*.

Two elements in particular relate this film to its prewar moment. The first is the emphasis on the fracturing of the family circle. Not once but twice, Ford includes heart-breaking scenes of the Morgan sons bidding farewell to their parents and slipping away into the darkness. Not once but twice, we see a major character widowed—Bronwyn suffers the loss of Ivor, Bess loses Gwilym. *How Green Was My Valley* almost seems to be whispering to contemporary viewers, "Sons will lose fathers; mothers will lose sons; wives will lose husbands. You know this will happen—and soon."

How are the viewers to cope? The second theme is the exaltation of memory as a way to defeat reversals or death. Huw's voiceover narration makes this explicit: "Memory. Strange that the mind will forget so much what only this moment has passed, and yet hold clean and bright the memory of what happened years ago, of men and women long since dead . . . So I can close my eyes on my valley as it is today and it is gone, and I see it as it was when I was a boy. Green it was, and possessed of the plenty of the earth. In all Wales, there was none so beautiful . . . Men like my father cannot die. They are with me still. Real in memory as they were in flesh. Loving and beloved forever."

The conceit that memory can counter loss is (not coincidentally) echoed in the song that won an Academy Award that year, "The Last Time I Saw Paris." Oscar Hammerstein's lyrics, set to Jerome Kern's melody, argue that although the Nazis have occupied that beautiful city, the singer will always remember Paris as she was when her heart was young and gay. By October America was on the brink of war, its innocence and peace tangibly slipping away, but still the past could be held fast by those who will remember. Memory and willpower are posited as additional weapons in our arsenal against our country's enemies.

■   ■   ■

In February of 1942, *How Green Was My Valley* won Best Picture, infamously beating out *Citizen Kane* for that honor. One might suspect that Hollywood's pique at Welles's brashness had some effect, or that Hearst's campaign against him bore results, but I agree with Andrew Sarris's analysis: "The awards to Ford were sincerely granted. People at the time genuinely believed that *How Green Was My Valley* was a better movie than *Citizen Kane*. It was warmer, more disciplined, less flamboyant and less self-indulgent, in short, a repository of the classical virtues in contrast to the romantic vices of *Kane*" (107). *How Green Was My Valley's* values—self-sacrifice, romantic love, loyalty to family, hard work, memory—were more appropriate to the time than *Kane's* ambition, self-assertion, irony, and mockery.

On the morning of 7 December, the biggest crisis Hollywood thought it was facing was the Legion of Decency's unhappiness with MGM's *Two-Faced Woman*, particularly Garbo's décolletage. On 18 December, through the smoke of Hawaii and the Philippines, while reciprocal declarations of war were still flying across the globe, Roosevelt explicitly enlisted the film industry by establishing the Bureau of Motion Picture Affairs as part of the Office of War Information. Now there was a war to be fought. Like Horace Pike in *The Lady Eve*, Hollywood left its merriment behind.

1942

Movies and the March to War

STEVEN JAY SCHNEIDER

On 1 January, the United States and twenty-five other Allied nations signed the Declaration of the United Nations, which stated that each government, "being convinced that complete victory over their enemies is essential to defend life, liberty, independence and religious freedom . . . [is] now engaged in a common struggle against savage and brutal forces seeking to subjugate the world." This engagement was specified in a pledge by the Allied nations to employ their "full resources, military or economic, against those members of the Tripartite Pact and its adherents with which such government is at war." Not surprisingly, the tension inherent in popular American filmmaking throughout its history, between reflecting current social, cultural, and political concerns and anxieties on the one hand, and providing a brief but effective respite from those very same concerns and anxieties on the other, was more apparent this year than ever before (and perhaps after).

Along with America's sudden engagement in World War II, the year presented a time of marked innovation and change as the country marched to battle. *Archie* comic books were first published, with the figurative mini-battles of teenage high school ego and defense; and to save fabric, for the duration of the war women's skirts became shorter. Sex instantly became meaningful now that shells were flying: Wilhelm Reich published *The Function of the Orgasm*. The first electronic computer was created and magnetic audiotape was introduced in the United States. Not surprisingly, the term "G.I. Joe" entered the language, but to certain consternation in American towns and cities the office of Civil Defense was established. America's fortunes in the Pacific arena were mixed: the Japanese lost the battle of Midway, but Manila fell to them, forcing General Douglas MacArthur to retreat to Bataan. The daily defeats and the personal humiliations of military life were accurately portrayed in George Baker's comic strip *Sad Sack*. On the radio, to distract them from agonizing news accounts, Americans could listen to "The Adventures of Mr. and Mrs. North," "The Whistler," "Red Ryder," "The Frank Sinatra Show," and "Fibber McGee and Molly," which topped the airwaves. Lloyd C. Douglas's novel of faith, *The Robe*, hit the bestseller charts, along with *King's Row* by Henry Bellamann and Pearl S. Buck's *Dragon Seed*; all three would later be made into films. The top jukebox hits of the year included "A String of Pearls" by the Glenn Miller Orchestra, "White Christmas" as sung by Bing Crosby, and "Don't Sit under the Apple Tree" by the Andrews Sisters. Eastman Kodak introduced Kodacolor film for the amateur photographer, although most of it wound up being used by the military for propaganda or surveillance use.

In this year we find such seemingly disparate movies as *Cat People*, in which the generic codes of horror cinema associate female sexuality and assertiveness with monstrosity and death. *To Be or Not to Be*, a sparklingly witty anti-Nazi farce, raises social and political awareness all the while providing "serious" entertainment. *Flying Tigers*, a massively popular propaganda piece, helps ready the American public for war and motivates even more young men to sign up with the armed services. And *The Palm Beach Story*, Preston Sturges's zany romantic comedy, gives American moviegoers some much-needed relief from the numerous melodramas and combat flicks dealing with World War II themes. The sheer variety of genres represented onscreen reveals the surface heterogeneity of America's cinematic landscape, from fantasy/adventure (*Arabian Nights*) to espionage thrillers (*Berlin Correspondent, Madame Spy*), domestic comedies (*The Bashful Bachelor, The Man Who Came to Dinner, Maisie Gets Her Man*), westerns (*Apache Trail, Bad Men of the Hills, Come on Danger*), war movies (*Atlantic Convoy, Wake Island*), and animated children's features (*Bambi*) . . . to name just a few.

Through the employment of a wide array of styles, themes, and generic conventions, all the films singled out for discussion in this chapter— Michael Curtiz's *Casablanca*, Irving Rapper's *Now, Voyager*, Orson Welles's *The Magnificent Ambersons*, Alfred Hitchcock's *Saboteur*, William Wyler's *Mrs. Miniver*, Sam Wood's *The Pride of the Yankees*, Curtiz's *Yankee Doodle Dandy*, and George Stevens's *Woman of the Year*—support the notion of America becoming a full-fledged participant in World War II, the country's cinematic output constituting a paradoxical effort to acknowledge while avoiding the terrifying implications of the war effort. In a sense, this trend in the movies can be seen as a metaphor (or mirror) for the U.S.A.'s grudging detachment from the spirit of isolationism, as Japan's 1941 attack on Pearl Harbor effectively dashed any lingering hopes America had of avoiding alliances with other nations. As James Cagney, playing legendary song and dance man George M. Cohan, noted in *Yankee Doodle Dandy*, "Seems it always happens. Whenever we get too high-hat and too sophisticated for flag-waving . . . Some thug nation decides we're a pushover, all ready to be blackjacked.

And it isn't long before we're looking up, mighty anxiously, to be sure the flag's still waving over us." As America marched to war, the films I discuss here showed over and over how we were looking up anxiously to find that waving flag.

▪▬▬▬▬▬▬ The Glowing and the Fading Past: *Yankee Doodle Dandy* and *The Magnificent Ambersons*

What better film to give voice to and simultaneously provide respite from wartime anxieties than Michael Curtiz's *Yankee Doodle Dandy*, a dynamic, nostalgic, unabashedly patriotic musical biopic that celebrates the rags-to-riches career of George M. Cohan, early twentieth-century composer and entertainment icon whose enormous repertoire of hit songs included "You're a Grand Old Flag," "Give My Regards to Broadway," "Over There" (America's best-known World War I anthem), and "Yankee Doodle Boy"?

The film's convenient if unimaginative flashback structure has an aged, still sprightly Cohan (James Cagney) narrating his entire life story to President Franklin Roosevelt (Jack Young), who has summoned him to a private meeting in order to give him the Congressional Gold Medal. This was the first award of this medal to a songwriter, and acknowledged Cohan's contributions of "Over There" and "You're a Grand Old Flag"; but in reality, Cohan, though he played Roosevelt onstage, had come to loathe the president and put off receiving the award for four years. Roger Ebert, for one, has called this set-up "one of the most implausible flashbacks in the history of musical biographies—a genre famous for the tortured ways it doubles back to tell showbiz stories" (Ebert 1), but it lets us know right from the start that Cohan's particularly populist brand of flag-waving musical entertainment carried significant weight in the White House, and that it possessed no small measure of political value when it came to rallying U.S. troops abroad and their families at home.

This strategy also allowed Curtiz to map the personal, albeit extraordinarily public, real-life tale of a particular individual directly over the charged social and political landscape of the first few decades of the 1900s. By focusing on the First World War rather than the Second due to the film's flashback structure, Curtiz taps into contemporary anxieties while still providing viewers with relatively light cinematic entertainment set in the past. However, as Murray Pomerance has elegantly pointed out, powerful emotions lurk just beneath the film's shiny surface:

> [There is] something surprising and touching and grand that runs through *Yankee Doodle Dandy* like a clear river, and that is James Cagney's magnificent

James Cagney sings about the red, white, and blue in *Yankee Doodle Dandy* (Michael Curtiz, Warner Bros.). Courtesy Jerry Ohlinger Archives.

> sincerity in the title role. This is evident in his way of embarassedly smiling to punctuate his thoughts; in his soft and civilized speaking voice; in the astonishing virtuosity of his dancing which is persuasive and original in style, unrelentingly athletic while also being childish, playful, and beautifully meaningless; and in something we rarely see onscreen anymore since alienated distance has overtaken Hollywood performance, and that is Cagney's complete and loving belief in everything he does.   (Pomerance 190)

Centered on Cagney's *tour de force* performance, *Yankee Doodle Dandy*'s dynamic song and dance routines serve to mitigate its occasionally over-the-top patriotism. Though heavily fictionalized in *Yankee Doodle Dandy* for maximum emotional impact, Cohan's life was very much the stuff of legend. After the opening scenes culminating in his visit to the Oval Office, Curtiz traces Cohan's early years as a gifted but arrogant child star—part of the famous Cohan family's traveling vaudeville act—through his ascension to become one of Broadway's most prolific and successful auteurs (producer, writer, and star of some forty shows, and author of hundreds of songs), through his initial struggles on Broadway, his marriage, the death of his father, right up to his retirement from the theater and successful comeback in *I'd Rather Be Right*, a musical hailing FDR as war approached on the horizon, with Cohan himself as the president/star.

Crucially, the only real Cohan flop we witness in *Yankee Doodle Dandy* is his one self-consciously "serious" work, *Popularity—A Drama in 3 Acts*, which alienates his audience and closes almost immediately after opening. What Cohan learns from this rare failure in his near-perfect professional career is that his gifts as an entertainer of the masses are best used generating spectacular, glossy, lightweight musicals; and that this talent should be embraced rather than eschewed (a similar lesson was learned onscreen only a year before by self-involved movie director John L. Sullivan [Joel McCrea] in Preston Sturges's *Sullivan's Travels*). In a sense, *Yankee Doodle Dandy* itself may strike viewers as a George M. Cohan production, offering appealing musical eye candy that taps into patriotic urges while keeping the focus firmly on our "inevitable" success rather than the horrible realities of war.

Yankee Doodle Dandy premiered on Memorial Day. Special screenings had been planned for Cohan's alleged birth date, Independence Day, but because Cohan was terminally ill with cancer the release date was moved up. The film became the year's top box office hit, and Warner Bros.' most successful production to date. But *Yankee Doodle Dandy* was also a critical sensation, eventually rewarded with eight Academy Award nominations: Best Actor (Cagney), Best Sound Recording (Nathan Levinson), Best Scoring of a Musical Picture (Heinz Roemheld and Ray Heindorf), Best Picture, Best Supporting Actor (Walter Huston, who plays Cohan's father), Best Director, Best Original Story (Robert Buckner), and Best Film Editing (George Amy). Cagney—best known for playing gangsters in films such as William Wellman's *The Public Enemy* (1931) and Michael Curtiz's *Angels with Dirty Faces* (1938)—would become the first actor to receive an Oscar for a musical performance (the only Oscar-winning role in Cagney's long and storied Hollywood career).

Another somewhat underappreciated screen personality was Orson Welles. The severely cut and criminally unrecognized follow-up to *Citizen Kane* (1941), Welles's *The Magnificent Ambersons* was the second movie made by the director as part of his extraordinary contract with RKO Pictures (one that allowed him what the studio called "total creative freedom," albeit within relatively tight budgetary constraints). As the film was going into pre-production, RKO hired Welles to go to Brazil to make a documentary intended to foster relations between the United States and South America (the film was never finished, but would later be released as *It's All True* [1993]). With Welles out of the country, *The Magnificent Ambersons* was shown in its entirety—running more than two hours—to select test audiences, to overwhelmingly negative response. Perhaps its downbeat mood and original bleak ending did not sit well with an anxious public, looking for escapist, or at least reassuring, motion picture entertainment during the early stages of World War II. RKO executives promptly took Welles out of the loop and asked editor Robert Wise to cut the film down and shoot new scenes, including the relatively happy ending that is typically shown today. Welles could do little but stand on the Brazilian sidelines and watch, and the resultant debacle arguably derailed his career in Hollywood for good. The final version of *The Magnificent Ambersons* stands at just eighty-eight minutes. Forty-four minutes of footage were removed and lost; they have never been found. Indeed, the lost footage of *The Magnificent Ambersons* has become one of the holy grails of the cinema, its loss denying viewers a look at Welles's masterpiece in its original, unadulterated form.

Based on the Pulitzer Prize–winning novel by Booth Tarkington, and set meticulously in the turn-of-the-century small town world he remembered from his own youth in Kenosha, Wisconsin, *The Magnificent Ambersons* was an even more personal project for Welles than *Citizen Kane*. The film centers on George Amberson Minafer (Tim Holt), the charismatic but arrogant and unpopular offspring of an aristocratic family, who eventually receives the "comeuppance" everyone wishes for him. Though *Kane* generally receives credit as Welles's most ambitious work, the first hour of *The Magnificent Ambersons* holds its own against its far more famous predecessor. Welles must have been tempted (and everyone must have expected) him to play George—the parallels between the two men are striking—but Welles wisely cast Holt as the lead and restricted his own role to that of offscreen narrator, using his familiar, well-trained voice to open the film with a memorable (if tongue-in-cheek) sermon on the history of male fashions.

Instead of *Citizen Kane*'s director of cinematography Gregg Toland, Welles decided to work with veteran Stanley Cortez (whose later films included Charles Laughton's *The Night of the Hunter* [1955] and Samuel Fuller's *Shock Corridor* [1963]). The resulting film is as visually striking as *Kane* in its use of sharp, deep-focus photography, but *The Magnificent Ambersons* also evinces a sweet, melancholy nostalgia for social visits, sleigh rides in the snow, rides in the early automobile and horse carriage, and other aspects of early twentieth-century pastoral social life. The film's melancholy aspect comes partly from its exposé of classbound society in early twentieth-century America, epitomized in the way the ambitious inventor and entrepreneur Eugene Morgan (Joseph Cotten) is forced to give up his upper-crust love Isabel (Dolores Costello)—George's mother—to a dolt from a prominent family, even as the wealth and luster of the Amberson clan slowly fades away.

At the heart of *The Magnificent Ambersons* lies a conflict between two different and disparate cultures. The horse-and-buggy culture, characterized by old money and rich, aristocratic families living an unhurried life in the country, clashes with the new and rising automobile culture, the latter emphasizing urban life and social mobility. At another level, the film explores the conflict between generations, between the Old World and a new one struggling to take its place. Time is at the center of this struggle. As the months and years pass by, the horse-and-buggy culture continues to decay, eventually to be swept away in the tide of a new society—a society that would rely on the development of industry and technological advances in the global fight for freedom.

Not unlike the seductive voice of a hypnotist, Welles's opening voiceover narration slowly and methodically praises the past way of life. He explains that "back when there was time to do everything," people were not in a hurry to get where they are going as they are today. It was a time for socializing, for parties, for serenades. Everyone ("everyone," as invoked in this film, is the white Anglo-Saxon ruling class) was happy, and everything was as it should be. While the narrator lulls us into believing that this was a genteel and ideal era, the images we see are anything but idyllic. Even in its supposed heyday, the Amberson household is slipping into a state of decline, slowly rotting from within. The family's investments do not pan out, and no new income is generated. Once the proudest family in town, the Ambersons set the fashions and had all the social power. But failing to adapt to the changing culture around them, they are inexorably swallowed up by the passage of time. That contemporary audiences did not react to *The Magnificent Ambersons* as Welles and RKO expected, even after the "happier" ending was inserted, may have been caused by the film's interlacing of nostalgia and ambivalence: for example, the rise of automobile culture (to which his viewers were completely accommodated) is seen by Welles as inevitable, not desirable.

Two sequences in particular are visually and narratively stunning, in the best tradition of Welles's cinematic genius. The Ambersons are having a soirée, with music wafting into the nocturnal street from the brightly lit gingerbread mansion, carriages pulling up sedately to deposit guests in tuxedoes and long gowns. In one long amazing sequential shot, the camera proceeds from outside, up the walk, onto the veranda, through the front door, into the swirling crowd of champagne drinkers, gossipers, businessmen, and giddy young people, twisting among dancers and executing a complete 360-degree sweep while taking in feature after feature of social interaction that reveals a sharp edge of character, a tension between people, an anticipation of the action that is to come. At another moment, young George is having a spat with his matronly aunt (Agnes Moorehead), who queries his possessiveness about his mother's love interests. They are in the immense Amberson kitchen, a platoon of pots and pans around them. Through the long scene, she busies herself tipping green beans while he wheedles her, the depth of focus keeping both in focus and establishing the tense relationship between them.

As a tale of enduring love and a morality lesson, according to which characters who desperately need to be humbled end up getting what they deserve, *The Magnificent Ambersons* should have been enormously heartening to American audiences in the throes of World War II. But it was not. Perhaps, as James Cobo points out, "*Ambersons* is not a romantic paean, or a homily to humility—it is a parable about the side of progress which damns the progressor and makes his world unfamiliar and cold" (1).

The Dominant and the Dominated Woman: *Woman of the Year* and *Now, Voyager*

George Stevens's savvy romantic comedy *Woman of the Year* was the first of nine film collaborations between stars Katharine Hepburn and Spencer Tracy (others include Frank Capra's *State of the Union* [1948], George Cukor's *Adam's Rib* [1949] and *Pat and Mike* [1952], and Walter Lang's *Desk Set* [1957]). The illustrious acting couple actually fell in love during the shooting of the picture, initiating a relationship that would last more than a quarter-century, until Tracy's death in 1967. With debates over the role of women in the war effort a popular and heated topic of discussion, *Woman of the Year*'s sharp, witty battle-of-the-sexes screenplay (penned by Michael Kanin and Ring Lardner Jr.) was bound to be of interest. Lardner had observed firsthand the incendiary relationship between his famous sportswriter father and celebrated *Herald Tribune* newspaper columnist Dorothy Thompson.

Glamorous, high-profile foreign affairs columnist Tess Harding (Hepburn) and brash, down-to-earth sports reporter Sam Craig (Tracy) both work at the *New York Chronicle*. An avid and devoted sports fanatic, Sam becomes irate when he hears a radio address in which Tess audaciously declares that the game of baseball should be cancelled until World War II is over. Sam voices his displeasure in his weekly column, provoking an equally barbed response from Tess. The two go back and forth trading insults in print until their mutual editor, Clayton (Reginald Owen), brings them together in an effort to make peace. There is a powerful sensuality to the scene in which they first meet in Clayton's office. Sam walks through the vestibule and we see a medium shot of him opening Clayton's door. Suddenly he looks down. We cut to a pair of women's crossed legs: black high heels, knee-length skirt. Following his eye, the camera moves up the legs and torso to discover Tess, who returns his gaze. He moves to back out the way he came but Clayton urges him to come in. He tries to retreat. We cut to Tess's face as she gives him a once-over. As Clayton addresses Sam, and Sam approaches his desk, Tess slides up behind him, peering over his shoulder to try for a glimpse of the paper he's holding. As she leans over, her arm happens to touch his. He looks at her and hands her the paper.

The dynamics of their interaction suddenly undergo a radical change, as their mutual attraction becomes immediately apparent. In a scene that became an instant classic, Sam takes Tess to her first baseball game, where she quickly ingratiates herself with the fans in attendance by showing more passion for the game than he does. Tess shows up wearing a huge white flouncy hat, and the two are sitting in front of an avid fan who alternates between screaming at the umpire and shuffling to get a view of the field past the hat. Sam, meanwhile, gives a perfunctory—and totally incomprehensible—explanation of baseball to Tess. Time passes, shown with a field shot in which the scoreboard is superimposed. When we return to Sam and Tess, she has stopped paying attention to him and is screaming at the umpire along with her new friend behind. To the surprise and disquiet of their co-workers, Tess and Sam continue their courtship, the romance between these seeming opposites quickly deepening.

When they make the decision to wed, Sam finds his wish for a traditional, old-fashioned ceremony superseded by the demands of Tess's hectic schedule, which requires that the wedding take place right away. The struggle to balance a high-profile journalistic career with spousal responsibilities and domestic bliss proves incredibly taxing for Tess, and Sam grows more and more frustrated with her lack of commitment to their marriage. He ends up getting too drunk to write his column, and the sports-ignorant Tess is forced to write it for him (perhaps in a comedic echo of the scene from *Citizen Kane* where Kane finishes Jedediah Leland's pan of his wife's operatic debut, then fires him). The outcome is calamitous, since Tess is no better a sportswriter than she is a housewife. The film's irony reaches a peak when Tess learns that she has been voted "Woman of the Year," while mulling over whether to stay with her husband. But when her father remarries, Tess becomes deeply moved by the reading of the vows, ultimately returning to Sam with a new passion for married life.

Known for her mixture of compassion and egotism, the larger-than-life Hepburn bore a striking similarity to her character in *Woman of the Year*. She is also, arguably, the film's true auteur. Having obtained the rights to the story herself, she managed to convince MGM studio head Louis B. Mayer to purchase the script and give her final say over who would direct and co-star. She also demanded and received a $100,000 salary, along with a $10,000 commission fee for serving as script representative, $1,000 for moving expenses to Hollywood, and $100,000 for screenwriters Lardner and Kanin (Marill 63). Hepburn thought Tracy would be the perfect choice as her leading man, and for director she selected the proven and reliable George Stevens (*Annie Oakley* [1935], *Swing Time* [1936], *Gunga Din* [1939]), with whom she was rumored to be romantically involved, and who had previously directed her in *Alice Adams* (1935) and *Quality Street* (1937).

At her first face-to-face meeting with her co-star, Hepburn famously commented, "I'm afraid I'm a bit tall for Mr. Tracy," to which the film's producer, Joseph L. Mankiewicz replied, "Don't worry, he'll cut you down to size" (Marill 65). The screen's most famous romantic pairing was underway at last.

Much like that of *The Magnificent Ambersons*, the original ending of *Woman of the Year* was altered after a sneak preview garnered some less than thrilling evaluations from viewers. Anne Edwards discusses the reason for this change, in her biography of Hepburn:

> The original ending of the Lardner-Kanin script had Tess Harding take an honest interest in baseball (her husband's passion) and become more enthusiastic than he at the game, which implied not compromise but growth and love. But [producer Joseph L.] Mankiewicz and Stevens were concerned that "the average American housewife, seated next to her husband, staring for two hours at this paragon of beauty, intelligence, wit, accomplishment, and everything else, [could not] help but wonder if her husband [wasn't] comparing her very unfavorably with this goddess he sees on the screen." (92)

Together, Mankiewicz and Stevens decided that Tess must be given some comeuppance. As in *The Magnificent Ambersons* and *Yankee Doodle Dandy*, neither talent nor charisma are excuses for arrogance on the part of the protagonist; only here there is the added issue that the protagonist is a woman making serious waves in the workforce. Because Kanin and Lardner were unavailable, John Lee Mahin (who had previously done some uncredited writing on William Wellman's *A Star Is Born* [1937] and Victor Fleming's *The*

Wizard of Oz [1939]) was tapped to prepare a different finale in line with the new, male-chauvinistic specifications of the film's producer and director.

Hepburn herself expressed concern that her sophisticated, upwardly mobile female character would be too threatening for viewers (of both sexes), despite a brave new feminist-inclined world where more than 350,000 women were donning military uniforms and six million more had taken jobs in defense plants and offices as part of the war effort. She even helped come up with the film's new ending, in which Tess dons an apron in an effort to woo back her husband, revealing herself to be a total klutz in the kitchen in the process. Despite the complaints about its compromised ending, *Woman of the Year* proved to be a critical as well as commercial success.

One of Hollywood's best-loved melodramas, and quite possibly the ultimate "makeover" movie, Irving Rapper's *Now, Voyager* owes its enduring popularity to star power, unselfconscious emotional climaxes, and, perhaps most important, the pleasure viewers obtain watching Bette Davis transform herself from ugly duckling to beautiful swan in one of her very finest performances. The film's title was taken from Walt Whitman's famous 1892 poem "Leaves of Grass," specifically, the section entitled "The Unknown Want": "The untold want by life and land ne'er granted / Now, voyager sail thou forth to seek and find." Casey Robinson's screenplay was adapted from the novel by Olive Higgins Prouty (who also wrote the novel *Stella Dallas,* superbly filmed by King Vidor in 1937).

Now, Voyager tells the complex and deeply moving tale of spinster Charlotte Vale (Davis), the repressed, frumpy, overweight daughter of a tyrannical Boston matriarch, the socially prominent Mrs. Henry Windle Vale (Gladys Cooper). The sympathetic and cosmopolitan Dr. Jaquith (Claude Rains), introduced in the film as "the foremost psychiatrist in the whole country," liberates Charlotte by prescribing a stay at his respected sanitarium. Davis's sojourn with Jaquith is literally a smashing success: her cure is indicated by the doctor's dramatic breaking of her eyeglasses, signaling her social and spiritual rebirth (set to Max Steiner's lush, romantic score) as a beautiful, well-dressed, perfectly manicured, single (and therefore available) woman.

The confident, resplendent Charlotte celebrates her new image by embarking on a sea cruise, where she promptly falls in love with unhappily married architect Jerry Durrance (Paul Henreid, best known for his role as a husband with different sorts of marital problems in *Casablanca*). A shipboard romance ensues, with Charlotte discovering for the first time a sense of passion and self-knowledge that has previously been denied to her. Days and nights of stolen romance intensify their forbidden relationship as they

Paul Henreid lights up Bette Davis in *Now, Voyager* (Irving Rapper, Warner Bros.). Courtesy Jerry Ohlinger Archives.

head for Rio de Janeiro. Indeed, the romantic scene there in which, by moonlight on a balcony overlooking the city, Jerry casually places two cigarettes in his mouth, lights them both, and then passes one to Charlotte, is one of the most enduring images in the cinema.

Returning home from her trip, Charlotte stands up for the first time to her overbearing mother, but ultimately resigns herself to a boring future with a drab Boston millionaire, Elliot Livingston (John Loder). But eventually Charlotte realizes she will never really be happy with Elliot and breaks off the engagement, much to her mother's dismay. Her mother sees Charlotte's new independence as a definite threat to her authority. The two women quarrel, and Charlotte's mother, never a well woman, conveniently dies of a stroke. Charlotte suffers a relapse and is again admitted to Dr. Jaquith's sanitarium. Gradually, she realizes that she alone controls her will and pulls out of her depression. She also befriends another of Jaquith's patients, the young and withdrawn Tina Durrance (Janis Wilson), Jerry's neurotic daughter. Nursing Tina back to normal mental health, though with more tenderness and less cold professionalism than Jaquith had with her,

Charlotte finds a new sense of social responsibility and bonds with the child as a maternal figure. Tina's home life, it turns out, is as miserable as her father's; she tells Charlotte frankly, "My mother doesn't want me at home. That's why it's helping father for me to be here." Seeing herself in earlier times in the awkward young girl, Charlotte makes Tina's reclamation a personal quest.

When she is dismissed from the sanitarium, Charlotte takes Tina with her and throws a coming out party for the young girl, inviting Jerry and Dr. Jaquith as her guests. Both men are amazed at the transformation in Tina. Seeing that his daughter has blossomed under Charlotte's care, Jerry agrees to leave her with Charlotte, as "their child." Thus, at the film's end, Charlotte has inherited her mother's property, wealth, and social position, but she decides not to pursue anything more than a platonic relationship with Jerry. Charlotte and Jerry drift toward the window in the living room. Gazing out at the night sky, Charlotte utters the memorably mysterious line, "Oh Jerry, don't let's ask for the moon. We have the stars."

As a prototypical "woman's picture" offering war wives a couple of hours of tear-jerking diversion from the all-too-real anxieties at home, *Now, Voyager* manages to have its cake and eat it, too: even while affirming the virtues of marriage and motherhood, it makes a strong case for romance outside the constraints of the domestic sphere. It could be argued that, by giving Dr. Jaquith so much of the credit for Charlotte's transformation—not unlike the creepy Dr. Judd's short-lived psychiatric success with the neurotic Irena in *Cat People*—the film is guilty of reestablishing the primacy of the patriarchy, as a substitution for Charlotte's domineering mother. In fact, though, as Barbara Leaming argues, *Now, Voyager* "shows us that a woman is capable of changing the path she seems to be on; she can head in a different direction and perhaps find an entirely new existence. Sex and love are possible outside of marriage, and a fulfilling life can be made without a husband and children of her own" (140). The only requirements are that one must have financial resources of one's own; and that whatever one was to begin with, in the end one must become "beautiful."

■ Hoopla and Propaganda: *Pride of the Yankees* and *Mrs. Miniver*

Sam Wood's touching and entertaining sports biopic *The Pride of the Yankees* owes most of its success to Gary Cooper's standout performance as Lou "The Iron Horse" Gehrig, the New York Yankees' remarkable first baseman during the 1920s and 30s. Known for playing stoic cow-boys, Cooper proved ideal for the role of Gehrig in both looks and disposi-tion. Through skillful underplaying for the camera, Cooper manages to give life and realism to Gehrig's notoriously bland personality, portraying him as a humble everyman with superhuman baseball skills, a gentle smile, and a healthy dose of "aw-shucks" charm. The only problem was that Cooper was right-handed, while Gehrig was a lefty (film editor Danny Mandell, who received an Oscar for his work here, solved this dilemma by having Cooper bat right-handed, then run to third base instead of first; the scenes in ques-tion were flipped left-to-right during the editing stage, with sufficiently believable results).

After a childhood spent playing stickball in the streets and smashing windows with impressive shots, a young and prodigiously talented Gehrig enrolls at Columbia University. At first he prioritizes his engineering stud-ies over baseball, in an effort to fulfill the wishes of his anxious immigrant parents (known simply as Mom and Pop Gehrig in the film, and played respectively by Elsa Janssen and Ludwig Stössel). But Lou's skill as a ballplayer soon asserts its dominance, and the local press make bets on his future career in the majors. When his domineering mother falls ill, Lou takes the opportunity to sign a contract with the Yankees. After serving some time in the minor leagues, he is eventually called up to the big-league team, where he joins a squad already filled with baseball legends such as Babe Ruth, Bob Meusel, and Bill Dickey (all of whom play themselves in an inspired bit of literal all-star casting).

When veteran first baseman Wally Pipp (George McDonald) is injured, Gehrig finally gets his chance to play, thus initiating a then-record string of 2,130 consecutive games as a player in major league baseball. But consid-ering how often *The Pride of the Yankees* is mentioned as one of the best base-ball movies of all time, it is surprising how little screen time the film devotes to showcasing Gehrig's prowess on the diamond. Instead, we get an in-depth look at Lou's courtship with wife-to-be Eleanor Twitchell (Teresa Wright), their storybook romance and eventual marriage, the last six years of Gehrig's professional career, and his two years suffering from amy-otrophic lateral sclerosis (later known as "Lou Gehrig's Disease"). The scene showing Gehrig's final appearance at Yankee Stadium—and in baseball—is especially powerful. As he steps out to home plate from the dugout, leav-ing his wife behind, the soundtrack pumps out "Auld Lang Syne." As Gehrig is being presented with awards, a wide-angle lens is used which reveals substantial portions of the adoring crowd behind him (in shots notable for a distinctive vertical reach up to the third tier of seats). When he addresses the crowd, shot from below in normal angle, a strange echo is produced as his voice speaking at the microphone is reflected by his voice from a radio broadcast just off-synch. Babe Ruth is standing behind his shoulder. The magnification of Gehrig/Cooper as he speaks; the adulating hush of the crowd; the rehearsed quality of the staccato articulation of his voice; and the contrived imagery in his text all make this sequence somewhat similar, in its use of film for public relations purposes, to what could have been seen in *Triumph of the Will*. Finally, we grow to love Gehrig not because of his amazing baseball skills—though these are certainly admirable—but because he is such a good husband and upstanding individual, such a noble American especially under the worst personal duress. If his body has decayed, his mind and spirit are whole and staunch against the greater enemy. The game will go on—and we will be victorious. Gehrig, however, will not "cross the plate." As he returns to the dugout, the daylight cut by the roof of the dugout etches a perfect curtain line on his vanishing body.

The critical and commercial success of *The Pride of the Yankees* testifies to the importance of baseball for entertainment purposes and distracting minidrama in wartime America. It was the highest-grossing picture made by producer Samuel Goldwyn to that point and it received eleven Academy Award nominations, including Best Picture, Best Actor (Cooper), and Best Actress (Wright). Perhaps the fact that the film presents Gehrig as a person rather than a ballplayer is at the heart of its success; despite the baseball title, *The Pride of the Yankees* isn't really a sports film, but rather the saga of one man's fight against the trials and adversities of life. This was a theme that wartime audiences could easily relate to, with the uncertainty of daily existence a constant concern. Moreover, the decision to focus on Gehrig's personal life was wise from a strategic and public relations standpoint. Considering how many of the country's men were headed into various branches of the military, any movie primarily concerned with celebrating the comparative triviality of baseball as a national pastime for healthy young men would have been deemed inappropriate at best, if not utterly insensitive and indefensible.

William Wyler's *Mrs. Miniver* is an uplifting wartime drama that highlights the resiliency of the British people in the face of terror and adversity. At the center of the story is Kay Miniver (Greer Garson), a warm, resourceful middle-class housewife in the small town of Belham, who is faced with the challenge of keeping her family together at the start of World War II. Her oldest son, Vin (Richard Ney), enlists as a pilot and defends England in the Battle of Britain. Kay's husband, Clem (Walter Pidgeon), meanwhile, works with a civil defense unit, and assists in the evacuation at Dunkirk. Through love, intelligence, courage, and sheer force of will, Kay holds her family together, even as England threatens to collapse due to the powerful effects of a devastating war.

In one of the movie's most memorable scenes, Kay manages entirely on her own to capture a downed though still dangerous German flyer (Helmut Dantine) who dares to invade the domesticity of her kitchen. *Mrs. Miniver* thus depicts the home front as a battlefront, and the family unit as an institution worth defending. The importance of this message is twofold: not only would it encourage those staying at home during the war to become more alert, motivated, and proactive; it would remind those in combat that this fight would not be fought in the trenches alone, that they had better do their job abroad so they could get back home and take up arms with their wives and even their children if necessary.

During German bombing raids, the Minivers repair to their homemade bomb shelter and wait out the attack with a typically British stiff upper lip. But *Mrs. Miniver* is also at pains to show the personal losses suffered in war, most emphatically when Kay's innocent daughter-in-law, Carol (Teresa Wright), is killed in an air raid. Eventually the Miniver home itself is bombed, and the town church is reduced to rubble. But the people's spirit receives a lift when the vicar (Henry Wilcoxon) delivers a powerful speech and the annual flower show goes on. As the vicar notes: "This is not only a war of soldiers in uniform. It is a war of the people, of all the people, and it must be fought not only on the battlefield, but in the cities and in the villages, in the factories and on the farms, in the home, and in the heart of every man, woman, and child who loves freedom."

It has been claimed that *Mrs. Miniver*'s propaganda value for Britain was so great that it influenced America's decision to join the war. Public and political response to the film was indeed amazing, with no less an admirer than Winston Churchill (whose 1940 "We shall fight" speech is so clearly echoed by the vicar) claiming that it "was propaganda worth a hundred battleships" (Herman 235). Most impressively of all, at President Roosevelt's request, the vicar's speech from *Mrs. Miniver* was broadcast over the "Voice of America" throughout Europe, translated into French, German, and Italian, and air-dropped in leaflets over German-occupied territory by the millions (Herman 235–36). Wyler himself deeply believed in the film's message; and he left no doubt in an interview as to his own personal convictions about America's role in the war. "I was a warmonger," Wyler noted. "I was deeply concerned about Americans being isolationists. *Mrs. Miniver* obviously was a propaganda film" (Herman 234).

▪ Nazis Abroad and at Home:
Casablanca and *Saboteur*

Perhaps the most beloved movie of all time, Michael Curtiz's *Casablanca* offers viewers such timeless ingredients as romance, intrigue, lost love, mystery, and melodrama, all set against the backdrop of World War II. Max Steiner's mesmerizing musical score (and Herman Hupfeld's classic ballad "As Time Goes By") also played a major role in ensuring *Casablanca*'s success, as did the film's array of brilliant actors, including Humphrey Bogart, Ingrid Bergman, Claude Rains, Sydney Greenstreet, Peter Lorre, Paul Henreid, and Conrad Veidt.

Casablanca is portrayed as an exotic, multicultural locale in the North African portion of unoccupied France, where persecuted individuals desperately seek exit visas to escape from the Nazis. Thieves, ruffians, corrupt officials, and dubious fortune seekers all look to profit from the desperation of the refugees. Meanwhile, Victor Laszlo (Henreid), the leader of an underground resistance movement who has been chased across Europe by the Nazis, wants to buy two letters of transit on the black market for his wife and himself. These valuable letters have fallen into the hands of exiled American Rick Blaine (Bogart), a former freedom fighter, now a cynical self-preservationist, who runs the most popular nightclub in town. To Rick's great surprise, Laszlo's wife is none other than his own one-time love, Ilsa (Bergman), who ran out on him in Paris when the Nazis took over. Eventually Rick realizes what happened to Ilsa in France and why, and a great sacrifice (albeit one that opens up room for a new and "beautiful friendship") is made by Bogart's character in the end.

The film actually opened on Thanksgiving Day, a mere three weeks after the Allies had landed at Casablanca. Two months later, the leaders of the free world met in the same city for the so-called "Casablanca Conference," giving Curtiz's picture more free publicity. Much of the film's greatness comes from its willingness to eschew closure: just as it was made before the war was over, it dares to leave its characters literally up in the air or out in the desert and its audiences, then and now, to wonder what happened to these people during the next few turbulent years.

Among its many other accomplishments, *Casablanca* served to propel Bogart's star to new heights, adding a romantic dimension to his world-weary persona. It was the breakthrough role Bogart had been waiting for, and it is worth noting that the film was never projected to be a major success, but merely a typical "A" release of the period that transformed itself into something special once the cameras began to roll. *Casablanca* also gave

Bergman a tragic element to go with her healthy radiance, making her seem complex and emotionally fragile. The bleakest, most depraved wartime contingencies and sensibilities are here rendered palatably romantic, even enchanting, while at the same time maintaining their ability to inform audiences about the logic and merit of the struggle against Nazism. In a particularly stirring scene, German officers spending the evening at Rick's café must vocally battle against French loyalists in a choral war: "La Marseillaise" triumphs, spectacularly.

Casablanca caters now as it did then to a nostalgia for the romanticized, vanished world that hovered between the two great wars, a cafe culture brought to its knees by fascism, populated by civilized, urbane (if somewhat shady) men and women clinging to an era that no longer existed. But all of this is background. What was stunning for viewers at the time—and remains stunning today—is the crispness and political punchiness of Howard Koch's dialogue and that of Julius J. and Philip G. Epstein; the scathing character work by Claude Rains, Conrad Veidt, Peter Lorre, and S. Z. Sakall; the suaveness of Paul Henreid as Laszlo; and the galvanizing romantic restraint of a beleaguered Humphrey Bogart confronted with a vulnerable and dignified Ingrid Bergman. The final sequence at the Casablanca airport, as Major Strasser (Veidt) fails to prevent Rick from organizing the Laszlos' flight from the city, has a compelling, even breathtaking rhythm and is visualized in shots where the keylit principal characters, especially Bogart and Bergman, shine like diamonds in the mist. At the same time as we are caught in the aesthetic flow of the sequence, the film tells us effectively that personal considerations can be—and ought to be—sacrificed in the name of the greater human cause, in this case anti-Nazism. Individualism sacrificed for wartime victory is individualism redeemed and purified in the fire of combat. Max Steiner's symphonic score drives us to realize, however, that this sacrifice of individualism is a feelingful one, associated with hesitation, memory, absence, loss, and despair as well as the noble fight for freedom. The film is also a powerful allegory of the transmutation of isolationism into engagement, a vital message now that America was in the fray.

Alfred Hitchcock's *Saboteur* is one of the darkest wartime films from that most urbane of directors. The project originally started under the aegis of producer David O. Selznick, but Selznick and Hitchcock had clashed over editorial control. Still under contract to Selznick, Hitchcock worked with John Houseman and Joan Harrison, along with Peter Viertel and Dorothy Parker, to create the script. The plot is simple, yet another variation on Hitchcock's "wrong man" theme that permeated so many of the director's

Robert Cummings (center) and Norman Lloyd (r.) inside Lady Liberty's torch in *Saboteur* (Alfred Hitchcock, Frank Lloyd Productions/Universal). Courtesy Jerry Ohlinger Archives.

films. Barry Kane (Robert Cummings), a patriotic worker in a defense plant, is framed for arson by the aptly named Frank Fry (Norman Lloyd, a long-time Hitchcock associate), a Nazi saboteur. Realizing that no one will believe his innocence, Kane goes on a personal manhunt to prove it, falling in love with Patricia Martin (Priscilla Lane) in the process. After a nationwide search, Kane finally locates the mastermind behind the spy ring, Charles Tobin (Otto Kruger), an outwardly respectable and prominent social figure. Through a series of typically Hitchcockian twists, Kane manages to unmask Tobin and trails Fry to the Statue of Liberty, where Fry is about to engage in another act of sabotage. Kane chases Fry up the stairs of the statue, and after a protracted battle around the torch, Fry falls to his death in the film's most famous set piece, "the swooning, vertiginous fall of the saboteur from Miss Liberty's hand in the film's final moment" (Spoto 252).

Many observers consider *Saboteur* to be second-rate Hitchcock, and in many ways, they are right. Universal exercised great control over the casting, and Cummings, Lane, and Kruger are all peculiarly one dimensional, lacking any real personality or "eccentricities" to bring real presence to their roles (Spoto 252). Hitchcock resisted their casting, but in the end was forced to use all three actors, and set about making the film in his usual efficient, entirely preplanned fashion, using detailed storyboards to block out each scene in detail. When the film opened, Universal was surprised to discover that *Saboteur* was a genuine box office hit, although it garnered no awards or nominations.

There was also one official government protest associated with *Saboteur*'s production. To demonstrate the efficiency and danger of the Nazi threat, Hitchcock interpolated actual newsreel shots of the capsized S.S. *Normandie*, a former French ocean liner that had been requisitioned by the U.S. government and renamed the U.S.S. *Lafayette*, before it was destroyed in a "suspicious fire at a Manhattan pier" (Spoto 253), making the fire seem like an act of sabotage through the power of montage. As Hitchcock later explained, "I cut to the hulk of the *Normandie*. I cut back to a close-up of the saboteur, who, after staring at the wreck, turns around with a slightly smug smile on his face. The Navy raised hell with Universal about these shots because I implied that the *Normandie* had been sabotaged, which was a reflection on their lack of vigilance in guarding it" (qtd. in Spoto 253). But the sequence stayed in, despite the objections of the Navy, and Hitchcock's wartime saga of betrayal and sabotage made it to the screen intact, still one of the director's most popular films, due in large part to its riveting final sequence.

■ ■ ■

The films of the year depict a nation newly at war, a nation just recently awakened from the slumber of isolationism, eager to take on the task at hand and conquer the Axis powers of Germany, Italy, and Japan. Ahead lay years of struggle. The Nazis were on the march in Europe, absorbing whole countries as part of their blitzkreig, or "lightning war," and an Allied victory seemed anything but certain. Spies and fifth columnists were everywhere, it seemed, and the attack on Pearl Harbor made it painfully clear that American soil was not inviolate. Now, with the attacks on the World Trade Center and the Pentagon on 11 September 2001, we have some inkling of what it must have been like for American citizens of the 1940s to wake up on Sunday morning and discover that they were vulnerable, and that the entry of the United States into World War II was now inevitable. The future of the free world was in peril, and the outcome was far from assured. What would 1943 bring? Americans wondered and waited, flocking to movie theaters for escapism, news, and the heroic images of wartime propaganda, in the hopes that the years to come would bring a brighter future for all the citizens of the world.

1943

▣▢▢▢▢▢▢▢▢▢

Movies and National Identity

CATHERINE L. PRESTON

The war effort was now in full swing, both in Europe and the Pacific. Dwight D. Eisenhower was chosen to command the Allied forces in Europe. Race riots erupted in Detroit and Harlem, and the Congress for Racial Equality (CORE) was founded, signaling that African Americans were no longer going to settle for second-class status in American society. Jean-Paul Sartre published *Being and Nothingness,* and existentialism entered the language of critical discourse. Bop jazz spread from New York and Los Angeles throughout the United States, and brought with it the zoot suit and jitterbugging. Franklin Delano Roosevelt and Winston Churchill met in Casablanca, declaring that "unconditional surrender" would be the only terms the Allies would accept; in the meantime, American troops were defeated by the Japanese at Guadalcanal. The Nazis massacred thousands of Jews in the Warsaw ghetto uprising, and after a bloody battle, the Marines captured Tarawa from the Japanese. Hit records included "You'll Never Know" by Dick Haymes and "All or Nothing at All" by Frank Sinatra. The federal government ordered a minimum forty-eight-hour work week in major defense plants. Top-rated radio programs included "Jack Armstrong, All-American Boy," "Milton Berle," and the adventure serial "Terry and the Pirates."

The country had been at war little over a year, and films were still marked by innovative efforts in almost every genre. Studios sought to respond to the government's need for ideological mobilization while simultaneously producing popular quality entertainment. Yet most producers continued to follow the philosophy that "Hollywood should avoid controversy and keep people's minds off their troubles" (Neve 74). The western genre was relegated to B-picture studios, and the social problem film that had often been a critique of societal structures or norms morphed into the more blatant propaganda movie, an affirmation of foundational American values. Such films were not confined to one genre, and they cannot now be considered a genre in any stylistic or narrative sense. The films of this year constructed an ideological space in which viewers could recognize the most commonplace, general, and thus in many ways unquestioned aspects of American identity. Hollywood struggled to construct a national cinema for a country at war that was built on tried and true generic formulas such as the war film, the romantic drama, the musical, and the thriller. But these movies often contained a twist, a narrative or stylistic innovation that made the viewer reflect on current events, on what it meant to be an American—soldier or civilian—at war.

Hollywood and National Identity

Although Hollywood does not consider itself, nor is it usually examined as, a national cinema, "in its range and coverage of the field of national imaginings, the Hollywood cinema is in many ways an unparalleled expression of national culture, one that has molded the self-image of the nation in pervasive and explicit ways" (Burgoyne 6). While no single film or genre can be said to represent the entirety of national life, the genre system as a whole visualizes the national self-consciousness. In other words, those mythic beliefs in a shared foundational origin, a common status, and similar aspirations become the cinematic narratives that constitute a "vast *speculum mundi* that defines what passes as social reality in the United States" (Burgoyne 124). This national self-consciousness had diminished through the 1930s, as classes were pitted against each other, and the notion of "the people" was constructed as separate from the nation's corporations. The idea that Americans shared common origins, status, location, and aspirations thus needed to be reaffirmed (May, *Big Tomorrow* 140).

Benedict Anderson argues that a definition of nationalism should not start with commonly held political ideologies but with the cultural systems that precede them. Political ideologies grow out of, and are constructed in opposition to, reigning representational systems (19). In other words, the idea of the nation can be usefully understood as a symbolic construct, an "imagined community," as a system of cultural signification built up through the nations' representations of itself. Surely the most visible and vivid, if imagined, community during the Second World War was the cinematic one Hollywood created and invited the American public to inhabit.

Whereas each individual film creates an environment "where historically specific constellations of power are made visible" (Shohat and Stam 368), multiple films produced within a discrete space and time also provide a powerful environment in which a particular national identity can be discerned. Hollywood films typically encouraged identification with individuals by focusing on the psychological aspects of one character's story, but they shifted during the war to encourage identification with government, the military, and business institutions (May, *Big Tomorrow* 156). By visualizing the ideals of American democracy such as freedom of religion, racial tolerance, gender equality, and a classless society, and by evoking American symbols such as the flag and the western frontier, films represented these concerns as shared experiences and common aspirations. In addition, Hollywood was influenced by the proliferation of newsreels and documentaries as well as by the intervention of the Office of War Information (OWI). Studios became more involved in documentary production and moved simultaneously to increase the degree of realism evident in the fictional narratives and the representation of characters. They sought to create narratives that were directly related to the experiences of Americans during this time (Cook, *History* 440).

Several films served to illuminate and define the American "imagined community": the realistic combat film, *Guadalcanal Diary;* the combat film with a more personal flavor, *Destination Tokyo;* the homefront war film, *Tender Comrade;* the morale-boosting service musical, *This Is the Army;* and a film to appease the black population, *Stormy Weather.* The vast majority of fiction films made by Hollywood fell into these categories. Another film provided a dark contrast. It did not focus on or depict the war, but told the story of an American small town in the grip of an evil murderous insanity. It is Alfred Hitchcock's *Shadow of a Doubt,* a film that contributes to a quite different sense of wartime national identity.

Hollywood and the Office of War Information

The second year of American involvement in the war was marked by Hollywood's struggle to find a way to contribute to the war effort through topical films without suffering at the box office. Theater owners were communicating to industry producers that they were "finding audiences becoming increasingly apathetic to war films" (Pryor "News"). Most critics shared the sentiment of Bosley Crowther at the *New York Times,* who wrote of the relative and uncommon ease with which the New York Film Critics' Awards were decided: "It may be that most of the critics felt such vaster issues are being fought today that their own tiny disputation over pictures would be childish and vain. And it may also be that everybody was so lukewarm toward most of last year's fare that mental and physical violence seemed a foolish and useless waste. In this voter's private reflections, the latter was frankly the case" ("All for the Best"). Historians have credited the close relationship between Hollywood and the OWI with responsibility for the mediocre films of the year.

Elmer Davis, head of the OWI, said, "The easiest way to inject a propaganda idea into most people's minds is to let it go in through the medium of an entertainment picture when they do not realize that they are being propagandized" (qtd. in Koppes and Black, "What to Show" 157–58). Hollywood studios were offering support to the government in whatever way it thought best, in effect opening the door for the OWI's Bureau of Motion Pictures (BMP) to influence the production of fiction films. Early on, OWI advisers argued constantly with Hollywood's own Production Code Administration (PCA) about the onscreen depiction of various war-related issues and events (Schatz, *Boom*, 3). But after the spring, when Congress cut the budget of the OWI's domestic branch and the overseas branch became, in effect, the sole censoring agency, Hollywood sought to turn the situation to its advantage. Ulric Bell was head of the BMP Overseas Branch, and he convinced the Office of Censorship to follow his lead regarding film production questions. As Allied forces gained the advantage in Europe, Hollywood became increasingly willing to allow the BMP to influence its films. "The standard package the liberators handed out included food, DDT louse killer, and OWI-approved movies" (Koppes, "Regulating" 272).

As a New Deal agency the OWI hoped to use film to improve race relations, among other things. This effort failed, but the representation of gender won a short-lived victory because most of the script reviewers were women. There began to be an improvement in the number and quality of representations of women. As mentioned, OWI oversight of Hollywood also led to greater realism in war films. In fact, this was the result of several influences: the use of government-sanctioned newsreels and documentaries to educate the public about the war; the relationship with the government in terms of availability of documentary footage; the oversight of scripts by the OWI, whose perception was that people wanted greater realism; the assignment of military advisors to oversee production of combat films; and the unintentional effects of a shortage of actors in Hollywood. A newspaper critic remarked that the "eminent illusion of reality achieved in two current war films, *Sahara* and *Guadalcanal Diary*, is attributable largely to fresh faces in their casts" (Crowther "On Soldiers in Films"). "By the fall of 1943 Bell had convinced every studio except Paramount to let OWI read all their scripts instead of certain selected ones, and even Paramount agreed to discuss its scripts with OWI in general terms" (Koppes and Black, "What to Show" 166).

Guadalcanal Diary

The most compelling impetus for a nationalistic identification with war films, at least for homefront audiences, was the heightened realism coupled with the awareness that screen soldiers' real counterparts were overseas fighting and dying as the film played. War films are a premiere genre for evoking a national identity. Both representations of war combat and the western frontier are foundational narratives in American history. Mythical and iconic, they embody the meaning of America as a sovereign country fighting for beliefs and values on which the country is based (Burgoyne 7). *Guadalcanal Diary*, released on 27 October, focuses on the marines who fought on Guadalcanal and is based on the best-selling book of the same name by journalist Richard Tregaskis, published in 1942.

Guadalcanal Diary, an early example of the period's realism, actually shows less combat and more workaday details of military operations than one might expect. When Hollywood approached the U.S. Marine Corps for help in the making of the film, the Corps required a rewrite "along more accurate lines. Now the film will follow the book faithfully, departing from it only by centering the story around a single unit of marines instead of treating the entire action of the campaign" (Stanley "Hollywood Bulletins").

Guadalcanal Diary is structured largely through synecdoche, in which the one unit comes to stand for the entire campaign. As the film progresses, the work of the one unit comes to stand for the quotidian work of all soldiers. This mechanism allows the viewers knowledge of the fighting the war entails, through the visualization of a representative account. Using voiceover narration the "journalist" guides the viewer through the daily activities of one marine unit involved in the Guadalcanal battle, from their arrival in August to their departure in mid-December as they are relieved by fresh troops. The entire narrative and all the action of the film focus on the effort to capture the island from the Japanese.

Representation of the practice of religion was common in combat films and typically showed Christianity to suit all options. Freedom of religious expression, one of the four basic freedoms assured by the Constitution, was an economic device that could be used not only to show solidarity among the soldiers and create unity for audiences back home but also to distinguish the rightness of the American mission from the godlessness of the Axis powers. As *Guadalcanal Diary* begins, it is Sunday, and some of the soldiers are at the Christian church service on the deck of their destroyer. As the camera pans across the faces of the soldiers, we hear and see them singing a hymn. The camera stops on a couple of men. One remarks to the other, "Hey Sammy, your voice is pretty good." Sammy responds, "Why not? My father was a cantor in the synagogue." Two issues are implied in this Jewish soldier's response. First, although the men come from different faiths they can all worship together as Americans. Second, like the son of the cantor in *The Jazz Singer* (1927), there is a reassuring assumption that assimilation makes secular Americans.

Later, as the men sweat in their foxholes through a night of bombing, one working-class soldier says a simple prayer: "I'm no hero. I'm just a guy. I came out here because somebody had to do it. I don't want medals. I just wanna go home. I can't tell those bombs to hit somewhere else. It's up to someone bigger than me. What I mean is I guess it's up to God . . . I'm not going to apologize for all the things I've done, but if we get it, I hope He sees we've done the best we could, and lets it go at that." It was possibly the most secular prayer uttered onscreen during the war, and served the purpose of forging identification with this grunt in a foxhole as representative of American religious expression.

The trend toward encouraging identification with institutions rather than one's religion, race, class, or ethnicity served to create an idea of a national body to which many people could relate. One way this national body was created was through war films' intentional inclusion of a recognizable multiethnic, multiracial cast of instantly readable characters, so that the cliché platoon included a farm boy from the Midwest, a Jew from Brooklyn, a youngster trying to grow a beard, and a Hispanic; rarely, there was also a black soldier.

As film historians have commented, Hollywood and the OWI wanted to create the image of an inclusive national community (Doherty 5). But now the heightened tensions brought on by the Sleepy Lagoon Murder Trial and the Zoot Suit Riots gave Hollywood more cause to append the Hispanic rather than the black body to the national corpus. The Sleepy Lagoon Murder Trial was viewed at the time by many of all races as a travesty of justice. The body of a young Mexican American man had been found near Sleepy Lagoon, in southeast Los Angeles, the previous August, and 300 Mexican American youths had been arrested and 12 of them charged and eventually convicted of the murder in a corrupt trial with judge and prosecutors routinely disregarding the defendants' civil rights. In June, a group of 11 sailors on shore leave maintained that they were attacked by Mexican American pachucos (gang members). Over 200 uniformed sailors spread through the city attacking and stripping any "zoot suiter" (a popular clothing style worn predominantly by Mexican Americans but also by black men, made up of baggy pants narrow at the ankle, a short tie, a button-up shirt, and a knee-length coat, narrow at the hip and very wide at the shoulder). For the following five nights gangs of sailors roamed the city streets attacking "zoot suiters," accompanied by the police who arrested over 600 victims, while the media claimed the sailors to be heroes and declared a "Mexican Crime Wave." After five days, the military moved in and restored order, declaring the city off-limits to sailors. Eventually the murder convictions in the Sleepy Lagoon case were over-turned and the defendants released from prison.

In the opening scenes of *Guadalcanal Diary*, this intermingling of race and class is clearly present, as visually presented in the way in which the soldiers are arranged on deck. They lie on each other's chests and legs; some sleep, others talk. The impression is that the ship is overly crowded, but it appears that the soldiers are quite comfortable to take their leisure in such close confines. There is physical intimacy in this scene, as Richard Jaeckel (one of the "fresh faces") and Hispanic soldier Anthony Quinn (who also played a Hispanic in *The Ox-Bow Incident*) lean against each other, Quinn's head on Jaeckel's chest. Through the often humorous dialogue, some men admit their fear, while others boast of their desire for battle. They dance together to the latest popular tunes, and there is a sensitivity not found in previous war films. "There is no doubt that a certain love is occurring, a love that is no less stirring for not being sexual" (Plunkett). Scenes such as these, including later sequences in which men cry over the loss of their friends, promote a sense of interrelation for audiences both at home and overseas. The lone black soldier appears during the boat journey to the island, and then is not seen again. He is in the Navy, not part of the Marine unit going to Guadalcanal, and is called on deck to identify the American ships on the horizon for the "landlubber marines" (Doherty 218).

The sacredness with which the American body was regarded is evident in a controversy that erupted over one scene from this film. After a battle between a small unit of the Marine battalion and Japanese soldiers on the other side of the island, all but one soldier in the unit are killed. The sur-viving soldier (Quinn) retreats into the ocean and swims for his life. He looks back over his shoulder from a distance and sees Japanese soldiers attacking the dead American soldiers with bayonets. This scene prompted the OWI to call for a ban on showing the desecration of dead Americans, maintaining that if wide publicity was given to such atrocities the Japanese would be encouraged to continue to mistreat prisoners of war and the dead. Several critics saw this as a "tightening of Federal censorship of the motion picture industry," coming as it did shortly after a governmental warning that films treating the current juvenile delinquency problem would not be regarded as suitable for exhibition outside the country (Stanley "Don't Show It").

Both *Guadalcanal Diary* and *Destination Tokyo* use the cowboy song "Home on the Range" as a trope of national identity. The song is played on a harmonica by one soldier as others sit around writing letters home on the eve of a big battle. The use of this tune evokes a sense of the safety and security of home, and simultaneously creates a similarity between the winning of the West (or "Manifest Destiny") and World War II. It also brings to mind the American values of freedom symbolized by the frontier, and in that context offers these values as justification for war.

Finally, a sense of nationalism is evoked through the use of symbols, the flag being the most obvious. After landing on Guadalcanal and arriving at an abandoned Japanese camp, the soldiers swarm over the airfield accompanied by dramatic extradiegetic music on the soundtrack. An officer produces an American flag that appears to be about eight by ten inches, saying that a lieutenant who had a heart attack carried the flag through China and the Philippines, and it was his wish to see it fly at Guadalcanal. The officer orders two soldiers to run it up the flagpole. The soldiers lower a normal size Japanese flag and run the tiny Stars and Stripes up to the top. It is a strange moment, fraught with irony, because as the flag ascends it becomes smaller and smaller. Simultaneously, the camera descends into a foxhole and shoots up at the flag from the ground. The effect is to make this symbol of the armed forces appear impotent, compared to the monumental task before them. However, given that the audience knew the outcome of the battle, this scene can perhaps be seen as truly ironic; the tiny flag becomes a symbol of the power and righteousness of the United States, representing an immense and ultimately successful mission.

Destination Tokyo

Destination Tokyo, released on 31 December, was a box office hit and exhibited extensively overseas during and after the war. The narrative follows the U.S.S. *Copperfin*, a submarine commanded by Captain Cassidy (Cary Grant). He is given top secret orders, to be opened only when his vessel is safely at sea, that require him to sneak into Tokyo Bay and land a few men (including an intelligence specialist) who can report on the locations of munitions factories, in order to maximize the damage done by the first Allied bombing raid on the capital city, and then return to base. Several seemingly unplanned events happen along the way, such as the knifing of one of the torpedo men (Mike [Tom Tully]) by a Japanese soldier he is trying to save, an emergency appendectomy performed by a pharmacy mate, the sinking of a destroyer by the sub, and revelations about the crew's personal attitudes toward the Japanese. *Destination Tokyo* fulfills the requirements of the evolving genre. It is an action adventure film that also seeks to instruct American audiences on how to think about the Japanese people and their culture.

Religious expression and prayer are highlighted here as they were in *Guadalcanal Diary*. The normative religious institution is Christian and there is a Christian burial at sea for the torpedo man who was knifed by the Japanese pilot. But more significantly, there is a crew member who goes through a spiritual transformation from being an atheist to believing in the power of prayer. The representation of this transformation was useful within the bounds of the official line during the war, highlighting both the need for precision teamwork and the disavowing of difference in order to present a unified front. A similar transformation occurs in relation to another normative institution: marriage. One of the crew members, Wolf (John Garfield), so called because he is always boasting about women he has had, says marriage is not something he is interested in, but changes his mind after listening to a record sent by the dead torpedo man's wife. We see Wolf sit and listen to the woman speaking; he stares straight ahead, as if imagining what it would be like for someone to be waiting for him to come home. This focus on marriage and family also occurs in the other films I discuss here, especially *This Is the Army, Tender Comrade,* and *Shadow of a Doubt.*

The act of eating was an especially sensitive topic during the war because of rationing. Food was used as a symbol of both physical and emotional nourishment and aggression toward the enemy. *Destination Tokyo* provides good examples of both these functions. During preparations for the submarine's departure from San Francisco Bay on Christmas Eve, the cook reassures the captain that they have plenty of hot sauce on board. The captain asks if they have enough steaks to go with the hot sauce. The cook responds cheerfully, "Yes, sir!" On Christmas day, the cook fixes a huge meal for the crew. The ship's menu scrolls slowly up the screen, giving the audience plenty of time to read and remember their own Christmas dinners, just a week earlier than the film's official release. Many of these home-cooked meals would not have been so lavish. The display and discussion of food reassures the audience that the servicemen are in good care.

In another scene two soldiers talk about eating the enemy. They are fishing off the side of the sub. One fantasizes about catching a big fish with a "Jap" in it. "Fried Jap in Tartar Sauce," he muses, while the other soldier mumbles that he would prefer his "boiled in oil." The national body is nourished through this metaphor symbolically representing victory. But the OWI was concerned about growing complaints that the Japanese people were demonized in films and other popular representations. Thus, the OWI's "Manual for the Motion Picture Industry" advised producers to present an image of the Japanese people as victims of their culture and their leaders. After Mike is knifed by a Japanese soldier, dies, and is buried at sea, the captain consoles the men by telling them that he was a great father, that he bought roller skates for his five-year-old son. Promoting American consumerism as a cure for Japanese aggression, the captain tells the men Mike died because the Japanese give their sons daggers: "That's just what he died for, roller skates, including some for the next generation of Japanese kids." The audience is encouraged to see the Japanese as misguided individuals redeemable through a shift to American goods, rather than evil savages as they were portrayed in some media.

Documentary conventions were becoming increasingly familiar in war films, and *Destination Tokyo* begins and ends with them. In the first scene, voiceover narration explains that the submarine's secret mission to bomb Tokyo Bay is being planned behind closed doors in Washington, D.C. The camera, placed outside the window of the meeting room, shows a group of generals huddled over the plans. When one general hands the plans to a subordinate, the camera enters the room through the window and follows the soldier as he exits the door, walks down a hallway, and delivers the plans to the secret coding room. The camera goes where the civilian viewer cannot go—into the coding room guarded by rifle-carrying soldiers—thus making the viewer privy to secret military operations. As the camera focuses in close-up letter by letter, the operator types into the coding machine that the *Copperfin* is "ordered to sea with a full allowance of torpedoes." The camera zooms in on that sentence, highlighting its import to the audience.

A straight cut shows a stationary medium shot of a moving train. In a visual exclamation point, the boxcars pass rapidly and then suddenly the camera pans to follow the label "Explosives" on one of the cars. In the next combination of long and medium shots the torpedoes are delivered to the *Copperfin* under cover of darkness. We watch as they are moved by crane from boxcar to sub and then a close-up shows the crew below decks securing them in the ship. The effect of the movement from shot to shot and the continuous movement of the torpedoes within the shots is to indicate a highly orchestrated activity. The viewer is impressed with the finely tuned and fully integrated military operation, in which home-front industrial production is visibly linked and contributing to military readiness.

As in *Guadalcanal Diary,* the audience is prompted to make associations between culture and historical memory and the current conflict. As Captain Cassidy opens the secret orders in the solitude of his cabin, we hear an orchestrated version of "Home on the Range." That this is set up earlier in the film by a soldier thanking the captain for the recently installed sound system allows the music to emanate naturally from the space of the story, rather than being imposed through an extradiegetic soundtrack. By late in the year, Hollywood was sensitized to criticism of heavy-handed propagandizing in previous films. Similar to the scene in *Guadalcanal Diary* in which "Home on the Range" figures into a quiet moment of reverie on the eve of battle, the song speaks to a core national ideology about the peace and freedom of open spaces, where one can believe and do as one pleases. Use of the song in these two scenes is thus a moment of deep cultural resonance for the audience, and in *Destination Tokyo* a space is created in which the submarine, at "home on the range," stands metonymically for the values and belief system put in jeopardy by the Axis aggression. Another scene that cues cultural memory occurs when the soldiers who have been put ashore climb up the hill overlooking the bay. One soldier says to the other, "You know, we're kinda like the pilgrims on Plymouth Rock." It's a quaint remark from a working-class man struggling to articulate the meaning of his labor to himself. Nevertheless, it creates a sense of Manifest Destiny similar to that original landing, and provides a sense of national serendipity between past and present events.

There is considerable secret information that is not Cassidy's to divulge, and there are pivotal actions that he does not accomplish. He repeatedly relies on the expertise of other crew members for success in the mission. *Destination Tokyo* is not alone in this filmic convention. As mentioned earlier, even though this goes against the grain of the classical Hollywood star-driven narrative, most wartime films, including those not specifically about the war, highlighted the teamwork involved in getting the job done. Brian Neve writes, "Radical writers played a significant role in development of the wartime genres that emerged, in part in response to the encouragement of the OWI. Employed for their political expertise, these writers (many of whom were blacklisted after the war) contributed to the shift of emphasis that such films exhibited, from the individual hero towards the collective effort and teamwork needed for victory" (77).

This Is the Army

A film that carried the "collective effort and teamwork needed for victory" to the allegorical extreme was *This Is the Army*, released at the end of July, based on the successful stage show written by Irving Berlin. The stage version opened the previous summer, designed as a benefit for the Army Relief Fund. Warner Bros. acquired the rights to Berlin's musical for $250,000, and asked for only 50 percent of the profits after production costs had been covered. Soon after, the studio decided to donate all profits to the Relief Fund, while producer Hal Wallis, director Michael Curtiz, and several actors donated their services to the project.

The film version of *This Is the Army* has all the original songs of the stage show, with a thin narrative veneer centering on a group of fathers who performed in a similar show in World War I. When their sons go off to World War II, they decide to produce another stage show, which becomes *This Is the Army*. There is also a romantic subplot between Lieutenant Ronald Reagan and Joan Leslie, in which Leslie periodically tries to get Reagan to marry her. Over 300 soldiers, most of them carried over from the stage show, and a large number of recognizable actors, such as Reagan and George Murphy, performed in the film. Many of the songs featured lavish musical numbers, with hundreds of soldiers singing and moving in synchronized motion around the stage.

The musical numbers include songs about new inductees arriving at boot camp, not being able to sleep on combat duty, and missing women's company. There are also vaudeville numbers about bumbling, awkward privates on KP duty who nonetheless command respect because they are soldiers fighting for their country, as well as gymnastic acts of strength and balance. And there is a number performed by a group of black soldiers called "What the Well Dressed Man in Harlem Will Wear," featuring boxer Joe Louis. The opening night at the Hollywood Theater featured a street display of anti-aircraft guns, camouflage units, jeeps, trucks, and 400 marching soldiers. In addition, there were several fundraising dinners organized by various social groups leading up to opening night. Thus, as a benefit for the Relief Fund, it was also an opportunity for patriotic display on a level not previously seen in conjunction with movies, and valorized the cinema as an essential element in the war effort.

Obviously, the songs are a major aspect of the patriotism and national identity invoked throughout the film, in which the connection is continuously made between duty to one's country and duty to oneself. In fact, visually and aurally, the boundaries between nation and self, the United States and the world, are dropped. In a representation of the beginning of the war, a graphic map of Poland burns up from center to edges indicating it has fallen to the Nazis. The next scene is Kate Smith singing "God Bless America," thus forging an association between Poland and American involvement. Following this scene there is documentary footage of the bombing of Pearl Harbor, again encouraging the connection between this fictional representation of war and reality. *This Is the Army*, like so many combat films, represents everyone as being on the same patriotic page. As in *Guadalcanal Diary*, *This Is the Army* assumes that marriage is the inevitable destiny of men and women. Joan Leslie finally tells Ronald Reagan in no uncertain terms that his refusal to get married before he goes to war means he thinks America has already lost the war. Somehow, this argument convinces Reagan, and the couple are wed just before the spectacular finale.

The American flag makes several appearances throughout the film, in honor guards that open and close the show. It is also featured in the vaudeville skit featuring the bumbling private, as an officer reprimands him for being out of uniform and smoking. The private remains silent while the officer yells. Toward the end of the dressing down, the officer says, "How can you command the respect and attention of another soldier?" and the private magically makes several scarves become the Stars and Stripes through sleight of hand. Now the officer, caught off guard, abruptly stops yelling and comes to attention saluting the flag, while the onscreen audience rises to its feet in thunderous applause.

Although black soldiers are included in one performance, the stage is segregated in keeping with the reality of the military situation. The black soldiers perform their own number, leave the stage, and do not appear again. In this number the military uniform is extolled as the most appropriate form of dress for black men in Harlem. Behind the singers and dancers is a huge painted backdrop of three men in zoot suits. The painting is a garish caricature in which the figures look more like white men in blackface than African Americans. *This Is the Army* was released not two months after the Zoot Suit riots occurred in Los Angeles, and the mise-en-scène and performance offer a conflicted image of the black man, simultaneously patriot and threat. Although that event primarily involved the Hispanic population, black men also wore zoot suits and had been victims of the white sailors' attacks.

The grand finale of *This Is the Army*, with all 300 soldiers on stage, is a call to make this the last war by routing the enemy abroad and at home. To roars of approval, the soldiers sing that "This time we will all make certain/ This time is the last time./ This time we won't say 'curtain'/ until we ring it down IN OUR OWN HOME TOWN." Behind the soldiers, the curtain rises on a huge granite-like sculpted image of Uncle Sam, with his sleeves rolled up and an eagle on his shoulder. The audience erupts in applause, the music reaches a moving conclusion, and the film ends.

This upbeat war-related musical was just the kind of film that the nation's theater owners were continually demanding (Schatz, *Boom* 3). They wanted to support the war efforts, but worried that the depressing and seemingly endless fare of both fictional and documentary combat films combined with daily news reports from the front would drive people to other forms of entertainment. And the theater owners knew their audiences: *This Is the Army* was the biggest box office hit of the year, making $8.5 million.

Stormy Weather

As Clayton Koppes writes, during the war "some advances were made in improving what had been, with few exceptions, a dismal record" in the representation of race in film ("Regulating" 273). *Stormy Weather,* an all-black musical review, can be seen as one of these advances. It opened one week before *This Is the Army* and like that film had a very thin story line linking a group of disparate musical numbers. The narrative is a tribute to twenty-five years of contributions by the "colored race" to the entertainment world, with a special tribute to Bill (Bojangles) Robinson. The story is told in flashback, as Robinson and other black soldiers return from World War I and Robinson meets Lena Horne. *Stormy Weather* then follows their relationship as their paths cross in various shows. The couple seem headed for the altar, but cannot make their relationship work because of their close ties to show business. They agree to go their separate ways but meet again years later in the present when they appear in a show put on for servicemen. They reestablish their romance and a happy ending is reached. But the narrative is a thin veneer for the showcasing of the talents of Cab Calloway, Katherine Dunham, Fats Waller, the Nicholas Brothers, as well as Robinson and Horne.

In keeping with realism's conventions, *Stormy Weather* uses documentary footage of black soldiers returning from the First World War. That African Americans had served in World War I was a surprise to some white viewers. Additionally, in keeping with conventions of black stereotypes, the film stays within the bounds of permissible actions for black actors of the time period. For example, the lead female actresses are all light skinned, and the costumes worn in one of the numbers include hats with bug-eyed

Lena Horne (l.) and Bill (Bojangles) Robinson sing, dance, and fall in love in *Stormy Weather* (Andrew L. Stone, Twentieth Century Fox), but they must never kiss onscreen. Courtesy PhotoFest New York.

black faces. Although the story revolves around a romance between Bill and Lena, they never kiss onscreen.

What is important about *Stormy Weather* for the representation of an inclusive national identity is that there is not a single white face in the film. Thus whites were not the intended audience, and the film implicitly marks the ideology of inclusion. Hollywood made the film in large part to appease the huge black populations moving to the cities to take jobs made possible by the war. Because of discrimination in the wartime factories, the influx of African Americans to the cities began only early this year, as employers turned to black workers as a last resort. When this migration began, it brought problems as well as opportunity. Housing shortages, inadequate health services, hostile police, and other hardships greeted the African American migrant. As African Americans moved into the cities and near military bases, they came into contact with other races and ethnic groups. Due to the tensions brought on by close contact in the work place, in public transportation, and in neighborhoods, race riots broke out in the early summer in Detroit and New York (Jeffries 73, 114).

Stormy Weather, already in production during the riots, was an attempt to address low African American morale, which was closely monitored throughout the war by the government and the National Association for the Advancement of Colored People (NAACP). The present-day stage show that is represented in the finale of the film is performed for black soldiers on their way overseas. Writing that it is "better to violate cinematic grammar than disrupt the narrative conceit," Thomas Doherty notes that the musical finale is performed in a Broadway theater and bankrolled by black financiers and producers. The finale "plays for an audience that applauds and cheers wildly, an audience that on Broadway can only be white. The conventional 'cut away' reaction shot showing the appreciative crowd never comes" (Doherty 210). Compared to the wildly appreciative finale in *This Is the Army,* the absence of audience reaction shots is glaring. In *This Is the Army,* shots of the audience standing, cheering, and clapping wildly are as important to the creation of patriotic fervor as the rousing music on stage. In fact, the audience shots are part of what constructs the identification of the viewing audience with the action onscreen. Without those cutaway shots, the absence of the audience gives the impression that, although we can hear the audience, something is missing, and the sense of identification is different. This obvious absence gives the lie to the fabrication of an all-inclusive national identity.

Tender Comrade

Released on 29 December, written by Dalton Trumbo and directed by Edward Dmytryk, *Tender Comrade* featured women "perhaps more prominently than any other wartime film" (Koppes, "Hollywood" 33). The story focuses on Jo Jones (Ginger Rogers) and four other women who all work together at a factory. The women decide to live together, pool their earnings, and support each other emotionally and financially while their husbands are fighting overseas. They hire a German housekeeper, discuss rationing, comfort each other in their loneliness, and fawn on one of the women's husband who comes home on leave. The film is transparently designed to teach women how to be good American wives while their men are away. Through a series of flashbacks, scenes of Jo and her husband Chris's (Robert Ryan) life together are depicted as the couple confronts issues that many young marrieds were facing this year.

In the first flashback, Chris proposes marriage but Jo gives him a hard time of it. In the second flashback, Chris is working too much at the munitions factory and she feels neglected. In the third and final flashback Jo and

Chris talk about the responsibility of bringing children into the postwar world. Each flashback is triggered by an event in the collective household where the five women live together. The first is triggered on the night the women move into their new communal quarters, as Jo comforts the youngest woman of the group, who has just been married. The second flashback occurs after Jo fights with Barbara Thomas (Ruth Hussey), who is going on a date because her husband never responds to her letters. The third and climactic flashback occurs after Jo gives birth to her son.

Tender Comrade is both melodramatic and propagandistic. Events are dealt with as moral issues, and everything occurs as a series of checks and balances. When too much bacon is accidentally delivered to the house, it is a violation of wartime rationing, and the German American housekeeper (Mady Christians), whose husband is also serving in the U.S. military, emerges as the voice of conscience. Her character is a reminder to the other women and the audience that the war is being fought to bring freedom, including freedom from want, to all people. Little things become big things, she preaches, and while one or two pounds of bacon may not be big in itself, it adds up to food taken out of the mouths of people who need it. Prompted by this recent convert to the American Dream, another of the women admits to hoarding lipstick and agonizes over her lack of patriotism. With a target audience of stay-at-home wartime wives, *Tender Comrade* is so intent on its discussion of domestic issues, both in the flashbacks and in present-day scenes, that it seems more than anything else a manual on how to survive the war without your husband. Thus, in one scene, Jo encourages the newly married young woman to talk about her husband. "How are you going to know you're married unless you talk about it?" she asks rhetorically. Although this falls into stereotypical notions of women's need to talk about personal issues, it can also be seen to encourage and legitimate such activity.

Discussing the representation of gender in films produced during the war, Thomas Doherty notes that there were three "war-born versions of American womanhood" that emerged. In the first, traditional gender roles were maintained and simply moved into the military-industrial sphere. In the second, new associations emerged, and were combined with old significations that were then represented in a "calibrated equipoise." Such films as *Tender Comrade* fall into this category. "That the two visions of the one sex were in polar opposition did not prevent Hollywood from selling both versions," Doherty notes. Finally, there were representations showing women doing things that spoke of a changed place and status for women in society. Doherty notes that Ginger Rogers driving a forklift was a "jarring

Jo (Ginger Rogers) at the controls of a forklift in *Tender Comrade* (Edward Dmytryk, RKO): like a manual on surviving the war without a husband. Courtesy PhotoFest NYC.

and transforming" revision of how gender had been coded before the war (155–58).

As jarring as that sight might have been, it was the reality of many women. *Tender Comrade* visualizes the experiences that women were living through, legitimizing them at the same time as the narrative emphasizes that it is a temporary, unnatural situation, that patriarchy will immediately be reestablished upon return of the men. Each of the women has a photograph of her husband next to her bed that she talks to and wishes goodnight. When one husband comes home on leave, the women forklift drivers and airplane builders fall all over themselves in the kitchen making him their favorite recipes. The film thus revolves around not the women in the house but the absent men, focusing the women's motivations, discussions, and attention almost entirely on their phantom presence. Any advances Jo and the other women might make in believing in their own value as workers and their ability to stand on their own are undercut by their obsession with their absent husbands.

Finally, although Jo is defined as very capable and able to support herself emotionally and financially, Hollywood defines her strength as essentially masculine. In two scenes, she is encouraged to be a "good guy." In a fight with Chris, he admonishes her to be a "good guy" and tell him what she is upset about. Later, she is giving herself a pep talk, after learning that Chris has been killed in combat. Talking to herself, she asserts that "no matter how tough things are, no matter how bad they seem, you'll come through. C'mon Jo, head up, take it on the chin like a good guy, like a soldier's wife should." Doherty remarks that Jo's prewar self is "petulant, dependent, and childish, a whiny and infantilized contrast to the initiative, strength, and maturity of her war-tempered character" (155). That contrast, Doherty notes, makes *Tender Comrade* instructive for women in the viewing audience.

▰▰▰▰▰▰ *Shadow of a Doubt*

Another film came out earlier in the year that also featured a young woman who had similar qualities of strength, initiative, and maturity, and who played the lead, but in another kind of role altogether. This was Alfred Hitchcock's *Shadow of a Doubt*. According to Thomas Schatz, the early 1940s witnessed the advent of film noir, which as a cinematic style "first took shape before the war in dark, expressive dramas like *Rebecca* (1940), *Citizen Kane* (1941), and *The Maltese Falcon* (1941)." During the war, noir developed in two distinctive types of narrative marked by the familiar

Uncle Charlie (Joseph Cotten, l.) gives his niece (Teresa Wright) a ring she later suspects was stolen from one of his victims in *Shadow of a Doubt* (Alfred Hitchcock, Skirball Productions/Universal). Courtesy Jerry Ohlinger Archives.

dark style. *Shadow of a Doubt* is part of the "female Gothic" type. Schatz notes that "these noir films evinced the 'dark side' of the wartime experience, coexisting in dynamic tension with Hollywood's onslaught of war-related films" (*Boom* 3). *Shadow of a Doubt* introduced the chilling suggestion that the enemy is not only here at home, but exists as part of the family in small-town America.

Shot entirely on location in Santa Rosa, California, in order to adhere to the spending limit on sets required by the government (Schatz, *Boom* 144), the film tells the tale of Uncle Charlie (Joseph Cotten), beloved baby brother of Emma Newton (Patricia Collinge), who comes to visit Emma's family. Emma's daughter Charlie (Teresa Wright), named for her uncle, begins to get a sense that Uncle Charlie is hiding something. Through a series of chance discoveries, Charlie learns that Uncle Charlie has killed three rich widows on the East Coast. Two detectives, Jack Graham (Macdonald Carey) and Fred Saunders (Wallace Ford), are on Uncle Charlie's trail, and pretend to be doing a national survey on the average American family in order to gain access to the house. Before long, Uncle Charlie realizes that his niece has found him out and tries, on several occasions, to kill her. At the end of the film, he accidentally falls from a moving train while trying to murder her one last time. At his funeral, Jack Graham comforts Charlie, as they stand outside the church, the only two people who know Uncle Charlie's dark secret.

Shadow of a Doubt stands in direct opposition to the dominant message of films of this period, and is worth special mention because so few films diverted from a straightforward patriotic ideology. In fact, it can be argued that in this film Hitchcock challenges the entire mythos of middle America. Many films have taken on the subject of a secure family threatened by dark and violent outside forces. Usually there is a dramatic meaning to a portrayal of this kind. Blake Lucas notes that although this threat may result in affirmation of the family unit, in *Shadow of a Doubt* the dramatic meaning can be read as an interrogation of the family's values, resulting directly from the persuasiveness of the intruder's values. This is especially the case because Uncle Charlie, as the "dark intruder," is a trusted member of the family, and because young Charlie is positioned between the family and the intruder, whom she alone comprehends (Lucas 51). But actually, one can go further and argue that Uncle Charlie's values qualify not only as the family's values but also the sunny small-town values heralded at the film's beginning and in Santa Rosa's two most important institutions, its bank and its church.

Tension in the small town is set up before Charles gets there, with the constant jabbering of the two younger Newton children and Emma's distant and somewhat distracted presence. Joe (Henry Travers), the father, is also portrayed as a slightly offbeat character, whose hobby is getting together with his neighbor Herbie Hawkins (Hume Cronyn) to discuss various ways of committing the perfect murder. Joe and Herbie seem to be interested in murder primarily because their own lives are so utterly dull. When Charles arrives and speaks his mind, he tells some truth about the tedium of small-town life, even though *Shadow of a Doubt* is simultaneously setting him up as a sinister interloper. In talking about his and Emma's childhood, Charles notes, "Everything was sweet and pretty then, not now, not like it is now." Later, when Charles goes to Joe's bank to deposit a large sum of money (taken from one of the women he has murdered), he speaks in a loud, bragging voice, embarrassing Joe as he suggests to the bank's president that maybe people shouldn't trust banks so much. Reminding Joe of the many bank failures in the 1930s, he suggests, "We all know what banks are."

One morning, as Emma brings Charles breakfast in bed, he blurts out that all women are fools, "silly women" who don't know what the world is really like. Because of Emma's absent-minded flightiness the viewer is encouraged to agree with him. Emma sits at the head of the dinner table every night, while Joe sits on the side, but the seating arrangement is a statement not so much about women's new place in society as about a world turned upside-down. The war, though present, takes a back seat in *Shadow of a Doubt*. Some soldiers are seen walking on the street, and a poster behind the bank manager reads, "Buy a Share in America." But other than these passing references, the war, beyond mention, seems very far away from the small town of Santa Rosa.

Young Charlie is a very different kind of hero for this year. First, she is a woman with a masculine name that marks her as a "good guy." She is portrayed as cynical about religion, telling her sister who is saying her prayers, "Don't bless too many people, it's late." In addition, as previously noted, she stands outside the church at the end of the film during her Uncle Charlie's funeral while the service is going on inside. Charlie is an outsider in 1940s wartime American society, smarter than those around her, quicker to pick up on clues and telltale hints.

As Jack tells Charlie at the end of the film, "The world needs watching. Sometimes it just seems to go crazy, like Uncle Charlie." Coming at the end of such a dark film, this line sounds like capitulation to the OWI, but here, too, Jack's authority to utter the line is called into question by his previous behavior. In a crisis, Jack proves unreliable; although he gives Charlie several phone numbers to contact him, he is not to be found at any of them when Charlie needs him most. And for all his efforts, it is not Jack who catches Charles but Charlie herself, although she is almost killed in the process. The rest of the Santa Rosa community will continue to regard Charles as an affable relative who somehow made good; Charlie knows better.

Democratic values are voiced at several points in *Shadow of a Doubt*, yet they are always undermined through off-hand or cynical treatment. Charles's rights to privacy and freedom are frequently invoked, and because we suspect him of murder the question of whether such freedoms should automatically be granted is broached. Charlie defends her uncle's right to privacy from the detectives when they arrive and want to take his picture. "When people ask for privacy they should have it," she avers. In a similar vein, Charles admonishes Jack, "Don't take any more pictures of me. Rights of man, you know, freedom?" But Charles is abusing the privileges he seeks, and threatens the lives and social welfare of those who love him the most. In this figure Hitchcock creates a very human monster, a homefront murderer who hides his true intent behind a bland mask of cynical amusement and seeks safety and shelter in the small-town America that millions of soldiers are fighting to protect.

During this year Hollywood shifted away from social problem films and toward films that showed a singularity of purpose in support of the war. Similarly reflected in the advertising of that year, the primary strategy of Hollywood's contribution to support of the war was to sell "The American Way of Life." "We can keep idealism alive, nurturing appreciation of the values of Peace . . . pointing up the rewards which arise from our way of life" (Keysser and Pozner 111). And certainly, "The American Way of Life" is in full view throughout *Shadow of a Doubt*. However, the narrative and iconography of the film operate to query that way of life and thus undermine it.

* * *

Hollywood was the government's best weapon against questioning the motives and operations behind wartime activities because people were reassured by the narratives and especially by the narrative closure that there was some ultimate purpose behind all the sacrifice and death. "The cinema's institutional ritual of gathering a community—spectators who share a region, language and culture—homologizes, in a sense, the symbolic gathering of the nation . . . the movie audience as a provisional 'nation' forged by spectatorship" (Shohat and Stam 368). This is the remarkable power of *This Is the Army*, and, for black audiences, *Stormy Weather*. But it was equally true of the combat films with their heightened realism, which read like a newsreel and felt like entertainment. And true, too, of the very instructive, consoling, and empowering—although very dark—women's films, as well as Hitchcock's Santa Rosa nightmare. What kind of world were the soldiers coming home to? What were they really fighting for? These questions were beginning to bubble under the slick narrative surface of the American cinema, and would burst forth in a torrent in the postwar years to come.

The author wishes to thank William T. McClain for his help in the research and writing of this essay.

1944

Movies and the Renegotiation of Genre

NICHOLAS SPENCER

The year's historical events were dominated by World War II. Optimism regarding an Allied victory in Europe greatly increased. Concurrently, American society began to shift toward a postwar orientation, and new forms of alliance and tension became apparent in numerous areas of American culture and society. Whereas the Pacific campaign was characterized by steady westward progress across the islands of the Central Pacific, the European engagement witnessed a dramatic and sudden change in fortune. The Americans' European campaigns commenced with limited success. Major success in the European conflict came, of course, with Operation Overlord, the D-Day landings of 6 June. By establishing a second front against the Germans, D-Day greatly increased the likelihood of an Allied victory in Europe. However, as William L. O'Neill notes, Overlord was "a high risk operation" and its success was by no means certain (343): the weather over the English Channel was uncooperative, and the German forces were numerically and technologically superior. By August, Allied forces had liberated Paris and were moving successfully through German lines, even though at the battles of Huertgen Forest and the Bulge late in the year, Americans suffered tremendous casualties.

The course of war greatly influenced the political events and social issues of the day. Franklin D. Roosevelt's fourth presidential election victory reflected America's wartime commitment to unity and continuity. Integration also occurred on the world stage with an international conference at Bretton Woods, New Hampshire, in July leading to the creation of the International Monetary Fund and the World Bank. Driven by Roosevelt's convictions, plans for the United Nations were significantly furthered at the Dumbarton Oaks conference in August. However, Roosevelt's commitment to international engagement was not unqualified. As Robert James Maddox notes, the president "deliberately refrained from holding out inspirational visions" in wartime and instead portrayed the war as "a disagreeable but necessary task" that relied on the contributions of individual citizens (184). Despite Roosevelt's rhetorical restraint, his policies provoked a renewal of isolationist resistance in America. Also, Roosevelt's health was in decline, and he vacillated on key issues, such as the extent to which details of the Manhattan Project should be shared with Allies. As well as by stability, political events were therefore characterized by conflict and the wavering of authority.

The social issues of the year also involved varying and sometimes opposing tendencies. The rapid decline of the national murder rate suggests a degree of social unity, but social conflict was equally real, and indeed the antithesis between utopian unity and existential conflict is central to an understanding of the year. The Servicemen's Readjustment Act, or the G.I. Bill, was passed by Congress in June. As well as reflecting the postwar orientation that was evident in many areas of American society, this bill gave veterans many new opportunities in employment, education, and housing. But the promise of peace had different implications for women. At the same time that the wartime female labor force peaked, employers began to withdraw job opportunities for women in anticipation of postwar demobilization. The first female air stewardesses were hired, this providing evidence of the return to traditional gender roles for women in the workplace. The decline in wartime production also increased the power of management in labor relations and led to the outbreak of wildcat strikes. Such industrial conflict registered the transition from a society of public production to one of private consumption.

The civil rights of ethnic Americans underwent some improvement. Japanese Americans continued to be interned, but in December, the Supreme Court set limits on which individuals could be detained. Japanese Americans who resisted the draft were eventually pardoned. The status of race relations was perhaps best captured by Gunnar Myrdal's *An American Dilemma*. In the book, Myrdal acknowledged white American racism against African Americans, but he advocated assimilation as the best way to overcome racial strife. In June, the Supreme Court ruled that African American citizens were eligible to participate in all elections, and in July, the desegregation of the U.S. Army commenced. Still, African Americans continued to be arrested and jailed for challenging segregationist laws. It was a time of division, which called into question the most idealistic visions of the American future.

William Graebner defines American culture in the 1940s as "The Age of Doubt" (144), identifying two broad trends in the culture of the decade. On the one hand, culture was characterized by nostalgia, sentimentalism, a belief in scientific progress, and a pervasive yearning for what he calls a "culture of the whole" (69). On the other hand, it was a time when irony, historical contingency, a feeling of historical exhaustion and cultural fragmentation, and an attraction to existentialism borne of a sense of meaninglessness were evident in many areas of culture. For Graebner, the "culture of the whole" refers to the ideal of a unified national culture characterized by shared values, an optimistic view of historical progress, and the utopian assumption that society is not divided by race, gender, and class. What Graebner calls "contingency" is directly opposed to the idea of the culture of the whole because it emphasizes the random and accidental nature of events. Contingency is further associated with an absence of historical structure or guidance and a sense that individuals and groups are brought together by haphazard means and thus do not constitute a unified social body. For him, social bodies that are formed by contingency are prone to conflict and division.

Throughout the culture, then, nostalgia, progressivism, and sentimentalism were matched by irony and exhaustion. The former were illustrated by the songs of Bing Crosby, such as "Ac-cent-tchu-ate the Positive," by books such as *Susie Cucumber: She Writes Letters,* and by serious music like Aaron Copland's "Appalachian Spring." The commitment to technological progress is especially evident in the establishment of both Project Hermes, a U.S. Army initiative to develop missile and rocketry technology, and the Jet Propulsion Laboratory in California. There is also ample evidence of the second of Graebner's trends. Exhaustion and irony could be seen in the founding of Dwight Macdonald's journal *Politics,* an important moment in American intellectuals' shift away from Marxist affiliations and movement toward the end of ideology. As Howard Brick argues, Macdonald's political views had existential tendencies in that they combined a negation of theories of progressive history with a belief in "pure moral will" (121). That the year saw the translation into English of Søren Kierkegaard's *The Concept of Dread* and the first production of Jean-Paul Sartre's *No Exit* underscores the significance of the existentialist theory of contingency at this time.

Also, key works such as Jackson Pollock's *Totem Lesson I* reflected a shift toward abstract expressionism in American art. The meeting of Jack Kerouac, Allen Ginsberg, and William Burroughs at Columbia University was an instance of the stirring of American counterculture. The inaugural publication of *Seventeen,* beyond exemplifying the growing importance of popular culture in the shift away from the demands of wartime production, reflected the presence of youth consumer culture and thus provided further evidence of the divisions within American society. And with such films as

Murder, My Sweet, The Uninvited, The Miracle of Morgan's Creek, Jane Eyre, The Lodger, Gaslight, Going My Way, Hail the Conquering Hero, National Velvet, None But the Lonely Heart, and *Since You Went Away,* Hollywood was urgently working to entice the American public with a model of an optimistic and undivided nation.

■ Movies of the War: *To Have and Have Not* and *Lifeboat*

Military developments were prominent in many genre films, yet the most renowned war movies of the year took an indirect approach to military engagement and, in so doing, portrayed the war experience as one of conflict and ambiguity. Howard Hawks's *To Have and Have Not* exemplifies these characteristics of the war movie. As Bernard F. Dick notes, American war movies frequently made use of "the resistance" (*Star-Spangled Screen* 147)—the civilians who were moved to oppose Axis forces—as a means of encouraging audience identification with protagonists. *To Have and Have Not,* set in Martinique in 1940 shortly after the Germans took the island from the French, shares the emphasis noted by Dick. However, the movie is distinctive because it portrays characters who are extremely reluctant to join the resistance.

Harry Morgan (Humphrey Bogart), a professional fisherman, is approached by members of the French resistance who wish to hire his boat. Following his initial wariness, Harry eventually sides with the French cause, and much of the narrative concerns the transformation in his attitude and behavior. Toward the beginning of *To Have and Have Not,* he meets Marie "Slim" Browning (Lauren Bacall), an independent American like himself. The progress involving the French resistance plot is mirrored by the unfolding romance between the two Americans. Both plots are informed by the tension between fragmenting detachment and holistic commitment.

Indeed, the ambiguity of the movie's title highlights the extensive nature of this tension. In the title, "having" refers to both one's independence and the possibility of personal or political commitment; conversely, "not having" suggests both the absence of autonomy and the lack of social connection. Of course, the movie ultimately invokes the benefits of commitment, but the protagonists retain their bristling personalities and express their newfound loyalties in oblique terms. For example, Harry and Slim's conversations are characterized by ironic comments and an absence of romantic proclamations. Similarly, Harry is sometimes aggressive toward the French characters and is often impatient with them.

By telling Johnson (Walter Sande) how to catch fish, Harry (Humphrey Bogart) commences his involvement in other people's struggles. *To Have and Have Not* (Howard Hawks, Warner Bros.). Digital frame enlargement.

To Have and Have Not is an allegory of the decision to commit U.S. military forces to the Allied liberation of France from German occupation, this reflecting abandonment of a hitherto-prevailing isolationist position toward the European theater of World War II. Harry's individualism is associated with both the justification of war in Europe and the isolationist sentiments that were roused in this presidential election year.

The need for commitment emerges from the relations between Harry and the other American characters, especially Johnson and Eddie. By showing the differences between these characters, the movie also evokes divisions in American society and distances itself from overly heroic or propagandistic narrative. When at the outset Johnson (Walter Sande), an American tourist, pays Harry to take him out fishing, for example, Johnson proves to be a hopeless amateur. In militaristic language, Harry tells him when to attack the fish, but Johnson does not know when to strike and loses Harry's rod and reel. Later, Johnson tries to cheat Harry out of the money that he owes him. Just when Harry is about to reclaim his money, Johnson is accidentally killed by the crossfire from a gunfight between Vichy and resistance forces. Johnson's role is to highlight Harry's combative skills in such a way as to suggest that they should find direct employment.

In other words, Harry's shift from a proxy position to an active one in the fishing trip with Johnson evokes a similar need for his participation in political events. His marginal existence in Martinique represents a rejection of American society. Along with his ironic disdain for Johnson, such a rejection of social norms suggests that Harry embodies the existential irony of the burgeoning counterculture. Similarly, his manual skills and physical toughness identify him with the vigor of the working class.

The theme of solidarity is emphasized in Harry's relationship with Eddie (Walter Brennan), an old friend who accompanies him on fishing trips. A "rummy," Eddie is forgetful, ineffectual, and apparently weak, repeatedly asking others if they have ever been bitten by a dead bee. His image of the dead bee that stings becomes a metaphor for the Vichy occupation of Martinique. Slim's repetition of this line after she and Harry have been detained by Vichy authorities for questioning underscores the relevance of Eddie's refrain to the theme of the occupation of French territory. When asked by Slim why he doesn't bite the bees back, Eddie replies, "I ain't got no stinger." In terms of the metaphorical role of the dead bee image, Eddie's impotence evokes, first, the limitations endured by those living in occupied territory and, second, the need for Americans to obtain a "stinger" and fight the Germans. Harry's loyalty to Eddie highlights the importance of being true to one's allies when they are in trouble. Later in the movie, Eddie accompanies Harry on a journey by boat at night to pick up two members of the French resistance. As well as providing a model of American unity in the cause of liberation, this scene reflects Eddie's transformation from incompetent alcoholic to freedom fighter. Such a transformation exemplifies the American turn to military engagement that the movie advocates. That Eddie turns out to be handy with a rifle and able to endure interrogation suggests that the proposed military turn will be successful.

If the need for a unifying commitment comes to light in the relations between these characters, the process by which such commitment is realized is communicated through Harry's interactions with Slim and the French resistance. The details of this process in the narrative are closely linked to key aspects of American history. Each point in Harry's progress toward political involvement is characterized by the haphazardness that is generally apparent in American culture. In other words, over and over a disconnected sequence of unpredictable events leads Harry to rethink his disposition against involvement. When he is initially asked to participate in the resistance, Harry replies that he does not wish to get involved in "local politics." As evidenced by his reference to the "small war" on the island, he is able to justify his non-involvement by separating the conflict on the island from the larger context of World War II. This separation of American interests from a "European war" that Harry expresses was one of the tenets of isolationism.

Referring to Harry's involvement in French liberation, the resistance tries to convince him to join them: "When things are changed, it would mean a great deal to you." Because comments such as these lead Harry to reconsider his detachment, the movie evokes postwar economic advantage as a justification for war. At the same time, Harry's romantic inclination toward Slim seduces the audience into an equivalent commitment to European war.

On the boat trip, Harry tells Eddie that the resistance has asked them to pick up "a couple of guys." The realization that M. and Mme. De Bursac (Walter Molnar, Dolores Moran) are their charges gives further rhetorical force to the seductive coupling of romance and war, as Harry is led to assume an active role in the struggle through the signal incapacity of the French. When soon after they are met by a Vichy patrol boat, De Bursac is "anxious to give up," but Harry shoots the patrol boat's light and enables their escape. De Bursac is shot, and on returning to Martinique it seems that Harry is the only person who can remove the bullet from his wound. Harry is therefore obliged to take the initiative in aiding De Bursac. When he refuses payment for giving further help to the resistance, it is clear that Harry's progress toward military commitment is complete. Yet the fact that his true interest is Slim suggests that isolationist sentiments have not been fully eradicated from him, or from the film.

The Atlantic Ocean had become an important battlefield in the war. From the earliest days of hostilities, the German navy had attempted to cut off Britain's maritime supply lines, and by the first months of 1942 German U-boats had destroyed many American merchant ships bound for Britain. It is this phase of the Battle of the Atlantic, which the Allies had won by May 1943, that Alfred Hitchcock's *Lifeboat* specifically dramatizes. The movie also attempts to resolve in symbolic terms those conflicts associated with American foreign and domestic affairs.

The film opens with the image of a sinking Allied freight ship. It soon becomes clear that the ship has been torpedoed by a German U-boat. A lifeboat is occupied by the famous journalist Constance "Connie" Porter (Tallulah Bankhead), and she is soon joined by a number of other survivors of the attack. As well as British and American characters, the survivors include Willy, the captain of the U-boat (Walter Slezak). As in several movies of the year, the journey eastward in *Lifeboat* is a metaphor for American participation in the Allied landings on mainland Europe. Isolationist reservations about eastward commitments are incarnated in the character of Alice McKenzie (Mary Anderson), an American military medic who is reluctant to go to London because of the complex and unhappy relationship that awaits her there. However, such discord is a minor element in *Lifeboat,* and the movie represents transatlantic unity in the fight against the Germans. Following the opening images of the sinking ship, for example, the movie shows a box with "Amcross Great Britain" stamped on it. We also see Mrs. Higgins (Heather Angel), a British woman who has given birth to a child in New York and is returning to England. On discovering that her child is dead, she commits suicide.

Images and sequences such as these represent the suffering of the British and the need for the massive Allied offensive of D-Day. The romantic attachment between Alice and Stanley "Sparks" Garrett (Hume Cronyn), the only British person who stays on the lifeboat, argues for the effectiveness of the American and British alliance. For example, it is these characters who realize that Willy has a compass and is leading the lifeboat off course (in order to effect a rendezvous with another U-boat). Whereas there was significant conflict between British and American commanders during the year, the relationship between Miss McKenzie and Sparks constitutes a symbol of unqualified transatlantic solidarity and capability.

In addition to Anglo-American relations, *Lifeboat* justifies military involvement by evoking the characters as models of unity, however continually fractured. As the characters decide what to do about Willy, the movie celebrates the democratic process, with their vote reflecting the ideal of a culture of the whole that was expressed by many cultural texts this year. However, the presence of George "Joe" Spencer (Canada Lee), an African American, creates uncertainty in the democratic process. The characters' deliberations are interrupted by their realization that the vote might also include Joe. In the silent moments that follow this realization, the embarrassment that the characters feel as a result of Joe's uncertain status in the democratic process is palpable. The invitation to Joe to join in voting on Willy's fate is in keeping with the Supreme Court's contemporaneous ruling that African Americans were now eligible to vote. Yet Joe's decision not to participate in the vote highlights the contemporary reality of racism and segregation. When Joe is asked to steal Willy's watch because of his background in crime, the movie propagates the stereotypes that informed racism in this period. *Lifeboat* attempts to counter such racist tendencies by making Joe a reformed Christian, but religious belief is barely valued in the narrative and thus the marginalization of Joe is not seriously undone.

At other times, the movie actively uses references to ethnicity and nationality in order to promote military opposition to Germany. John Kovac (John Hodiak) is from Chicago, but he is of Czech descent. As he reminds the others of Nazi Germany's invasion of Czechoslovakia, the movie asks the viewer to relate to Kovac and identify American and Czech interests as synonymous. In contrast, Gus Smith (William Bendix) is used to suggest that the American commitment to war can be based on the rejection of one's ethnic background. Born with Schmidt as his last name, Gus has shorn himself of his German heritage and argues as strongly as anyone for the hostile treatment of Willy.

Just as *Lifeboat* articulates a conflict over the role of ethnic background, so too is its opposition between German deviousness and Allied fairness informed by a tension between the virtues of democratic fair play and a combative loathing of Willy. The movie negotiates this tension by distributing various sentiments among its characters: some view the German as a subject with legal rights, and others objectify him and thus need not qualify their violent disposition. According to Clayton R. Koppes and Gregory D. Black, *Lifeboat* differs from many other movies about World War II in that it addresses the issues of how the Allies would treat defeated Germans (*Hollywood* 309). The post-1945 orientation that Koppes and Black ascribe to the movie was evident in many spheres of American society. Additionally, the issue of the treatment of Willy is used to justify the military actions of the year. Upon realizing that Willy has hoarded water and encouraged Gus to commit suicide, the marooned survivors attack, kill, and throw him overboard. These events suggest the ultimate need for violent confrontation, such as that epitomized by Operation Overlord.

The most sustained threat of division within the unity of *Lifeboat* involves the issue of class. The tenuous accord between American labor and capital is embodied in the class relations of the movie. Kovac, the most overtly working-class character in the movie, is the focus of these class relations. Most of his dealings with Charles D. "Ritt" Rittenhouse (Henry Hull), a wealthy owner of shipyards and other concerns, are cordial in nature. That Ritt plans to honor his poker debt to Kovac represents the ideal of unity among workers and owners in wartime America. Yet Ritt ultimately turns on Kovac and accuses him of cheating. The emergence of antagonism between these two men reflects the breakdown of harmonious labor relations that was evident in the wildcat strikes of the year, but the sense of class antagonism is even more pronounced in the dynamic between Connie and Kovac. For much of the narrative these characters are in conflict, and one of the central aspects of *Lifeboat* concerns the possibility of overcoming the divisions between them. At the outset we see Connie recording images of the shipwreck with a film camera. Kovac is incensed by her dispassionate objectification of others, and he inadvertently knocks the camera into the water. The conflict between Kovac and upper-class Connie is exacerbated by several factors. She taunts him because she believes that he has communist sympathies; he suspects her of treachery because she speaks German with Willy. When Kovac proclaims himself the skipper of the lifeboat, Connie accuses him of being a dictator. In scenes such as this, Connie gives voice to the need to restrain labor and left-wing radicalism in the context of wartime production.

Yet Kovac is not a dictator, and he concedes to the wishes of others regarding the course of the lifeboat. Such developments portray labor as a robust and worthy source of anti-fascism. The conflict between Connie and Kovac is seemingly resolved by the romance between them. But uncertainties remain. Kovac disputes Connie's claim that she too is from the stockyards of Chicago, and he tells her to "quit slumming." The discord is finally overcome when Connie gets rid of her expensive bracelet, which to Kovac is a constant reminder of class inequality. That the movie resorts to a symbolic image as a means of overcoming class division reflects the uneasiness that informs key aspects of the unity that it seeks to represent.

Renegotiating the Musical: *Pin-Up Girl* and *Meet Me in St. Louis*

Despite their frequently indirect allusions to military engagement, the war movies of the year offer a broadly supportive vision of America's participation in World War II. In other movie genres, representations of American culture as a unified whole engender more overt support for involvement in war. The Hollywood musical *Pin-Up Girl*, directed by H. Bruce Humberstone, epitomizes this unabashed militarism. Here, Lorry Jones (Betty Grable), a celebrated pin-up girl, works at a United Service Organizations (USO) depot in Missoula, Missouri, and gives away signed copies of her photograph to numerous servicemen. Lorry and her friend Kay (Dorothea Kent) are transferred to Washington, D.C., to work as stenographers for the U.S. Navy. Dreaming of stardom, Lorry goes to New York and befriends Tommy Dooley (John Harvey), a navy hero who has just returned from Guadalcanal. Lorry becomes a successful nightclub singer, and she and Tommy fall in love.

The primary conflict in *Pin-Up Girl* concerns the dynamics between romance and war. The movie evokes the romance between Lorry and

Tommy as the centerpiece of a society that is united in its commitment to both war and stable gender relations. At the same time, the movie suggests that the exigencies of war put pressures on romance and refashion gender roles. In an attempt to resolve the conflicts associated with war and romance, the movie makes insistent and reflexive reference to its own genre as "musical comedy" and resorts to fantastical elements. In the opening scene, for instance, an impossibly large number of servicemen exit a car at the USO depot. The interiors of the nightclubs that are shown are also unbelievably vast. In one of these spots, Lorry and Kay fraudulently claim that they are singers in a Broadway show entitled *Remember Me*. When asked to sing a song from this show, Lorry is magically able to do so. *Pin-Up Girl* strives to portray American society in uniform and homogeneous terms, but the narrative departures from realism suggest the strained nature of this project.

The drama begins with Lorry's imminent departure for Washington. The men of Company B protest Lorry's upcoming journey because she is their favorite pin-up girl and they want her to stay in Missoula. Just as her move eastward evokes the deployment of American forces in Europe, so too the protests of Company B regarding her new assignment reflect domestic anxieties about American commitments to the European theater. With the men left behind as the woman departs for the East, this conjunction of movement and anxiety is also an instance of gender reversal. Lorry is so popular because she is a pin-up girl, and her distribution of signed photographs highlights the shift from disciplined production to mass cultural consumption that was evident in American society.

The appearance of the infamous and iconic image of Betty Grable underscores the movie's invocation of the power of popular culture. This image also exemplifies "the crotch shot" that Nadine Wills describes as a key feature of the Hollywood musical (121). For Wills, the crotch shot represents "an excessively delineated femininity" that "attempt[s] to naturalize the often unstable relationship between gender (femininity) and sex (female)" (121, 122). Wills's argument is highly pertinent to *Pin-Up Girl*. At various times in the movie, Lorry is portrayed as pin-up girl, stenographer, and nightclub singer. Her identity is therefore divided in the narrative. The famous crotch shot image of her in various contexts attempts to overcome such divisions by reducing female identity to exaggerated femininity. However, the gender variations that are associated with Lorry's different identities are not so easily dispelled. She tells the men of Company B that she is going to star in a USO show, but of course she is to work in the Navy office. This lie told by Lorry exemplifies the issue of gender variation because stenographer and USO star are portrayed as incompatible female gender identities. Also, Lorry's insistence on her role in the USO show suggests a desire to reaffirm female gender roles in the context of women's working obligations, which are exemplified by her office position.

This gender division is reiterated when she and Kay go to New York and claim to be stars in show business. Lorry does become a singer. That she is known by both her stage name of Laura Lorraine and her everyday name of Lorry Jones amplifies the impression of divided identity. The complex treatment of gender reflects American social developments, with women being expected to continue to work in manufacturing and other economic sectors while they were also to prepare themselves for a return to a more rigidly gendered postwar social existence.

At the Club Chartreuse they meet Tommy, and Lorry bluffs her way through the conversation by falsely stating that a song that is played reminds her of her time in Paris. That Tommy is a returning hero of Guadalcanal evokes the victory and celebration associated with the Pacific campaign, but these French motifs make sober reference to both the American military's involvement in the European theater and the need for further military action.

Pin-Up Girl's desire to integrate its gendered and patriotic aspects is evidenced by the continuance of Lorry's singing career in Washington at the Club Diplomacy. While Lorry's nightclub act promotes the gender attribute of female objectification, the name of the club and its Washington location suggest the patriotic struggles of wartime. The conversations in which Tommy talks to Lorry about the difficulties of maintaining romance in a wartime situation have a similar purpose. At the movie's conclusion, the integration of Lorry's three identities is an attempt to show that the divisions of wartime can be resolved into a unity.

In this film, songs both reiterate and deviate from many of the themes of the drama. In the opening title song, the conjunction of female gender roles that characterized American women's lives this year is treated explicitly. The female waitresses at the USO who sing "Pin-Up Girl" state that they take on a mothering role for the servicemen. But the waitresses are also objects of sexual desire, and the servicemen regard them as pin-up girls. The necessity of both aspects of the mother/sex object conjunction is explicitly stated in the waitresses' response to the servicemen. The waitresses state that they understand the amorous overtures of the servicemen, but that they serve the maternal role of providing food for the men. Gender issues are further complicated by the portion of the opening song in which Lorry reads aloud a letter written by a serviceman to his romantic female partner at home. The letter suggests that pin-up girls are simply surrogate objects that represent true loved ones, but Lorry's assumption of the male voice reflects the wartime gender reversals that threaten to subvert the stability of domestic romance. As well as highlighting conflict, the songs fragment the movie by departing from dramatic themes. Whereas the drama focuses on Lorry's pursuit of Tommy and a singing career, the songs express solidarity with military endeavors and directly appeal to the American public's sense of patriotism. Songs such as "Don't Carry Tales" reflect the individualistic basis upon which Roosevelt asked for Americans' support in wartime. "Yankee-Doodle Hayride" has a similar purpose, and the inscription of "1944" on the barn shown during this song emphasizes the historical specificity of the movie's sentiments.

The patriotic tendency of the movie culminates in the final instrumental scene. In this sequence, Lorry is dressed in uniform and leads a unit of female soldiers in a grandiose spectacle of military parade. Having finally attained the status of feminine singing icon, Lorry can now fully (and silently) celebrate militaristic values. The conclusion therefore suggests that the best way to overcome the divisions of wartime is to support the war effort and not let the exigencies of wartime subvert stereotypical gender roles.

Hollywood musicals of the year typically portray American culture in holistic and homogeneous terms, but their relation to events of war is often varied. Whereas *Pin-Up Girl* is an overt treatment of the impact of war on the American home front, Vincente Minnelli's *Meet Me in St Louis* mediates these concerns through a nostalgic rendition of turn-of-the-century St. Louis. That the ostensible conflicts of this light-hearted romantic musical are false or trivial only enhances their significance as allegories of wartime events. As in *Pin-Up Girl,* the military aspects of *Meet Me in St. Louis* are associated with the contrast between Missouri and New York.

In *Pin-Up Girl,* the enthusiasm with which the characters move from Missouri to New York reflects the ardor of Operation Overlord. Settled with her family in St. Louis, Esther Smith (Judy Garland) in *Meet Me in St. Louis* is unhappy to learn that her father Alonzo (Leon Ames) has a career opportunity that may take all of them to New York. The family's anxieties reflect contemporary concerns about the eastward movement of American armed forces, but such sentiments are offset by the enthusiasm associated with the imminent departure of Esther's brother, Lon (Henry H. Daniels Jr.), to college at Princeton.

Other story lines deal more explicitly with the resolution of conflicts associated with New York and the East. At the start of the movie, Esther's sister Rose (Lucille Bremer) awaits a phone call from Warren Sheffield (Robert Sully) in New York. Rose believes that he will use the phone call to propose marriage, but when the call arrives no such proposal is made. The sense of disconnection between the Smith family and the East is reiterated when Warren is accompanied by Lucille Ballard (June Lockhart), who is described as an "eastern snob," at the Christmas dance in St. Louis. However, at the dance Rose is united with Warren and Lon pairs with Lucille Ballard.

As well as referring to these romantic partnerships, Lon's announcement that "the plans have changed" expresses America's commitment to the Allied cause in the European theater of war. The ideals represented by these romantic pairings are complemented by the sentiments of "Have Yourself a Merry Christmas." Esther sings this song to her younger sister Tootie (Margaret O'Brien) in an attempt to give her the strength to face the upcoming move to New York. The song appeals to the need for stoicism until the arrival of a moment of reunion. While the sisters' strength is rewarded by their father's decision not to relocate the family in New York, the song asks that commitments in the East be faced with courage.

In addition to the overarching issue of the execution of Operation Overlord, many other aspects of war are mediated through the narrative of *Meet Me in St. Louis*. A discussion about the French and English pronunciations of St. Louis evokes the conjunction of American and French concerns that informed the D-Day landings. The dusty streets of St. Louis and the many "dead" dolls that Tootie buries suggest the horror of European battlefields. Tootie also figures in the most explicit war reference in the narrative. On Halloween night, she and her sister Agnes (Joan Carroll) wish to participate in the pranks of the neighborhood boys. Tootie courageously walks on her own through the night to the house of Mr. Braukoff (Mayo Newhall). When he answers the door, she throws a bag of flour at him. Instead of defending against this intrusion, Mr. Braukoff's dog licks up the flour. Mr. Braukoff's Germanic-sounding name suggests that this sequence can be read as an allegory of American military confrontation with Germany, and the ineptitude of Mr. Braukoff's guard dog reflects American confidence in victory.

The experience of war on the home front is also intimated in the narrative. In the opening scene, two women prepare the family dinner. Both the relation between the women and the structure of the family are initially unclear. As the story unfolds, we learn that the scene involves Anna Smith (Mary Astor) and Katie the maid (Marjorie Main). Because the initial uncertainty about their identity suggests a lack of class conflict or even dif-

The scene of Anna Smith (Mary Astor) and Katie the maid (Marjorie Main) preparing dinner together suggests an absence of class conflict and the domestic absence of males in *Meet Me in St. Louis* (Vincente Minnelli, MGM). Digital frame enlargement.

ference, it is possible to view such scenes as advocating social unity in the face of imminent labor conflict. As in all the early sequences in the movie, Alonzo Smith is absent in the opening scene. Mr. Smith's absence reminds us of the family divisions caused by military mobilization, and his frequent deferral to the decisions of the women in the family reflects the domestic independence of women in wartime.

Meet Me in St. Louis is also informed by some of the current conflicts in American politics, expressing them through its representation of the past and future. Occurring between summer 1903 and spring 1904 and culminating with the opening of the World's Fair in St. Louis, the nostalgic events of the narrative evoke both militaristic and isolationist sentiments. *Meet Me in St. Louis*'s nostalgia is almost exclusively domestic in nature, and this domestic emphasis is a significant way in which the narrative departs from the conventions of the Hollywood musical. In one sense, the movie's domesticity also functions as a counterweight to the dispersal of American soldiers in wartime. *Meet Me in St. Louis* depicts a family that is constantly together and at home, and even the movie's extra-familial social relations barely extend beyond domestic confines. Esther falls in love with John Truett (Tom Drake), a young man who has recently moved in next door, and her first song, "The Boy Next Door," intertwines John's virtues with his proximity in the neighborhood. Yet such nostalgic domesticity is also associated with the isolationist sentiments that the combination of war in Europe and a presidential election were making prominent.

As well as being nostalgic for a domestic American past, the movie anticipates the postwar era. The World's Fair symbolizes the international postwar world that was being ushered in through agreements to form the United Nations and other organizations. Jane Feuer states that *Meet Me in St. Louis* is distinctive among Hollywood musicals because it does not portray traditional stages and instead makes all the "world" of the narrative into a stage (23). The representation of the World's Fair deepens the identification of world and stage and evokes the postwar international scene as the stage of American power.

Such American dominance is also suggested by the lyrics to the title song. Referring to St. Louis, these lyrics insist on the role of the United States as the exclusive center of postwar internationalism. The scene in which the family takes the trolley to the future site of the World's Fair evokes excitement about the technological future. Yet at other times the movie is wary of technological innovation. The trolley tracks are associated with danger, and the telephone makes human communication difficult. Such ambivalence about technology reflects the dualism of the movie's nostalgic and progressive perspectives. However, the movie consistently advocates American unity and power.

Renegotiating Noir: *Double Indemnity* and *Laura*

Unlike war movies and musicals, American film noir is a product of the 1940s and its issues. According to Andrew Spicer, the noir movies of this year, such as Billy Wilder's *Double Indemnity* and Otto Preminger's *Laura,* enabled the "major phase" of American film noir between 1944 and 1952 to be realized (27). Like other films, *Double Indemnity* inflects contemporary concerns through a treatment of the recent past. Set in Southern California in 1938, the film narrates how Walter Neff (Fred MacMurray), an insurance salesman, and Phyllis Dietrichson (Barbara Stanwyck) murder Phyllis's husband (Tom Powers). The motive is financial. Walter and Phyllis intend to collect the accident insurance policy that they have opened in Dietrichson's name. They make Dietrichson's murder seem like an accidental fall from a moving train so that the policy's double indemnity clause will be activated. Their plot becomes unraveled as Barton Keyes (Edward G. Robinson), Walter's boss, figures out how the murder was committed. Walter and Phyllis start to argue, and he kills her. In the melee, Walter is also shot by Phyllis, yet before dying he is able to confess the whole story to Keyes.

One of the distinctive features of *Double Indemnity* is its dynamic between the representation of the year in which the narrative takes place and the events of the year in which it was released. Following the Supreme Court's determination that insurance was commerce, this was the first year in which the insurance industry was subject to federal regulation. From this perspective, *Double Indemnity* emphasizes the role of individual instincts, reckless negotiations, and, in Walter's case, corrupt practices in the unregulated past of the insurance industry. Through Walter's death, the movie symbolizes the end of this unregulated era. Also, the Federal Aid Highway Act was passed by Congress this year. This legislation facilitated the large-scale construction of highways and thus had an especially strong impact on Southern California, as had rail routes since the early part of the century. *Double Indemnity*'s portrayal of urban streets and train stations, such as the one in Glendale, evokes the transportational milieu of 1938 as being both distinct from that associated with the new legislation and conducive to crime. At the same time that it condemns the criminality of 1938, however, the movie treats this earlier moment of California history in romantic and nostalgic terms.

As the title of the movie suggests, there are many examples of doubling in *Double Indemnity*. For example, Walter doubles as Dietrichson on the train, and Keyes has an internal "little man," a double who warns him of fraudulent insurance claims. More significant, the movie's narrative has a double focus in that it evokes the national culture of 1944 as well as that of 1938. The culture of contingency that Graebner attributes to the 1940s is much in evidence. The importance of contingency is suggested by the film's credits, where a shadowy male figure on crutches looms across the screen. It is an image of both Dietrichson, who injures his leg prior to leaving for Palo Alto, and Walter, who disguises himself as the injured man. As well as exemplifying the many unforeseen factors that obtrude upon Walter and Phyllis's murder plan, Dietrichson's accident significantly contributes to Keyes's reconstruction of the details of the murder. Specifically, Keyes realizes that given the speed of the moving train, a person with Dietrichson's injury could not realistically die from an accidental fall onto the tracks. Therefore, the iconic image that opens the movie represents the negative effects that contingency brings.

The issue of contingency is closely related to that of the culture of existentialism that was evident during the year. The seemingly random and chaotic unfolding of events in *Double Indemnity* denies the possibility of larger commitments or systems of belief. As well as being single, Walter and Keyes mock the notion of serious personal relationships. Of course Walter is attracted to Phyllis, but the emotional content of their relationship soon evaporates. As Paula Rabinowitz argues, Phyllis's anklet is a "destabilizing" fetishistic symbol that betokens the conjunction of sex, death, and discord in her relationship with Walter (72). Engraved with her own name, Phyllis's anklet also represents the narcissism and isolation of noir characters. The suspicion and paranoia that result from such isolation are embodied in Nino Zachetti (Byron Barr), a former medical student who befriends Dietrichson's daughter, Lola (Jean Heather), and is then involved in a secret liaison with Phyllis. Led by adverse circumstances to an existence that is restricted to the margins of society, Zachetti always seems afraid to be seen by others and thus his actions appear illicit.

The doubling that occurs between Walter and Phyllis is portrayed as a form of life imprisonment: having committed a murder together, they can never be free of each other. Linked to this existentialist contingency is the representation of consumerism in *Double Indemnity*. As we have seen, the year saw the increased importance of consumption over production in the economy. In the movie, Walter and Phyllis frequently meet in a busy supermarket. Just as they attempt to overcome the difficulties they face in these scenes, so too consumerism is indirectly portrayed as a form of meaning that attempts, in this case futilely, to overcome existential angst and ennui.

The isolated nature of the characters in *Double Indemnity* and the social divisions that are apparent between, for example, Walter and Phyllis counter a sense of social unity and thus illustrate the considerable extent to which the movie is antithetical to the idea of a culture of the whole. Lola Dietrichson represents division in the family and the emergence of oppositional youth culture. She lies to her father and complains to Walter about conflict at home. Isolation also brings with it an individualism that prevents class unity. Although Walter and Phyllis broadly share the same class background, the conflict between them is signified at the outset of the movie by class differences. When Walter and Phyllis first see each other she rests at the top of the stairs in her home and Walter stands at the bottom. Phyllis's position represents the elevated class status that she has attained by virtue of her marriage to Dietrichson. Her drinking of iced tea and her ignorance about what is in the icebox are among the several examples of Phyllis's performance of her bourgeois class role. The recalcitrance of her servant, Nettie (Betty Farrington), suggests the superficiality of Phyllis's class pre-

As Phyllis (Barbara Stanwyck) tells Walter (Fred MacMurray) that Dietrichson has had an accident, the influence of contingency is asserted in *Double Indemnity* (Billy Wilder, Paramount). Digital frame enlargement.

tensions, and when she and Walter meet "without that silly staircase between us," it seems that class unity may be realized. But the unfolding of the narrative shows that these initial divisions are more real than any putative connection between the protagonists.

In the struggle between unity and contingency, it is clear that the latter prevails in *Double Indemnity*. The lack of social unity is exacerbated by the absence of authority. Roosevelt's poor health and the labor resistance to management both exemplified the weakening of authority this year. As David R. Shumway argues, Walter's final return to the insurance office indicates that he is a "disciplined individual" (97), a character who both transgresses and identifies with the authority structure of business. However, Walter's desperate attempt to restore morality and authority is at odds with most of the narrative. The opening image of Dietrichson on crutches evokes the family patriarch in a state of weakness, and his death furthers this impression.

Law enforcement is wholly absent, and the crime is investigated and solved wholly within the ambit of the insurance business. The boss of the insurance company, Norton (Richard Gaines), appears to speak with authority, but his view of the Dietrichson case is inaccurate. Also, Keyes tries to persuade Walter to accept promotion to "claims man," a position he describes as that of "a doctor and a bloodhound and a cop and a judge and a jury and a father confessor all in one." Walter's refusal of the offer is in keeping with the movie's lack of patriarchal authority and its romanticization of powerless existence.

The Sophisticated Noirism of *Laura*

If *Double Indemnity* is a definitive example of film noir, then *Laura* illustrates the extent of the genre's renegotiation. Here, Mark McPherson (Dana Andrews), a detective, investigates the death of Laura Hunt (Gene Tierney). The prime suspects are Waldo Lydecker (Clifton Webb), a famous journalist, and Shelby Carpenter (Vincent Price), a youthful dilettante. Both men are in love with Laura. After discovering that Laura is alive and that a different woman has been shot, McPherson deduces that Lydecker is the murderer. At the close of the movie, McPherson and Laura are together and in love.

Several aspects of *Laura* are in keeping with noir's generic conventions. The scenes that occur at Laura's country home are filled with images of suspicious and surreptitious nocturnal movements. McPherson's periodic returns to the dark and cavernous basement of the police station also serve to restate noir motifs. McPherson himself is in some respects a quintessential noir figure. Having arrested a gangster who killed three police officers on Long Island, he has experienced the dangerous urban confrontations that define the genre. He speaks in the clipped brogue of the noir hero, and his disposition toward Lydecker and Carpenter bristles with potential violence.

As in *Double Indemnity*, the noir elements of *Laura* exemplify a widespread culture of existential uncertainty. However, *Laura* is more concerned with irony than contingency. Through his narcissistic and unsentimental commentary on narrative developments, Lydecker is the most insistent source of irony in the movie. Since his interjections also introduce levity into the narrative, irony takes on a dual role: it is both an accent of the existential qualities of noir and a sign of *Laura*'s renegotiation of genre.

Jans B. Wager argues that noir is often "transgeneric" (76), but *Laura* is distinctive because it contains opposed generic qualities. As if to protect Laura's image from the attributes of noir femmes fatales, such as Phyllis Dietrichson, the movie continually reminds us of the extreme virtue of the titular character. Also, the setting of *Laura* inverts many of the conventions of noir films. Whereas *Double Indemnity* represents the nighttime sprawl of

Los Angeles, *Laura* takes place in the tightly knit and brightly lit world of New York society. The film's lightheartedness and illuminated interiors represent a departure from noir's portrayal of societal decay.

Laura's deviations from the conventions of noir engender thematic dualism and conflict. The characters in *Double Indemnity* are isolated and dispersed, but *Laura* is dominated by its character ensemble. For example, McPherson conducts his initial investigations with both Lydecker and Carpenter in tow. These group scenes suggest that *Laura* shifts toward a representation of a unitary culture. In Graebner's analysis, the holistic aspects of American culture in the 1940s were antithetical to the cultural tendencies associated with film noir. For Graebner, the "culture of the whole" is associated with homogeneity, sentimentalism, centralization, and optimism.

A contrasting cultural trend is identified with apprehension, "moral ambiguity" (Graebner 26), division, and social disorder. The presence of both unity and irony in *Laura* indicates that this movie responded to the period's diverse sensibilities. Such divisions are evident in the generic aspects of the movie. In his first discussion with Lydecker, McPherson refers to one of the journalist's book reviews. In stating that Lydecker's review turned into a description of a murder case, McPherson makes a reference to generic hybridity that is also relevant to *Laura*. The hybridity of *Laura* concerns the conjunction of noir and romantic elements. The first firm evidence of the romantic aspect of the movie occurs as McPherson looks around Laura's apartment. It is an extended sequence that indicates McPherson's romantic interest in the case. The revelation that McPherson has placed a bid on a portrait of Laura from her apartment solidifies this impression. Also, he interacts with Bessie (Dorothy Adams), Laura's faithful maid, in such a way as to suggest that she is also his servant.

The romantic impetus of *Laura* is accelerated by Laura's return. As she reappears, McPherson awakes from sleep. The movie suggests that the prior murder narrative was simply a dream. That noir motifs also increase at this point in the narrative underscores the movie's hybridity. In the police station, McPherson interrogates Laura under bright lights. It is a classic noir moment. Yet it is also at the police station that Laura calls McPherson by his first name and thus makes explicit the movie's romantic trajectory. The realization of the romantic ideal of a unitary culture in the confines of the noir setting typifies the interpenetration of the dual tendencies of the film.

In addition to the movie's overall generic dualism, *Laura* also renegotiates the intersection of class and culture that is associated with noir. In noir movies such as *Double Indemnity*, the social milieu is dominated by popular culture and lower-class characters. In contrast, *Laura* represents class and cultural conflict. Proud and forthright, Bessie sets the tone for the advocacy of working-class culture that we see in the movie; through his constant playing of a pocket baseball game and his use of slang, McPherson is identified with popular culture and the working class. In contrast, the representations of Carpenter and Lydecker as sophisticates are used to critique the pretensions of high culture.

Carpenter aspires toward high culture, but his ignorance about the program of a classical music concert illustrates the superficiality of his interests. He understands that Laura appreciates a popular song, but he cannot share such a perspective because he lacks a clear cultural and social identity. As the spokesperson for upper-class pretensions and high-culture tastes, Lydecker is a more robust character than Carpenter. He disdains McPherson and uses the arguments of cultural and class snobbery in an attempt to persuade Laura to have nothing to do with him. Yet his views can be quickly compromised. When he first sees Laura, for example, he states that he only writes with a goose quill and therefore will not endorse the advertisement for pens that she has designed, but subsequently he reverses his decision, endorsing her advertisement and becoming close friends with her. As illustrated by Lydecker's capitulation to Laura's wishes, the movie portrays the defeat of the cultural values that he represents.

All these examples are relevant to American history in 1944. As we have seen, this year was an important moment in the transition toward the postwar culture of consumerism. The treatment of popular culture in *Laura* affirms this transition. In contrast, Lydecker, as illustrated by the reference to his apoplexy as "an old family custom" and McPherson's assault on his antique clock, is identified with the moribund traditions of the past. The shift to postwar consumerism is also associated with the decline of industrial production and the influence of labor. *Laura* compensates for these developments by suggesting that working-class identity should be associated with the consumption of popular culture. The movie also compensates for decreases in female manufacturing jobs by portraying consumer culture as a source of upwardly mobile employment for women. Laura may be an independent career woman, but her feminine virtue means that she barely challenges gender roles and her active involvement in consumerism affirms the broader culture of the whole.

■ ■ ■

Despite generic variations and often considerable mediations, the relation between historical events and American film this year shows remarkable patterns of consistency. The historical phenomena that are repeatedly apparent in war, musical, and noir movies are usually those that are contentious or dramatic. This statement is especially relevant to the representation of World War II in these film genres. Because it required significant rhetorical justification and involved the decisive D-Day landings, American involvement in the European theater of World War II is widely represented onscreen.

For the most part, American war, musical, and noir films provide rhetorical justification for the commitment of American troops to the European theater. Movies intimate the postwar consumerist gains that the United States might obtain through military commitment, and the ultimately victorious nature of the war is never in doubt. However, isolationist reluctance to engage in a European war is often inflected through these justifications of military involvement. Also, movies' allusions to war are inseparable from their representation of social issues at home. Issues of class, gender, and race were in flux, and many of these developments were due to the new realities of World War II.

At the same time as they interrelate social and military changes, movies this year engage with divergent cultural tendencies toward wholeness and contingency. The narrative and thematic conflicts that are produced by the combination of these factors impact the generic features of war, musical, and noir films. Because the year's recasting of film genres had an effect on American movies that lasted well into the late twentieth century, it is no exaggeration to say that the historical events of 1944 made an abiding contribution to the definition of American cinema.

1945

☐☐☐☐☐☐☐☐☐☐

Movies and the March Home

KRISTINE BUTLER KARLSON

As the year opened, the Allied Forces were planning offensives on Japan, Italy, and Germany to bring the war to an end. President Franklin D. Roosevelt was inaugurated into office for a fourth term in January, and at the same time Russian soldiers were crossing the Oder River into Germany; within six weeks, they had pushed almost as far as Berlin. The United States First Army eventually managed to push back the Nazi forces to east of the Rhine, and the Allies succeeded in breaking the German defenses on the western front. In the Far East, American forces landed in Iwo Jima, finally taking it on 16 March. During the first three months of the Okinawa campaign, 12,500 Americans were killed, and thirty-four naval craft were sunk in intensifying kamikaze attacks. It seemed that the offensive there might go on indefinitely.

In February, FDR, Winston Churchill, and Josef Stalin had met in Crimea for the Yalta Conference, where they ratified the new Polish-Soviet border and where Stalin agreed to get involved in the war against Japan. Both Roosevelt and Churchill recognized the reality of a Soviet power stable enough to allow Stalin to negotiate two extra seats in the newly emerging United Nations, whose charter, signed on 26 June by fifty countries in San Francisco, promised "to save succeeding generations from the scourge of war, which twice in our lifetime has brought untold sorrow to mankind" (Dickson 4). Stalin did not hold free elections in Eastern Europe as promised, and American opinion turned increasingly hostile to Russia as the year wore on.

On 12 April, the day of FDR's death, American troops succeeded in liberating the Nazi concentration camp at Buchenwald and saw for the first time the unimaginable atrocities committed by the Germans. Very soon later, Mussolini and his mistress were captured and shot, and Hitler, realizing he could no longer hope for victory, committed suicide in a Berlin bunker with his mistress and wife of one day, Eva Braun. Once news of Hitler's suicide was announced, Germany surrendered quickly. By 8 May, the Allies could announce V-E Day, signifying the end of war in Europe, and by summer, it seemed life had returned to normal: the first postwar civilian passenger automobiles rolled off the Detroit assembly lines; rationing and shortages were slowly ending. The long-awaited resumption of production of consumer goods in the United States dovetailed with an explosion of new technologies developed during the war, now available for civilian use. The rage for new products at the beginning of the postwar period would result in a more convenient lifestyle for the middle class and would spark the beginnings of a disposable economy with environmental ramifications unforeseen by those participating in it.

But hostilities in Japan continued. From 17 July to 2 August, newly sworn-in president Harry Truman met with Churchill and Stalin at Potsdam, a suburb of Berlin. Stalin delayed communication to his partners of Japan's desire for peace, hoping to be able to join the war before it ended and thereby gain an advantageous negotiating position in the Far East. This delay, which ultimately put off settling the Japan question, would contribute to the decision by the United States to drop the atomic bomb on Hiroshima and Nagasaki. It was decided at this conference that Germany would be administered by an Allied Control Council, that Stalin would have 25 percent of West German industry, that Nazi leaders would be tried as war criminals at Nuremberg, and that Korea would be divided. In August, the attention of the Allies turned once again to ending the war with Japan once and for all. On 6 August, America dropped the first atomic bomb on Hiroshima, a twenty-kiloton uranium bomb, nicknamed "Little Boy," which killed 80,000 people. Three days later, Nagasaki was hit by a second A-bomb, a twenty-two kiloton plutonium bomb, dubbed "Fat Man," which killed an estimated 70,000. President Truman jubilantly called the atomic bomb "the greatest thing in history"; with its launching came the immense possibilities of nuclear energy and the specter of unfathomable horrors in a new, nuclear age. On 14 August, Japan agreed to the terms of unconditional surrender, and Emperor Hirohito made his surrender broadcast on 15 August, V-J Day. The Japanese signed the surrender terms aboard the battleship Missouri in Tokyo Bay on 2 September. World War II was over. American and Russian soldiers met in the middle of Germany and celebrated victory over a common enemy, but mere months later, the Cold War would make enemies of these same soldiers and their two countries for decades.

After years of turmoil and change, the future of postwar America was difficult to predict. The collective energies that for years had gone into the war effort would turn toward a desire for material abundance and success in domestic and economic life. In the years during and directly after the war, movies were at their all-time height of popularity. A medium wrapped in the very fabric of social existence, cinema's influence on the public, and thus its role in forming a sense of self and country, was at its zenith as people looked for models in postwar society.

The studios were in transition from a war economy to a postwar economy. Films released during the year, whether thrillers or musical comedies or dramas, evoke this economic and social transition in a variety of ways, reaffirming, recasting, and complicating the roles of individuals in the couple, the family, and the community. The soldier's return and his successful (or not-so-successful) reintegration is a frequent theme. *The Clock,* directed by Vincente Minnelli, casts Robert Walker as soldier Joe Allen, who meets Alice (Judy Garland) on a two-day leave in New York City. They fall in love and decide to get married before Joe has to return to base. In the stylish and star-studded *Weekend at the Waldorf,* one of the multiple plotlines involves a battle-weary "walking wounded" soldier (Van Johnson) looking for one last romance with a stenographer (Lana Turner). In the musical *Thrill of a Romance,* Esther Williams marries a successful businessman whose obligations take him away during their honeymoon. When she meets war hero Captain Milvaine (Van Johnson), she must choose between either financial and marital comfort or passion.

The importance of the couple and, by extension, the family is stressed in all these reintegration plotlines. Even movies that do not directly refer to the war reaffirm the strength of the couple in the face of adversity. *State Fair,* a remake of the only Rodgers and Hammerstein musical written for the screen, is a nostalgic affirmation of prewar midwestern tradition and American values through a love story that evolves during an Iowa fair. The unforeseen blockbuster *Mom and Dad,* a sexual hygiene film that made unexpected millions, warns of the dangers of not discussing sexuality with young girls through the story of a teenage girl who gets pregnant by a pilot who then dies in a plane crash. In the love story *The Valley of Decision,* a Pittsburgh coal mine strike threatens to come between a young maid (Greer Garson) whose family works in the mine and the son of the mine's owner (Gregory Peck). Alfred Hitchcock's *Spellbound* is the story of a psychiatrist, Constance Petersen (Ingrid Bergman), who falls in love with the new director of the sanatorium in which she works, a Dr. Edwardes (Gregory Peck). When it becomes apparent that he is in fact not Edwardes but an amnesiac who has assumed the doctor's identity, Constance faithfully stands by and helps to cure him, in the process solving the mystery of what happened to the real Edwardes. Though not explicitly about the war, the film recalls the difficulties facing women whose husbands were coming home from the war in a fragile mental state. *The Picture of Dorian Gray*, based on the novel by Oscar Wilde, has the handsome but corrupt Dorian Gray's painting aging and growing more ugly with each sin, beginning with the suicide of his rejected fiancée. Throughout the film, though he grows ever more wicked, even this debauched character still has one pure love: Gladys, the daughter of the painter.

The celebration of American legends characterizes many films as well. America as the land of opportunity flourishes in *The Dolly Sisters*, which casts Betty Grable and June Haver as the two real-life Hungarian sisters whose uncle Latsie brings them to New York in the early 1900s. To pay his card debts they go into vaudeville and meet with unexpected fame. *Dillinger* tracks the main character's rise from petty criminal to Public Enemy Number One. Jimmy Cagney as Nick Condon in *Blood on the Sun* is the embodiment of America as intrepid and honest. Condon, a journalist working in Tokyo, refuses to cooperate with the anti-democratic imperialist government and must live by his wits to avoid being killed. In *A Bell for Adano*, Major Joppolo (John Hodiak) and his men are assigned to restore order to the war-torn Italian town of Adano at the end of World War II. His role is to obtain the trust of the villagers and help them regain their spirit and unity, symbolized by the film's stolen town bell. It is replaced in the tower in time to ring for Joppolo's departure, a ringing hope for the future.

The films examined in this chapter portray a country on the brink of profound change, but not quite certain yet about where it was headed. The thrill of triumph, evident in many earlier war films, was now tempered by a more realistic portrayal of military life in films such as *A Walk in the Sun*. Greater psychological complexity and the sense of ambivalence common to soldier and civilian alike were now allowed. Some films reflect the transition to peacetime for women who had entered the workplace to aid the war effort. *Mildred Pierce* indirectly comments on the status of working women, strongly encouraged by the government and social pressure to go back to their roles as wives and mothers and to give their jobs to the men who had come back to claim them. Social problem films such as *The Lost Weekend* and *A Tree Grows in Brooklyn* raise the specters of alcoholism and psychological disorders in the postwar context. The spy thriller *The House on 92nd Street* capitalizes on the audience's taste for suspense, its interest in wartime intrigues, and its desire for films showing an organized and vigilant American government and citizenry. Though set just before the war, it offers a reassuring read of the vigilance and technological skill of the FBI in protecting the American people from ever-present threats to democracy. The domestic thriller *Leave Her to Heaven* offers a disturbing picture of the postwar domestic sphere, yet ultimately proffers a triumphant reconstruction of the couple. Finally, it is impossible to ignore musicals such as *Anchors Aweigh* and the highest-grossing film of the year, *The Bells of St. Mary's*, the tale of an easy-going priest and a hard-headed nun who lock horns as they run a Catholic school. The film addresses fears of juvenile delinquency and broken homes as a result of war, repairing the threatened nuclear family and offering a reassuring, humorous, and optimistic look at postwar society that is as much about looking back with nostalgia toward traditional prewar values as it is about looking forward.

Within a short time after Pearl Harbor, Hollywood was invested in promoting the war effort, due in large part to encouragement by the government. The industry, like so many others, was quickly converted to war production, and a number of government bodies influenced film production, particularly the Office of War Information (OWI) and its Bureau of Motion Pictures (BMP). These organizations worked "to enhance public understanding of the war, to coordinate the war information activities of all federal agencies, and to act as the intermediary between federal agencies and the radio and motion picture industries" (Koppes and Black, "What to Show" 279–80). Within days of the country's entry into the war, cinema genres began to be reformulated to reflect this engagement:

> Spy, detective, and crime thrillers . . . were easily reformulated (perhaps too easily) into espionage thrillers or underground resistance dramas. . . . The musical and woman's picture were recycled for war production. . . . The backstage musical was recast to depict groups of entertainers putting on military shows "for the boys," while working-girl sagas and melodramas of maternal or marital sacrifice were ideally suited to war conditions.
>
> (Schatz, *Boom* 204)

By 1945, the wartime relationship among the OWI, the BMP, and the studios was coming to an end, but the influence of these bureaus would be felt for years to come.

▪ A Walk in the Sun

Throughout the war, the Pentagon asked for "war films which exulted in America by creating mythical—ethnically, regionally, and occupationally heterogeneous—platoons, to personify American democracy" (Quart and Auster 17). The BMP had stressed multi-ethnicity as one of America's great strengths in order to counter propaganda from Germany and Japan that the United States was a country of undisciplined mongrels. As late as 1945, this filmic imperative makes itself felt in films such as Lewis

The "melting pot" of Caucasian America: Dana Andrews (l.), John Ireland (center), Lloyd Bridges (r.), and Richard Conte (right rear) in *A Walk in the Sun* (Lewis Milestone, Twentieth Century Fox). Collection Kristine Butler Karlson.

Milestone's *A Walk in the Sun*. The opening voiceover, by Burgess Meredith, creates a mythic melting pot of Caucasian America.

> There was Tyne, who never had much urge to travel. Providence, Rhode Island, may not be much as cities go but it was all he wanted; a one-town man. Rivera, Italian American. Likes opera and would like a wife and kid, plenty of kids. Friedman, lathe operator and amateur boxing champ, New York City. Windy, minister's son, Canton, Ohio, used to take long walks alone and just think. Sergeant Ward, a farmer who knows his soil, a good farmer. McWilliams, first aid man, slow, southern, dependable. Archimbault, platoon scout and prophet, talks a lot but he's all right. Porter, Sergeant Porter. He's, well, he has a lot on his mind, a lot on his mind. Tranella, speaks two languages, Italian and Brooklyn. And a lot of other men.

The accompanying image track shows a hand turning the pages of the book on which the film is based, written by Staff Sergeant Harry Brown. Each "page" reveals a different character or set of characters, with the actors' names accompanying the image. Unlike many earlier movies of its genre, this opening sequence presents this group of soldiers as a psychological as well as ethnic mix. Moreover, this socially diverse group is not a closed unit; there are "a lot of other men" as well—ultimately, as many as served in the war.

A Walk in the Sun recounts the 1943 invasion of Italy by the Texas Division of the U.S. infantry, which lands on the coast in Salerno and then moves inland to take a fortified farmhouse. The film, unflinchingly realistic in the treatment of the soldiers' experience, portrays their struggles to keep up morale, conveyed by an emphasis on dialogue unusual in combat films. The first man dies in the first five minutes—a new guy who leans over the boat to look through his binoculars and gets his face blown off by a shell. Despite this bloody beginning, there is very little actual combat. Much of the film consists of waiting, as the soldiers talk, prepare themselves mentally, and are suddenly thrown into bursts of battle. The use of tight close-ups during conversational exchanges conveys the cramped closeness of the soldiers and emphasizes their individual psychological struggles. Night-for-night photography in the opening dialogue sequence on the landing barge allows strong contrast and gives the soldiers' faces an almost ghostly quality. The darkness heightens the tension for the audience, who cannot see any better than the soldiers what awaits them.

Although the film avoids overblown heroism, it seeks to make the common soldier into the stuff of legend. The opening voiceover states that the events took place "way back in 1943. . . . Here's a song about them. Listen." What follows is an original ballad, written by Millard Lampell and performed by Earl Robinson. Milestone conceived the ballads as a way to dramatize certain events in the film and give it a unifying element lacking in the dialogue-heavy script. When the ballads proved unpopular with his colleagues, he reduced the number but refused to eliminate the device altogether. The finished film has only four, down from the original eleven intended. To a contemporary viewer the ballads seem an intrusive, patently unrealistic element, but they do create an aura of legend and thus liken the struggles of the Texas Division to the everyday heroes of American folk songs: common people who struggled against overwhelming odds, often dying in the process.

A Walk in the Sun is not about the glorious cause of democracy, but about the common foot soldier and his quiet devotion to duty. No one in the film is immune to death or madness; there is no heroic leader to keep up morale with near-superhuman strength. When Captain Tyne (Dana Andrews) is killed, Sergeant Porter (Herbert Rudley) must take his place; he subsequently breaks down and must be replaced himself. The possibility of cracking under pressure is presented as something common to all soldiers. Thus, Private "Windy" Craven (John Ireland) consoles Porter as he lies sobbing in the dirt: "We understand." Each infantryman deals with his fate differently; Windy's spoken letters to his sister "Frances" are a means of whistling in the dark against fear, the soldier's constant companion. The common soldier's curse is never to know what is happening, as is made palpable by the visual absence of the enemy. The soldier is not privy to the larger picture, the clear objectives known by those at the top—a fact that ultimately questions the logic of these same objectives. This gloomy message pervades many other war pictures, such as *The Story of GI Joe, They Were Expendable,* and *Objective, Burma!,* which celebrate the defeats of early days in anticipation of the victory that lay just ahead.

Mildred Pierce

The sheer number of women involved in the workforce during World War II made it one of the most dramatic periods of change for women in American history. Employment opportunities—particularly for white women—increased, continuing a trend that began during the Depression. Between 1940 and 1945 the proportion of all women who were employed increased from 27.6 to 37 percent. In 1940 only 15 percent of married women were in the labor force; by the end of the war one of every four wives was employed (Hartmann 16–21). During the war, women were granted unprecedented freedoms by a country increasingly ambivalent about the costs of these freedoms to society as a whole. Autumn 1945 saw the return of thousands of American soldiers, and the drastic reduction of employment opportunities for women. Many would face readjustment to the presence of a spouse and a return to full-time homemaking.

Hollywood had played an important role in shaping attitudes about the war and women's place within it. The BMP, whose reviewing staff was composed largely of women, was concerned to portray women contributing to the war effort, in both the public sphere and at home, in their efforts to raise children and make ends meet. Hollywood films, as well as women's magazines (such as *Good Housekeeping* and *McCall's*), had played a crucial role in encouraging women to take on war work. Now these same media urged women to return to the home (Ohmer 53–68).

Mildred Pierce, directed by Michael Curtiz, combines complicated and contradictory discourses about women's place that have fascinated and troubled many film scholars. Part maternal melodrama, part film noir, *Mildred Pierce,* based on the novel by James M. Cain, is at once a crime film and the story of a woman (Joan Crawford) struggling to make a way for herself as a single career woman. The film begins with the murder of Mildred's second husband, Monte Beragon (Zachary Scott), gunned down in the couple's beach house by an unknown assailant. His last word, "Mildred," implicates her in a crime that it will be the film's job to resolve. Scholars have called attention to the stylistic changes that accompany the progression of Mildred's story. Early in the film, after Monte's murder, Mildred walks through the dark, her face half in shadow, toward a bridge where she contemplates suicide. An evocative musical score by Max Steiner and dark, expressionistic lighting convey her desperation and the nightmare her existence has become. This lighting suggests that Mildred is a femme fatale. However, as the film progresses, early flashbacks of her life before her separation from her husband are brighter, more evenly lit, and correspond more to 1930s melodrama. These early scenes portray a more domestic Mildred and complicate the femme fatale reading. In the first analysis, the difference between these two styles seems incongruous. Mildred's version of the story (her flashbacks) would seem to be pitted against the film noir juridical discourse, which bookends and recasts her story, appropriating it and thus controlling the "real" truth of the events. Though the film arguably seeks to repress the woman's version of the story, the strain of such a repression is apparent at key points in the narrative. This tension suggests a larger social tension made evident in the film—that between celebration of women's greater presence and success in the workforce during the war and emphasizing the postwar priority for women to return to the home.

In a pivotal essay, Linda Williams correctly addresses the film's temporal and stylistic ambiguities. Although the war is never specifically mentioned and events in the film are not directly connected to the war, the story encapsulates that period and there are allusions to the war in the dialogue. While courting Mildred, Monte expresses happiness that "nylons are out for the duration," a clear reference to shortages and rationing. Later in the film, Mildred's business partner, Ida (Eve Arden), reacts with surprise when Mildred's first husband, Bert Pierce (Bruce Bennett), gets a job in a defense plant: "Manpower shortage must be worse than we think." The war, then, is present if not explicit. The timeframe of Mildred's separation from her husband up to the murder also seems to mirror the timeframe of the war. The story that Mildred recounts took place over four years, as she says to the detective while trying to explain why she divorced Bert: "It's taken me four years to find that out. But now I know I was wrong." Four years prior to the date of the film's release would be 1941, the year of U.S. entry into the war. Mildred divorces Bert, in part because of his failure to get a job, in part because of fears that he is having an affair with their neighbor Mrs. Biederhoff, a woman obviously married but whose husband seems to be conspicuously absent—perhaps away at war? As Williams points out, there are conflicting indicators of the temporal location of these events. Mildred and Bert could have split up at the end of the Depression, or perhaps during wartime. The film does not give us a clear explanation as to why Bert is out of work. It does, however, suggest that Bert is discouraged and perhaps depressed. The economic situation of the film does seem to reflect a wartime period of want. Mildred explains that Bert had been in a successful real estate venture with his partner, Wally Fay (Jack Carson), until "suddenly, everybody stopped buying; the boom was over." Bert loses his job, and the bills pile up.

Though it is true that "we are not encouraged to read (Mildred's) newfound independence in the context of a collective national experience of wartime" (Williams 21), we ultimately are encouraged to read Mildred's divorce of Bert, and her recognition four years later of this as a mistake, as a readjustment narrative. That Bert is not a returning soldier does not negate this, as he is secondary to the narrative obviously pitched for a female audience. Had Bert been a soldier, we must imagine that Mildred's leaving him would have been patently unacceptable to audiences. His lack of motivation allows Mildred some degree of justification for the divorce. Bert's inability to find a job may or may not be justified—a quandary that the film does not resolve for the viewer. However, that he is a concerned parent reaffirms his worth as a father and his ultimate recuperability. His disapproval of Mildred's desire to give her children, Veda and Kay (especially the older Veda, played by Ann Blyth), "the best" puts Mildred's judgment into question to the benefit of his. Her obsession with Veda and relative lack of concern for Kay will be revealed as increasingly dangerous and unnatural. Bert's worth is further affirmed at the police station in the second present-tense sequence, when Mildred is informed that he has been charged with Beragon's murder. Mildred objects, saying that Bert is too good and kind to have murdered anyone. The detective sardonically replies by asking why she divorced him. To clear him of the crime Mildred must continue her narrative of the past. The entire sequence of events leading up to the murder is thus offered as an exculpation of Bert.

Striking out on her own, Mildred had taken a job as a waitress, and eventually managed to open her own restaurant in a property owned by

Mildred Pierce (Joan Crawford) clutches her daughter Veda (Ann Blyth) as ex-husband Bert (Bruce Bennett) looks on: the breakdown of the middle-class family in *Mildred Pierce* (Michael Curtiz, Warner Bros.). Collection Kristine Butler Karlson.

rich playboy Beragon. As her restaurant prospers, gender dynamics become increasingly ambiguous for all save Bert himself. Mildred becomes, as she herself describes it, "hard." She becomes involved with Beragon, who has never worked a day in his life; thus Bert's period of unemployment is no longer a justification for Mildred's having left him. Mildred hires Ida, an aggressive and mannish former colleague, to help her run the restaurant. Tomboy Kay, the "nice, normal little girl" who still has time to grow out of her boyish behavior (and thus poses no serious threat to the social order), dies of pneumonia, thus raising the specter of maternal neglect. Mildred and Veda are now left alone together. The relationship that develops between them is as much that of mistress/suitor as of mother/daughter. Mildred buys Veda expensive gifts and a fancy car to win her affection. When they are briefly estranged following Veda's blackmailing of a rich young man, Mildred redecorates the entire house and marries Monte to win Veda back, promising to give her the lifestyle to which she aspires. The unscrupulous Monte is now free to spend Mildred's money; he and Veda become lovers behind Mildred's back. The nuclear family has been completely perverted.

Mildred Pierce clearly demonstrates ambivalence about women's place in postwar society. The film's position regarding women's employment is based on a need-versus-greed dichotomy, but it is more complicated than that. Mildred is viewed as heroic in taking a waitressing job (seemingly below her middle-class status) to feed her children. However, in the context of the war and immediate postwar economy, her success as a restaurant owner and her pursuit of wealth would have been seen as excessive to contemporary audiences. Mildred and Ida's financial successes are thrilling, and channel for female audiences "the exhilaration of female independence . . . [which] was undoubtedly experienced by many women during the war but was unacceptable to the dominant ideology of national unity" (Williams 23). Yet Mildred's work ceases to be admirable, appropriate "women's work" when Bert gets a job. Her spoiling of Veda and Kay, the death of her younger child, and finally her lying to the police about Monte's murder to protect Veda (who shot Monte when he said he didn't love her) are all actions implicitly linked to her pursuit of excessive wealth. The end of the film restores order to the family structure and places Mildred back in a traditional role. The murder solved and Veda in jail, Mildred and Bert walk out of the Los Angeles Hall of Justice into the morning sunlight (the "new dawn" of the postwar). As they recede into the distance, two scrubwomen in the foreground clean the steps. The patriarchal law, represented in the imposing stone of the building, is once again solid ground for the middle-class couple. The working-class women are once again in their place. Mildred's business has been bought out by Bert's shady former partner, Wally Fay; the audience can assume that her business days are over. She is now free to go back to her husband and her home, sadder but wiser.

The Lost Weekend

When the United States joined the war, the OWI enjoined Hollywood to redefine the social health of America, emphasizing not the problems but the promise of a democratic society. Increasingly, protagonists with psychological difficulties were portrayed in war period films not as metonymic of society's ills, but as isolated cases in a country resolutely on the path to an ever better tomorrow. Topics such as unemployment, alcoholism, orphaned children, migrant workers, prostitution, even lynching, which had flourished in the "social problem" films of the Depression era and into the early 1940s, had been taboo during the war years. These films, which tended to critique the systems and institutions against which their protagonists struggled, were considered unpatriotic in the context of the war.

This was a watershed year for alcoholism in film, a moment in which the strictures of the Hollywood Production Code began to break down. In 1922, the Hays Commission had created a set of moral rules by which Hollywood filmmakers were to abide. This commission was a precursor to the Production Code of 1934, which put down in no uncertain terms what was not to be shown on screen. Section I, part 4: *"The use of liquor* in American life, when not required by the plot or for proper characterization, will not be shown" (Production Code, 139). Evolution in understanding of alcohol abuse contributed to a gradual easing of these regulations: the creation of Alcoholics Anonymous in 1935, the founding of the National Council on Problems of Alcoholism in 1937, and in 1944 the National Committee on the Education of Alcoholism, an offshoot of the National Council. The National Committee worked to increase awareness of alcoholism and three main principles: alcoholism is a disease; the alcoholic deserves help to treat the illness; alcoholism is a public health problem. National Council advocates lobbied Hollywood to produce films embodying these ideas. As a result, the period between 1945 and 1962 saw the production of close to thirty films that took the alcoholic and his or her drinking as their sole or primary focus (Denzin 5).

The Lost Weekend, directed by Billy Wilder, adapts Charles Jackson's 1944 novel, creating one of the top-grossing films of the year and the standard by which subsequent films about alcoholism would inevitably be judged. Alcoholism in the 1930s had been shown as primarily a problem affecting the entertainment industry, for "if problems with alcohol were going to be treated, such problems had to be located in a site far away from normal, everyday life; what better place than Hollywood's own backyard" (Denzin 43). *The Lost Weekend* marks a shift from this portrayal. Set in Manhattan, it was the first film to challenge restrictions on showing drinking on screen. The film follows the drinking binge of would-be writer Don Birnam (Ray Milland) as he turns to drink to escape his feelings of failure. We watch as he hides alcohol from his brother and girlfriend, Helen (Jane Wyman), steals from his cleaning lady, takes a purse in a nightclub and a bottle from a liquor store, tries to pawn his typewriter, pawns Helen's coat, and spends a night in Bellevue. The novel version of Don shares some traits of the 1930s film alcoholic: he is an aspiring writer with high notions of art and an affection for F. Scott Fitzgerald. The film creates Birnam in something of a similar vein: though Wilder had wanted to cast José Ferrer as the protagonist, Paramount insisted instead on the handsome and distinguished Milland, chosen in part for his accent (he was Welsh by birth) and demeanor. Though he has what Helen calls "flashes of real brilliance," his failure to be a productive writer and his self-doubt sets him apart from the creative loner hero of earlier films such as *A Star Is Born.*

The film opens with natural lighting as Don and his brother/roommate, Wick (Phillip Terry), pack for a long weekend in the country. The bedroom in which they pack is small and cramped, creating a claustrophobic feel that mirrors Don's desperation to escape from a weekend in which he will be away from drink. The camera tends to film him close, and the frame appears too small for him as he restlessly moves about the room. Don finagles a way to postpone their departure so that he can procure alcohol for the trip, convincing Wick to accompany Helen to a concert, promising to meet them later. Don immediately runs out to buy alcohol, then stops in a bar and fails to return to the apartment at the appointed time; Wick leaves him behind, and Don goes on a bender. Don progresses through many stages of drunkenness and desperation. At Nat's bar, Don is charming and witty. When he realizes he has missed the time to return home, he becomes frantic and desperate; accordingly, the camera style turns noir, using the coming nightfall to heighten the contrasts between light and dark. As the film progresses, certain scenes become positively nightmarish, aided by Miklós Rózsa's eerie music: Don's stay at Bellevue, where he witnesses firsthand other patients in the throes of delirium tremens, and Don's own bout with DTs in which he sees a bat swoop down and devour a mouse making a hole in the wall of his apartment.

The film cites the causes of Don's alcoholism as twofold. On the one hand is fear of failure and desire to escape the "ordinary"—the psychological problem of an unstable sense of self. On the other, Don's alcoholism is presented as a medical illness, and in this the film is truly a first. However, though *The Lost Weekend* portrays the causes and horrors of alcoholism with unprecedented realism, it fails to offer suggestions of treatment or cure. Finally, it is Helen's love that redeems Don. Her faith helps him to realize that he can write a novel telling the story of the alcoholic (a novel that probably closely resembles Jackson's). His therapy, as she says, will be to "put [the nightmares of the alcoholic's life] on paper. Get rid of them that way. Tell it all, to whom it may concern. It concerns so many people, Don" (Wilder and Brackett 109). This rather pat and unsatisfying ending, with the protagonist being "saved" by the love of a good woman, owes much to the conventions of the 1930s films of the Production Code era, and little to a modern, progressive view of the realities of alcoholism.

▰▰▰▰▰ ■ *A Tree Grows in Brooklyn*

A Tree Grows in Brooklyn, based on the 1943 novel by Betty Smith and directed by Elia Kazan, tells the story of a poor Irish American family in the tenements of Brooklyn in the 1910s. Though more melodramatic than *The Lost Weekend*, the film is ultimately more realistic regarding the eventual fate of the alcoholic. Here we are not in upscale Manhattan but in humble Brooklyn. Johnny Nolan (James Dunn) is an Irish charmer loved by everyone in his community. A singing waiter by trade, Johnny is not a Hollywood artist, but rather an ordinary guy with a creative nature. He is essentially a good man, but a hopeless dreamer. As in Wilder's film, alcoholism is not shown as provoked by any exterior elements. The family's poverty is part of the backdrop, but never suggested as a reason for Johnny's drinking. Set before the First World War, the film is pervaded by nostalgia for a simpler time, beginning with the first songs in the opening credits, such as "Oh, You Beautiful Doll" and "Take Me Out to the Ballgame." This earlier setting removes the film from association with the audience's immediate realm of experience. The causes of Johnny's drinking are never addressed, though his Irishness is implicitly a factor, emphasized by the Irish songs he sings. Like Don Birnam, Johnny cannot support his family; his wife, Katie (Dorothy McGuire), washes the stairways of their tenement building to make ends meet. Johnny also often makes promises in all earnestness, which those who love him know he will not keep. Johnny never has Don's moments of insight, at least not in front of the camera, and will not have a moment of redemption or recovery.

The film's focus on the Nolan family—particularly the women—suggests that alcoholism is an illness that endangers the stability of the home. The protagonist is young Francie (Peggy Ann Garner), who idolizes her father and is too young to fully understand what is happening to him. Though Johnny is never shown drinking, there are references to what he is like when he is "sick." The words "drunk" and "alcoholic" are used, though rarely, to describe him. The role of Francie's brother, Neeley, is relatively unexamined in the film; the family dynamic is represented instead in the trio of Francie-Katie-Johnny. The trio's relationship is eerily consistent with present-day research on alcoholics and their daughters and wives. Francie's intense love for Johnny is heightened by Katie's apparent hardness with him, leading to what psychologist Robert Ackerman terms "role confusion." In case studies of families with an alcoholic father, daughters often felt "that their mothers were emotionally absent and full of resentment toward their fathers. This situation caused the fathers to expect that their daughters

The Nolan triangle: Francie (Peggy Ann Garner, l.), Johnny (James Dunn), and Katie (Dorothy McGuire) from *A Tree Grows in Brooklyn* (Elia Kazan, Twentieth Century Fox). Collection Kristine Butler Karlson.

understand them and support them. In many ways the fathers responded to their daughters in what I call 'emotional incest'" (Ackerman 60). The photography in the film reflects this relationship and emphasizes that the real couple in *Tree* is Francie and Johnny. Johnny's first scene is not with Katie but with Francie, when he comes home to prepare for a job as a singing waiter for a wedding. As Francie irons his apron, they talk about the future, and her role seems to toggle between those of daughter and wife. At one point, the camera takes the two in close-up with soft lighting as Johnny comes from behind to embrace Francie and kiss her tenderly on the cheek. This embrace is made more ambiguous in the next shot, as Francie and Johnny move to the window to mourn the cutting of their favorite tree as "Lullaby and Goodnight" lilts in the background.

Ultimately, both *The Lost Weekend* and *A Tree Grows in Brooklyn* center on the alcoholic's success or failure to find his place in the social order. The love of a good woman is seen as crucial to the alcoholic's recovery. Unlike Helen, Katie's love is not sufficient to cure Johnny. In fact, the film suggests that this insufficiency pushes him over the brink. When Katie discovers she is pregnant for the third time, she attempts to stop being, as she says, so "hard." But, exhausted and pushed to the limit by Johnny's wild dreaming, she finally breaks. "Ya ain't got a chance. Who're we tryin' to kid?" This pronouncement pushes Johnny toward his death. He leaves the apartment on Christmas night and is not found until New Year's, dead of pneumonia and acute alcoholism from standing out in the cold waiting for work. The birth of the Nolans' third child, Annie Laurie, occurs after Johnny's death. This birth is an entirely female affair, as Katie's sister, Sissy, her mother, Mary, and Francie all work together. The nuclear family is reconstituted at the end of the film when Katie agrees to court and eventually marry the kind and recently widowed Officer McShane (Lloyd Nolan). Rather than offer Johnny's rehabilitation, the film thus replaces him with a good Irishman, reconfiguring the nuclear family and allowing the American myth of happiness, upward mobility, and prosperity to continue unchallenged by Johnny's exceptional case. As a result, this film is consistent with the wartime film industry's cultivated image of a society in which social problems are transitory, inevitably resolved in a resolutely democratic America.

The House on 92nd Street and Leave Her to Heaven

Espionage and crime films were by far the most popular with the major studios in the early days of World War II. Thomas Schatz suggests this is due to the ease with which B-grade espionage and sabotage films could be reformulated. G-men and police could "simply [turn] their sights from gangsters to foreign agents; the trappings of the story—props, sets, costumes, cast and plot structure—remained much the same" (Schatz, *Boom* 241). In the mid-forties, these films began to move away from a war context toward more domestic concerns. Henry Hathaway's *The House on 92nd Street* is a notable exception to this trend. In the film, German American William Dietrich (William Eythe) is hired by the FBI in 1939 to go undercover in a Nazi spy ring. Dietrich tries to keep up his cover with the Nazis while preventing them from sending atom bomb secrets to the German government. The opening credits are revealed by a hand turning the pages of what appears to be a classified FBI document. As we read, we learn that the story is adapted from cases in the FBI's espionage files. Patriotic music plays as we read the lists of cast and crew and the claims to veracity. Not only is footage shot on location in the cities concerned, but "with the exception of the leading players, all F.B.I. personnel in the pictures are members of the Federal Bureau of Investigation." A lengthy sequence follows, with voiceover narrative introducing the spectator to the background of "the Christopher Case" and the modern technological advances of the bureau.

This picture is exemplary of the mélange of documentary and fiction that developed in the late war years. The tone of danger having passed and effectively dispatched allows the film to present the FBI as a swift, efficient machine, similar to the nation's armed forces. The unmuddied purpose and clarity of the bureau's victory is unusual in a 1945 film; however, the ostensible year of the action is 1939, and the ultimate goal of the Christopher Case is to prevent information about "Process 97," the secret ingredient of the atomic bomb, from falling into the hands of the Germans. This story, the opening credits insist, "could not be released until the first atomic bomb was dropped on Japan." Less about combat than about the technology of the postwar, the "now it can be told" tone seems to be preparing the film's audience for the dangers (in the wrong hands) and wonders (in the right hands) of atomic defense.

Few crime films from this period are as ideologically uncomplicated as *The House on 92nd Street*. Many exhibit ambivalent and contradictory assumptions regarding society as a whole, marriage, and domestic life, painting a disturbing picture of the private sphere that would have been unacceptable to the OWI. Even when a relationship is portrayed as true blue, as in that between Al and Sue in Edgar Ulmer's *Detour,* that relationship is doomed from the beginning by forces out of Al's control. As Al says, "Fate, or some mysterious force, can put the finger on you for no good reason at all." This statement sums up well the psyche of the noir hero, always caught between forces he can't understand or control. Innocence makes no difference; good intentions are for naught. The domestic sphere of marriage is put in question in *Conflict, Leave Her to Heaven, Scarlet Street*, and other films of the period. Lack of love or excessive love on the part of a husband or a wife leads to more than one criminal act and the potential breaking apart of the romantic couple. In both *Conflict* and *Leave Her to Heaven*, excessive desire is equated with incest. In the first film, the forbidden love of the protagonist for his sister-in-law drives him to murder his wife. In *Leave Her to Heaven*, Ellen's excessive love for her husband, Richard, is seen as transference of her incestuous love for her recently deceased father. Ellen's active desire is monstrous on a much larger scale than that of *Conflict*'s protagonist; her husband's remark early in the movie is revealing: "If you'd lived in Salem a hundred years ago, they'd have burned you." Ellen is an example of female sexual desire in excess, always monstrous, the quintessential noir femme fatale. The psycho-social roots of Ellen's illness are clear: she desires Richard for herself, does not want to integrate into the family, and violently refuses the role of mother—both that of surrogate mother to Richard's brother, and of biological mother to her own unborn child—by killing them both. Ultimately, when Richard realizes the depths of Ellen's depravity, she commits suicide and frames her adopted sister Ruth to keep her away from her husband.

Dana Polan has asserted that "the forties horror film, then, becomes a site for the narrativization of a conflict between unbridled desire and the containing of desire within the limits of a stable rationality" (176). *Leave Her to Heaven* solves this conflict by removing the excessively desiring woman and replacing her with one more given to domestic pursuits (Ruth's love of gardening has earned her the nickname of "the gal with the hoe" by Richard). Ultimately, Richard and Ruth discover that they are indeed in love with one another. To save her, he implicates himself in Ellen's death and spends two years in prison. Dutifully, Ruth waits for him, and the film ends with their embrace on the dock of Richard's cabin in Maine. Ruth's replacement of Ellen in Richard's life escapes being incestuous in that she is not actually Ellen's biological sister but her cousin. The couple is thus recuperated, and Richard, for whom the familiar, *heimlich* haven of his family home had been transfused by the *unheimlich* menace of his wife, can now return with Ruth, the hold of the past broken.

The Bells of St. Mary's

One of the most famous movie couples of the year was not even a couple, strictly speaking. Father Chuck O'Malley (Bing Crosby) and Sister Mary Benedict (Ingrid Bergman) won American hearts in Leo McCarey's *The Bells of St. Mary's,* the sequel to 1944's *Going My Way.* Young Father O'Malley arrives at St. Mary's Church and School to take over its direction. He finds his energies pulled in three directions: he clashes with Sister Benedict on how to raise and educate the young people in their charge; he takes a young girl from a troubled family under his wing and takes it upon himself to help resolve the family's problems; finally, he must attempt to save St. Mary's school from extinction by convincing a cranky businessman (Henry Travers) to donate a new school building.

In the course of accomplishing these tasks, Crosby's character has time for a song or three. "Aren't You Glad You're You," "The Bells of St. Mary's," and "In the Land of Beginning Again" are integrated into the plot not as musical numbers per se, but rather as organically occurring opportunities for Father O'Malley to break into song. Unlike other musicals of the period, instrumental accompaniment is restricted to the pianos that O'Malley plays as he sings. There are no breakaway moments in which characters dance choreographed numbers. Rather, these songs are mere pauses in the action, seemingly motivated simply by the fact that there happens to be a piano in the room. The religious theme of the film, as well, motivates other musical pauses, such as Crosby's rendition of "Adeste Fidelis" with the school children around the piano. Song in *The Bells of St. Mary's,* from singing the old school song to intoning a Christmas hymn, is equated with the artless joy of living and with a simple, somewhat nostalgic, unfailing Christian faith in the future. Crosby's easy-going baritone conveys the soothing sense that all is well, or soon will be.

The narrative of *Bells of St. Mary's* does correspond in many ways to the musical genre. As scholars of the musical have noted, the primary narrative engine of the genre is the formation of the couple. Rick Altman and others have shown that musical protagonists are generally represented as diametrically opposed attitudes—two mutually exclusive terms that must somehow be reconciled by the end of the film. Here, O'Malley is unorthodox, easy-going, and more concerned with enjoying life than with rules. On his first day at St. Mary's, he immediately proclaims a holiday for the children. When a fight breaks out on the school grounds between two boys, O'Malley breaks it up, but instead of punishing the youngsters, he compliments one on his fighting technique and ruffles his hair. Sister Benedict, on the other hand, is rule bound, committed to upholding Christian doctrine and the standards of St. Mary's. She opposes fighting and has taught the second boy, Eddy, the virtues of turning the other cheek. Where Father O'Malley is realistic—St. Mary's is in decay and may need to be closed down—Sister Benedict is idealistic, believing firmly that the sisters' prayers will be answered and the rich Mr. Bogardus (Travers) will donate his brand new building next door to St. Mary's to serve as a new school. For the narrative to reconcile, the two protagonists must move toward each other, progressively abandoning their old ways to meet in the middle. Sister Benedict, realizing that Eddy is not being well served by her advice, buys a book on boxing and teaches him to fight. When the bully next approaches him on the playground, Eddy soundly trounces him (after waiting to be attacked first, of course), then offers friendship, which the bully accepts. Sister Benedict will also learn that the academic standards of St. Mary's have their limits when a star pupil purposely fails her year-end exams in order to stay at St. Mary's another year.

For his part, Father O'Malley takes on some of Sister Benedict's idealism in his negotiations with Mr. Bogardus, though he remains ever practical and unorthodox in his means. He convinces Bogardus's doctor to make the patient believe that his bad heart could be made better by doing good deeds. Father O'Malley thus engineers the "miracle" for which the sisters have been praying. By the end of the film, each has come toward the other's way of thinking, and the "couple" is formed. But of course, for a priest and a nun to fall in love is out of the question. Sister Benedict's diagnosis of tuberculosis provides a way to end the story and also to allow the narrative to climax in a way similar to that of the love confession. Though her doctor has instructed Father O'Malley to say nothing of why she is being sent away, he cannot bear her to think that he wants to get rid of her. In the last scene of the film, O'Malley calls her back just as she is leaving and reveals to her that she is being sent away because she is ill. Her response of ecstatic radiance, shown in an extended close-up, calls to mind that of a lover hearing a declaration of love for the first time. Narratively, this happiness comes from the fact that she now knows that she can come back to her children and her new school once she has been cured. This displacement of the love confession onto confession of a serious (but curable) illness provides for an eventual reuniting of the couple, a "happily ever after" that removes any overt sexual and marital aspects from the film. Indeed, formation of the couple and the nuclear family takes place when O'Malley succeeds in reuniting the parents of Patsy Gallagher, one of the students. Fears of juvenile delinquency corresponding to the reality of broken homes as a result of war are addressed here with an uncomplicated reconstitution story. Now that Father O'Malley has found Patsy's father and reunited her parents, things will be different. Patsy, who now has a stable family and no longer fears leaving St. Mary's, walks down the aisle to graduate in her pure white dress. Her parents look on proudly, seeing, like us, a vision of hope for the future.

Anchors Aweigh

Anchors Aweigh, as well, offers a vision of future happiness and success for young couples in love. This film celebrates the military with patriotic beginning and ending scenes on the stylized deck of a navy ship. Music director José Iturbi leads a military band playing a rousing choreographed version of "Anchors Aweigh" in the opening sequence, in which Gunner's Mate Joe Brady (Gene Kelly) and Seaman Clarence Doolittle (Frank Sinatra) receive the Silver Star. Following the ceremony, they and their shipmates are immediately granted four days' leave in Hollywood, which Joe intends to spend romancing a certain "Lola." He gets sidetracked from poor Lola trying to find a woman for Clarence. On their search, the two are picked up by the police to help return a young navy-obsessed boy to his home. It is then that they meet "Aunt Susie" (Kathryn Grayson), young Donald's guardian. Though Kelly tries to set up Aunt Susie and Clarence, he ends up falling for her instead.

Anchors is a spectacular musical comedy, combining Gene Kelly's dancing, Frank Sinatra's and Kathryn Grayson's singing, and José Iturbi's entertaining conducting and masterful piano playing, not to mention the dancing of Jerry the Mouse (of "Tom and Jerry" fame) in the celebrated animated sequence with Kelly. This highly entertaining film casts Kelly, once again, as a happy-go-lucky child-man out for a bit of fun, who falls in love with his opposite. In order for the formation of the Susie/Joe couple to happen, he must put his irresponsible "sea wolf" ways aside. As he tries to arrange a meeting with Susie and Mr. Iturbi, he will eventually forget about his egotistic pursuit of "Lola" and bit by bit assume the role of father figure to Donald. By the end of the film, gone is the Joe Brady who says, "If you like dames, what's the point in gettin' one that's different from all the other dames?" He has been converted now that he has found a woman "you wanna come home to." If in previous wartime films Kelly has played unpatriotic characters who had to learn the sense of duty to country (for example, *For Me and My Gal*), here his role is to come home from war and learn the patriotism of domesticity. The film is part readjustment narrative, with not only Joe but Clarence discovering the transformative powers of a good woman's love. At the same time, it reinforces Hollywood as a vision of American success and spectacle when Aunt Susie (Grayson) is finally discovered by Iturbi and makes her singing debut on board Joe and Clarence's ship. Interestingly, the film ends *before* her song begins, with a shot of the two couples (Joe and Susie, Clarence and "Brooklyn") embracing. In *Anchors Aweigh*, Hollywood is very much the place where dreams of celebrity, but more importantly of love, come true.

* * *

When President Truman disbanded the Bureau of Motion Pictures on 31 August, the organization had read 1,652 wartime scripts. Thus officially ended an unprecedented relationship between the government and Hollywood that proffered a model for future interaction during military conflicts. Such partnership, it was presumed, had helped to make the public understand the reasons for fighting and who the enemies were, to instruct the public about their important role in the war, and to construct a strong and unified vision of America both for Americans and for Axis and Allied nations alike. This careful construction of America rested on myths of American democratic values; gender, racial, and class harmony; and the carefully constructed vision of a world in which American values would become universal truths at the end of the war.

1946

Movies and Postwar Recovery

WHEELER WINSTON DIXON

The war was over but sunshine had not broken through. The Nuremberg verdicts were sentencing key Nazi leaders to death, and more was being learned about their complicity in war crimes. Though out of office, Winston Churchill was far from complacent: he came to America and coined the phrase "Iron Curtain," describing the postwar world, still threatened by totalitarianism, as haggard. On the domestic front, strikes of electrical workers, meat packers, steel workers, and others idled four and a half million people, but the culture was hardly idle: Wagon Lits/Cook, Scandinavian Airlines, Alitalia, Air India, and the International Air Transport Association were all created, and Americans took advantage by traveling around the world.

It was a year of new beginnings in many ways, with events and developments reaching into both the future and the past. With the invention of xerography, the world as simulacrum, or copy, sprang into a new dimension: costly Photostats were eliminated and it became a matter of relative ease to duplicate all manner of documents, be they legal, economic, or creative. The first meeting of the United Nations took place in London, inaugurating an organization that would try to undo the factionalism of modern history at a new round table. The United States began a controversial series of atomic bomb tests in the Bikini atoll. The discovery of the Dead Sea Scrolls brought ancient history to the dinner table, and home jukeboxes, which had sporadically appeared in roadside cafes since the early 1930s, went into mass production, turning anyone with a few nickels into a purveyor of contemporary music. The world of military and post-military life saw major changes: as returning soldiers made up for lost time and started raising families, the Baby Boom began; Dr. Benjamin Spock moved at the same time to revolutionize child rearing with his book *The Common Sense Book of Baby and Child Care*, which implicitly told parents to trust their own instincts when it came to guiding their young.

If returning veterans sought to pick up their lives where they had left off, there was a palpable feeling that society had been fundamentally altered. The ranch house came into prominence in the new suburban architecture, as returning veterans and their families abandoned apartment life for their own homes. Electric blankets were introduced, as was the Slinky toy, a giant coiled spring that seemed to magically walk down flights of stairs by itself. Timex watches, the bikini, vinyl recordings, and Estée Lauder cosmetics were all introduced to a receptive public. The ENIAC (Electronic Numerical Integrator and Computer), the world's first electronic digital computer, was developed at Harvard, using eighteen thousand vacuum radio tubes and plenty of electrical power.

It was a time of real social concerns. As one observer put it:

> Though the government had lifted most of the wartime price and wage controls (with the exception of rent, sugar, and rice), the public was repeatedly cautioned that the emergency situation might not yet be over. Many returning GIs found it extremely difficult to readjust to the mundane pressures of civilian life, just as many of the women who had taken wartime factory jobs to support their families now found it hard to resume their housewife duties. From penthouse dinner parties to corner bars, Russian Communism and the atomic bomb were the main topics of conversation.   (Epstein 18)

Spiraling inflation, widespread labor disputes, and an acute housing shortage caused many returning GIs to wonder whether or not the war had truly been won.

While the situation seemed alien and uncertain at home, on the screen the tensions between old comforts and new anxieties played out in full. The sedate Bing Crosby remained a potent box-office figure, thanks to the success of such films as Stuart Heisler's *Blue Skies,* and provocative Rita Hayworth triumphed in Charles Vidor's steamy melodrama *Gilda.* Alfred Hitchcock's *Notorious* featured the year's top female star, Ingrid Bergman, teamed with Cary Grant in a fast moving espionage thriller that blended suave romance with stolen fissionable uranium and Nazi spies. Tyrone Power was reintroduced to postwar audiences in Edmund Goulding's *The Razor's Edge,* based on the novel by Somerset Maugham, a film that marked a distinct change of pace from the actor's normal costume swashbucklers (Epstein 18).

The primitive wartime comedy of Abbott and Costello gave way to the more anarchic, garrulous routines of Jerry Lewis and Dean Martin, who on 25 July paired for the first time in Atlantic City. Irving Berlin's *Annie Get Your Gun* was a huge success on Broadway, with individual songs, like Perry Como's dreamy recording of "They Say It's Wonderful" and Dinah Shore's energetic rendition of "Doin' What Comes Naturally," becoming hit singles.

Born Yesterday, with Judy Holliday, triumphed in 1,642 performances. "The Christmas Song (Chestnuts Roasting on an Open Fire)" was heard for the first time, as was Edith Piaf's "La Vie en Rose." In more elevated culture, the Juilliard Quartet and the New York City Ballet were founded. Nat King Cole's trio clicked with their ballad "(I Love You) For Sentimental Reasons," while Charlie Parker and Dizzy Gillespie parted ways after a hugely successful and innovative two-month gig in Hollywood.

Despite the seeming frivolity of much popular culture, the films on the whole reflected a new, darker, profounder vision of human society. Edward Dmytryk's *Till the End of Time*, similar in structure to William Wyler's *The Best Years of Our Lives*, dealt with the difficulties of three war veterans in readjusting to postwar life, and featured actor Bill Williams as a Marine ex-boxer who had lost both his legs in the war. John Brahm directed the decidedly dark psychological mystery *The Locket*, which used multiple flashbacks within flashbacks to tell the story of Nancy (Laraine Day), a kleptomaniac who marries and destroys a succession of clueless husbands including painter Norman Clyde (a young Robert Mitchum) and psychiatrist Harry Blair (Brian Aherne), as a result of a childhood obsession with the eponymous locket. Jean Negulesco directed the oddly fatalistic *Three Strangers*, in which Sydney Greenstreet, Peter Lorre, and Geraldine Fitzgerald fight over a lottery ticket, with predictably disastrous consequences. Robert Siodmak brought Ernest Hemingway's short story *The Killers* to the screen, making a star of a young Burt Lancaster. Siodmak also directed the interesting psychological thriller *The Dark Mirror*, starring Olivia de Havilland in a dual role as identical twins, one of whom is a murderess. Bette Davis played a similar twin role in Curtis Bernhardt's *A Stolen Life*, appearing as identical sisters, both competing for the affections of Glenn Ford. Joan Crawford appeared in Jean Negulesco's *Humoresque* as a bored society woman who falls madly in love with violin prodigy John Garfield. Eventually, Crawford commits suicide, a victim of alcoholism and overpowering jealousy, as Garfield's transcription of Wagner's "Liebestod" is broadcast on the radio (Lewis 290).

Gregory Peck starred in Clarence Brown's *The Yearling*, a sentimental tale of a boy and his adopted pet deer, filmed in Technicolor on location in Florida. John Ford's *My Darling Clementine* offered Henry Fonda as the gallant Wyatt Earp, engaged in a showdown with the treacherous Walter Brennan and his sons at the famous O.K. Corral. Lewis Milestone's *The Strange Love of Martha Ivers* marked Kirk Douglas's screen debut—this was a noirish story of a town ruled by an aristocratic clan mixed up in murder and blackmail—while the soon-to-be-blacklisted Larry Parks convincingly portrayed singer Al Jolson in Alfred E. Green's *The Jolson Story*, a lavish Technicolor tribute to the singer whose performance in Alan Crosland's *The Jazz Singer* (1927) had launched the era of sound films. The film was the biggest hit up to that time, taking in almost $8 million at the box office (Lewis 292). All told, it was a year with something for everyone— including Stuart Heisler's *Blue Skies,* Vincente Minnelli's *Ziegfeld Follies,* and foreign films such as Jean Cocteau's *Beauty and the Beast,* Roberto Rosselini's *Open City,* and David Lean's *Brief Encounter*—although it is the darker films that seem to hold our attention now. The year also represented the peak for cinema attendance. Each week, 90 million Americans went to the movies, or more than 60 percent of the population (Lewis 288).

Optimism and Wariness: *The Best Years of Our Lives*

A curious blend of optimism and wariness that typified the year's key films was exemplified by the resoundingly successful *The Best Years of Our Lives,* based on MacKinlay Kantor's novel *Glory for Me.* Producer Samuel Goldwyn assembled an all-star cast, including Myrna Loy, Fredric March, Dana Andrews, Teresa Wright, Virginia Mayo, Cathy O'Donnell, and Harold Russell as the double amputee Homer Parrish. The structure of the film is deceptively simple: three men return from the war, expecting to be easily reassimilated into postwar society, but as events prove, nothing comes easily to any of them. The lambent atmosphere of relief that many Americans expected after the war fails to greet these returning soldiers; instead, they are plunged into different experiences of emotional, social, and economic trouble and darkness before they can find the light.

Fred Derry (Andrews), an ace bomber in the war, discovers that his wife, Marie (Mayo), is a cheap gold digger, more interested in spending his money than in helping him find a peacetime job. Smitten with the sight of him in uniform, Marie insists that he wear it when they go out to dine or dance, while Fred would simply like to forget the past and bury his uniform in a closet. When Fred's finances are exhausted, he is reduced to taking a menial job as a soda jerk in a downtown drugstore. He even loses this job when he punches a customer who suggests that the sacrifice of veterans may have been in vain, and soon after Fred discovers that Marie has been cheating on him. At the same time, he is falling in love with Peggy Stephenson (Wright), the daughter of a sergeant, Al (March), whom he met on the transport plane back to their hometown. Disconsolate with his job prospects and failing marriage, he walks through a graveyard of fighter planes about to be scrapped, and momentarily fantasizes that he is back in the thick of battle. A construction foreman rouses him from his wartime reveries, tells

Harold Russell (l.), Dana Andrews (rear), and Fredric March in *The Best Years of Our Lives* (William Wyler, Goldwyn/RKO). Courtesy Jerry Ohlinger Archives.

him that the bombers are being junked to make housing materials, and offers him a job.

Al Stephenson's rite of passage into postwar society is less dramatic than Fred Derry's, but still involves a considerable adjustment. Active and fit during the war, he comes home to discover his wife, Milly (Loy), expecting him to take up precisely where he left off in his old job at the local bank. But Al, bored, begins frequenting a neighborhood bar where he and his former comrades sporadically meet, becoming something of a genteel alcoholic. In one memorable scene, while he addresses guests at a formal banquet, Milly counts his drinks by marking the tablecloth; it is only the "least said, soonest mended" decorum of small-town American society that saves him from disgrace. When Al discovers that Fred has fallen in love with his daughter, he is furious. Fred, after all, is a married man. Yet as Fred's marriage to Marie crumbles and he finds a new job, the implication is clear that Peggy and Fred will marry and begin life anew.

Homer Parrish (Russell) has the toughest situation to deal with. He has lost both his hands and must rely on two metal hooks to eat, dress himself, and function as a useful member of society. Russell, a non-actor who had in fact lost both his hands in a training accident, was a natural performer and handled his scenes with such ease that veteran actor March became irritated. As William Wyler's biographer recounted:

> Russell's hooks caused some minor discord. March cautioned him that his hooks were stealing scenes. In one bar sequence, Russell had to pour a bottle of beer. After one of the takes, March rolled his eyes. "When I say my lines, keep those goddamned hooks down!" he commanded. "Don't lift that bottle because I want people listening to what I'm saying, not watching you drink beer!"
> (Herman 288)

In the film, Homer returns to his family but cannot bring himself to embrace his former sweetheart, Wilma Cameron (O'Donnell), fearing that his hooks will repulse her. Wilma, however, is a model of patience and understanding, as are Homer's parents, and in a touching and ground-breaking scene he explains his true feelings to Wilma, who remains unchanged in her devotion to him: presentation of intimate relations between able-bodied and disabled persons had never been so explicit onscreen before. Indeed, the scene—in which Homer explains to Wilma how he uses his hooks and how helpless he feels without them—was extremely difficult to film. As Wyler later wrote in a 1947 essay on the production of the film:

> We wanted to have a scene . . . in which Homer tells Wilma the reason he has been avoiding her is not that he doesn't love her, but that he doesn't feel it fair to her to marry her. "You don't know, Wilma," he says. "You don't know what it would be like to live with me, to have to face this every day—and every night." Wilma replies, "I can only find out by trying, and if it turns out that I haven't courage enough, we'll soon know it." This was intended to lead to a scene in Homer's bedroom in which, in order to prove his point, he demonstrates his difficulty in undressing, removes his hooks, and explains how helpless he is once they are off. . . . There were delicate problems in bringing a boy and a girl to a bedroom at night, with the boy getting into his pajama top, revealing his leather harness, which enables him to work his hooks, and finally, taking the harness off. . . . We solved the problems without the slightest suggestion of indelicacy, and without presenting Homer's hooks in a shocking or horrifying manner. As a matter of fact, we felt we could do quite the opposite and make it a moving and tender love scene.
> (qtd. in Herman 284)

The scene easily passed muster at the Production Code Administration, which realized that Wyler was interested in humanist realism, not sensationalism. Such realism permeates the entire work, and despite widespread industry predictions that a homecoming tale so downbeat would never sell tickets, the film became an instant critical and commercial success (Herman 291). It won numerous Academy Award nominations, although, oddly enough, not for the brilliant cinematography of Gregg Toland (who died shortly afterward of a heart attack) (Herman 291–92). In all, *The Best Years of Our Lives* is an authentic American classic, a powerful and deeply felt film about the difficulty of readjusting to the terrain of small-town life after the rigors of war.

▬▬▬▬▬ Escapism and Distress: *The Spiral Staircase*

Robert Siodmak was a remarkably efficient and adroit director of thrillers, a man who could bring sincerity and conviction to his *mise-en-scène*. When he was given a really good script (based on the novel *Some Must Watch* by Ethel Lina White) with an excellent cast, he effortlessly rose to the challenge. Superficially an "old dark house" thriller, *The Spiral Staircase* remains one of the most genuinely frightening and inventive horror films of the 1940s, as well as being one of the first serial-killer films: the murderer is driven by compulsions he cannot control, rather than a motive of anger, jealousy, or profit.

As *The Spiral Staircase* begins, a killer is on the loose at the turn of the century, strangling young women who suffer from some physical defect that apparently induces the homicidal frenzy. A mute servant girl in an enormous mansion, Helen Capel (Dorothy McGuire) is an obvious target, and young Dr. Parry (Kent Smith), the local physician, is rightly concerned for her welfare. He also hopes to cure her affliction, having determined that her mute state is the result of a traumatic incident rather than a physical disability. But Dr. Harvey (Erville Alderson), the older village physician, is suspicious of Dr. Parry and his motives. After all, Parry may raise false hopes in Helen or, worse yet, challenge the old man's diagnoses and cut into his monopolistic hold on the local patients.

The other members of the household are a spoiled and unsavory lot. Any one of them could easily be—or know the identity of—the killer. Professor Warren (George Brent) seems too meek and mild for anyone's good; Blanche (Rhonda Fleming) is a scheming adventuress; Steve Warren (Gordon Oliver) is a hell-raising ne'er-do-well; and the house's caretakers, Mr. and Mrs. Oates (Rhys Williams and Elsa Lanchester), are irresponsible and unreliable alcoholics. No principal character has real affection for any of the others. Indeed, all of them are engaged in a protracted deathwatch, awaiting the demise of the reclusive, eccentric, and bedridden matriarch, Mrs. Warren (Ethel Barrymore), so that they can inherit her considerable estate.

Dorothy McGuire in *The Spiral Staircase* (Dorothy McGuire) (Robert Siodmak, Dore Schary Productions/RKO/Vanguard Films Production). Courtesy Jerry Ohlinger Archives.

Though bedridden and given to periodic bouts of delusion, Mrs. Warren keeps a sharp eye on the proceedings. One thing she knows for certain: somebody in this family is a killer.

The narrative unfolds with grisly efficiency, presenting a murder within the first five minutes as a young woman is strangled in her rooms above an early motion picture theater while downstairs, on her day off, Helen raptly watches Edison's *The Kiss* (1896). When the murder is discovered, Helen and the rest of the audience are sent home to lock their doors. In a superbly edited sequence that affords the viewer only the barest glimpse of the killer, the murderer follows Helen to her front door. Now, although she has arrived home safely, she must deal with the conflicting demands of the various household members, most pressingly Mrs. Warren, who distrusts Nurse Barker (Sara Allgood), the caretaker hired for her by members of the family.

Continually entreating Helen to "leave this house if you know what's good for you!" Mrs. Warren slips in and out of consciousness, even as the murderer continues to strike with impunity and pile up victims all around. As the members of the Warren family are dispatched one by one, Helen finds herself alone in the house with the old invalid. Mrs. Oates dozes uselessly in the kitchen, dead drunk on brandy she has stolen from the family wine cellar; her husband has been sent on a fool's errand. Cut off from the outside world, unable to communicate with anyone or to summon help (the newfangled telephone in the front parlor is frustratingly useless), the mute young woman must face the killer alone in a climax that ranks as one of the most terrifying denouements in screen history. Central to it is Helen being confronted with an image of herself in a hallway mirror: the face has no mouth. At that very moment she finds herself face to face with the killer, who announces the logic behind the murders and is ready to dispatch her, too, until a quite unthinkable someone benevolently and powerfully intercedes.

All the cast members are masterful in their portrayals, and Siodmak's constantly moving camera, prowling the hallways of the darkened New England mansion in 1906, never lets the viewer relax for an instant. If there is one thing *The Spiral Staircase* excels in, it is atmosphere, audiences being induced to identify with the trapped Helen—so real and immediate is her plight. Shot at RKO, the film benefits strongly from Roy Webb's sinister music (making full use of the quivering, whining tones of the relatively new electronic instrument, the theremin) and Nicholas Musuraca's deep, mood-drenched, black-and-white cinematography that throws the house into a grim and foreboding darkness. The art direction, by Albert S. D'Agostino and Jack Okey, perfectly evokes the plush and claustrophobic splendor of turn-of-the-century interior decor, with Darrell Silvera's set decorations cramming every nook and cranny of the enormous sets with Victorian bric-a-brac, full-length mirrors (that never show what Helen desperately needs to see), and heavily upholstered furniture. In short, the film manages to engage our sympathies entirely for Helen. It thus works on a number of levels: as a straightforward thriller, as a parable of society's in-difference to weakness and affliction, and finally as a testament to self-empowerment in the crucial moment when all other remedies have failed.

▓▓▓▓▓▓▓■ Dark Love at Warner Bros.: *The Big Sleep*

Howard Hawks's *The Big Sleep* is also a dark and atmospheric film, shot almost entirely on studio sets at Warner Bros. An archetype of 1940s noir, this film suggests a vertically stratified social system riddled with corruption and decay yet at the same time florid, lascivious, appealing, and mysterious. As if the underlying tensions and fears that characterized the war had now been imported to civil society and hidden under the shiny veneer of class and success, the story placed Raymond Chandler's famous private eye Philip Marlowe (Humphrey Bogart) in a nest of scheming crim-inals operating in and around Los Angeles in a complex plot that teased away the gossamer veils of extreme wealth and flirted with love.

The Big Sleep has Marlowe trying to extricate Vivian Sternwood (Lauren Bacall), eldest daughter of a reclusive millionaire, and her drug addicted, nymphomaniac sister Carmen (Martha Vickers) from the clutches of gam-bler Eddie Mars (John Ridgely) and his gang, including one of the most ruthless killers ever depicted in any American film, the brutal Lash Canino (Bob Steele). In untangling the mystery, Marlowe runs afoul of the DA's office and his erstwhile pal, Chief Inspector Bernie Ohls (Regis Toomey), while also uncovering a pornographic book racket run by Arthur Gwynn Geiger (Theodore von Eltz), his homosexual lover Carl Lundgren (Tommy Rafferty), their sullen assistant Agnes Lowzier (Sonia Darrin), and the utterly unscrupulous Joe Brody (Louis Jean Heydt), who tries to muscle in on Geiger's racket. Naturally, with the motion picture code as enforced by the PCA in full force, much of this had to be suggested instead of stated out-right, but very little is left to the imagination.

The film had a long and troubled genesis. Production began in 1944, but it was not released until 1946, after extensive reshooting, recasting, and reediting. *The Big Sleep* reteamed Bogart with Bacall, an actress with whom he had clicked, both on- and offscreen, in Hawks's 1944 *To Have and Have Not*. Just nineteen when filming of *The Big Sleep* began, Bacall was a protégée of Hawks and his wife, the implacable Slim Keith. Hawks, indeed, regarded Bacall as little more than his personal property, a promising starlet to be groomed for international fame. Almost from the start Bacall, a woman with a mind of her own, rebelled. While she was perfectly willing to toler-ate the Warner Bros. publicity machine and to cooperate with newspaper

Humphrey Bogart and Lauren Bacall in *The Big Sleep* (Howard Hawks, First National Pictures Inc./Warner Bros.). Courtesy Jerry Ohlinger Archives.

columnists such as the notorious Walter Winchell for the sake of publicity (the vitriolic Winchell was so smitten that he dedicated an entire newspaper column to Bacall—an extremely rare gesture—entitling it "Bacall of the Wild"), in matters of the heart Bacall kept her own counsel. She had fallen for Bogart hard. Much to Hawks's displeasure (he threatened to demote her to the poverty row studio Monogram and ruin her career), Bacall turned in tears to Bogart for comfort and advice and Bogart angrily confronted Hawks, who did not deal easily with such insubordination from his actors. On *The Big Sleep* shoot, with Bogart and Bacall's offscreen romance still smoldering and Bogart enduring an unstable marriage to Mayo Methot, from whom he was living apart and trying to work out a divorce agreement (Behlmer, *Inside* 245), tempers were frayed from the start.

Shooting did not progress smoothly. Bogart was frequently absent from the set, and Hawks was continually rewriting. Obsessed with Bacall but tied to Methot, Bogart was drinking heavily. By the end of 1944, Hawks and his gifted co-writers Jules Furthman, William Faulkner, and Leigh Brackett thoroughly redid the ending with a last-ditch attempt to keep filming even in Bogart's absence. But the turmoil of shooting was far from over. Lauren Bacall's agent (and future producer) Charles K. Feldman, seeking to further his client's career, attended a preview screening of the film late in 1945 and saw to his dismay that Bacall's role had been substantially cut. He saw her future in jeopardy if the performance in *The Big Sleep* failed to click with audiences. Accordingly, on 16 November, Feldman wrote Jack Warner, head of production at Warner Bros., "as a friend" (Behlmer, *Inside* 249), imploring that certain scenes be reshot to build up Bacall's character and to showcase the undeniable chemistry between her and Bogart. Warner listened. He memoed his staff not to strike any prints of *The Big Sleep* and by 3 January roughly ten minutes of new footage—Bogart and Bacall bantering in a café, a love scene, and some other new material—had been shot and incorporated into the final print (249). To keep the running time down, several scenes of plot exposition were cut, making the film an almost incomprehensible roller-coaster ride of murder and mayhem. Hawks was dismayed, but Jack Warner was ecstatic. In a 9 January telegram to members of his New York office, Warner exulted that the retakes had definitely improved the finished film:

HAD FINAL SNEAK PREVIEW "BIG SLEEP" LAST NIGHT. THIS NEW VERSION WHICH HAS NEW SCENES PROTECTING BACALL COMES OFF GREAT, AND IN MY OPINION WE HAVE ONE HUNDRED PERCENT BETTER PICTURE.

(qtd. in Behlmer, *Inside* 249–50)

A particularly nasty piece of work in this film, evocative in many ways of the postwar thirst for, and presence of, desperation and darkness in civil life, is Canino's murder of the pathetic Harry Jones (perennial mopey fall guy Elisha Cook Jr.) by forcing him to drink poison. Hawks has Cook gulp it in with his hysterically fearful eyes before putting it into his mouth. Geiger's own demise depicts him being literally cut in half by his own men's machine gun fire as they mistake him for Marlowe in the climactic shoot-out. With a superbly atmospheric score by the gifted Max Steiner and moody cinematography by Sidney Hickox, *The Big Sleep* succeeds admirably as an engrossing crime melodrama, a noir of unimpeachable seediness, and a romance film of tortured and perverse feeling that culminated in Bogart and Bacall's marriage (following Bogart's divorce) not long afterward. Especially evocative is Christian Nyby's crisp editing: frequently, for instance, he uses lap dissolves to indicate a passage of only a few moments; he uses a brilliant seven-shot sequence studded with close-ups to show Marlowe's pickup of Carl Lundgren after the shooting of Joe Brody; and when Marlowe visits Eddie Mars's joint on Fontana Boulevard and sees Vivian Sternwood singing, he grasps their interaction by using intercut close-ups of their faces as they stand on opposite sides of the room. With its spicy performances, and its slick patter—

> *Marlowe (to cabbie):* There you are, sugar. Buy yourself a cigar.
>
> *Cab driver:* If you can use me again sometime, call this number.
>
> *Marlowe:* Day or night?
>
> *Cab driver:* Uhh, night's better. I work during the day.

—*The Big Sleep* is one of the key gangster films of the 1940s, an exercise in style and tough guy dialogue that remains as entertaining today as when it was first screened.

An Alien Land after the War: *The Blue Dahlia*

George Marshall's *The Blue Dahlia* is something else again, a no-nonsense crime thriller in a distinctly minor key. Scripted by hard-boiled author Raymond Chandler in a blind-drunk stupor (see Houseman 7–23 for more on this curious working method), *Dahlia* depicted the unhappy homecoming of war veteran Johnny Morrison (Alan Ladd) and his badly wounded compatriot, Buzz Wanchek (William Bendix). When Johnny's unfaithful wife, Helen (Doris Dowling), is murdered, suspicion falls first on Johnny and then on Buzz. In early drafts of the script Buzz was, in fact, to have been the murderer (he has returned from duty with a large metal plate in his head and is subject to frequent blackouts), but the War Department, still very much possessed of a strong voice in Hollywood, vetoed the idea and Chandler had to come up with another killer.

In the final, rather arbitrary scene, a house detective who has been skulking around various apartments throughout the film, "Dad" Newell

(Will Wright), is revealed as the true villain. In this way Buzz's character avoided the fate of being one of the screen's first psychotic killer veterans. *The Blue Dahlia* was designed by Paramount primarily as a vehicle for the "hot" team of Alan Ladd and Veronica Lake. The film propelled them both to international stardom; he, the cold-blooded ruthless killer; she, the slender, smoldering sexpot who manages to convince him to play on the right side of the law.

But what is most interesting about *The Blue Dahlia* is Chandler's vision of postwar America as both a social and moral wasteland and an emotional minefield. When Johnny first confronts his wife upon his return from the war, she is having a huge, drunken party at their home, transparently throwing herself at other men. Having been permanently damaged by the war, even the slightest incident triggers the considerable temper of Johnny's pal Buzz. When Johnny, Buzz, and another of their wartime pals, George Copeland (Hugh Beaumont), are drinking in a bar, Buzz is suddenly unnerved when the jukebox, spouting jumping jive, is turned up. Clutching his head in agony, Buzz pulls the plug on the jukebox to the annoyance of the other patrons, until Johnny explains Buzz's injury and momentary peace is restored. "Dad" Newell (Will Wright) is a particularly disturbing figure, a sort of hypersurveillant peeping Tom who does little but spy on the film's protagonists and issue vague threats from time to time. Although his identity as the real killer may have been the result of postwar censorship, it makes Newell a much more interesting character in retrospect. While throughout the film, he presents himself as the voice of morality and authority, in the end his character is the most corrupt of all. Indeed, his honorary title, "Dad," is a ghastly joke on the patriarchy itself. "Dad" is nobody's paternal figure; rather, he is a scheming killer who hides his guile behind a mask of benevolence. Chandler's message is clear: everyone is corrupt; everyone is on the take; no one can be trusted.

The Blue Dahlia is photographed in appropriately drab black and white—which perfectly suits the sordid world Chandler's characters are forced to inhabit—by the gifted Lionel Lindon. It stands as a supremely dystopian vision of postwar America, light years away from the relative optimism of *The Best Years of Our Lives*. At the film's end, Johnny's wife is dead, the house detective who was supposed to aid in solving her murder is revealed as the real killer, and Johnny himself faces an uncertain future. While *The Blue Dahlia* is really a nervous "A" picture—that is, a "B" picture with an "A" budget—whose creation was dictated primarily by the fact that Paramount needed a Ladd/Lake picture in a hurry, it still offers a compelling vision of life in an alien land after the war, where friends and acquaintances can no longer be trusted and where everyone is concealing something from public view. *The Blue Dahlia* is thus a crime thriller with a twist. It conveys a message about the pervasive immorality lurking in postwar American society just below the elegant surface of cocktail parties, swank restaurants, and the supposed normalcy of everyday social commerce.

Too Sweet for the Times: *It's a Wonderful Life*

It's a Wonderful Life, Frank Capra's paean to rural America, is another story altogether. The film's plot and characters are extraordinarily well known. Briefly: during the Christmas season, small-town banker George Bailey (James Stewart), convinced that his life is a failure and despondent over the loss of a considerable amount of money from the small savings and loan company he operates, decides to kill himself by jumping off a bridge. But as he leaps, Clarence Oddbody (Henry Travers), an angel trying to "earn his wings," saves him from destruction and shows him how corrupt Bedford Falls would have become without him—to wit, a typically 1940s noirish landscape of gambling, prostitution, and corrupt law enforcement. George realizes the error of his ways and is restored to the present, where his wife, Mary (Donna Reed), and caring neighbors chip in to help him recoup his losses and save the family firm. The film ends with the townspeople gathered in the front parlor of George's home, serenading George and his family with a rousing rendition of "Auld Lang Syne." Although it contains a strong undercurrent of darkness in its nightmarish depiction of how the little town of Bedford Falls would have gone wrong had George never been born, *It's a Wonderful Life* ultimately extols the virtues of community, faith, and charity, positing that all problems are solvable if a community puts its collective will to dealing with them. The tableau of Stewart, Reed, their children, and their friends gathered around one another at the Christmas tree made an icon out of optimism in America.

For many years Capra had been the primary Hollywood booster for the common citizen, the champion of small-town values over big business and corrupt politicians. But after the war he was a changed man. His work on the *Why We Fight* series of propaganda films for the allied war effort (discussed in the introduction to this volume) had exhausted him, and he returned to Hollywood transformed and saddened, much of his idealism gone. "When you make a picture today you are bucking a system, and no independent producer is big enough to lick it," Capra thought. "So, even if he has ideals and ideas, he has to compromise them if he wants to stay in business" (qtd. in McBride, *Frank Capra* 503, 505). Cinematographer Joe

Walker, who eventually shot much of *It's a Wonderful Life*, agreed that both Hollywood and Capra had changed during the war years: "I never saw any big change in Capra at all until he came back from the war. He was more anxious. He wasn't the . . . happy director on *Wonderful Life* that he had been before the war" (505).

Having decided against working again under Harry Cohn at Columbia, the only large studio that would offer him a contract, and having formed Liberty Productions (with loans from A. P. Giannini's Bank of America and in association with William Wyler, George Stevens, and Sam Briskin), Capra purchased the story that would become *It's a Wonderful Life*, Philip van Doren Stern's *The Greatest Gift*, from RKO for $50,000. After much difficulty, a screenplay was written by a tag-team of writers, many of whom detested Capra's ultra-right politics and his support of HUAC, including Albert Hackett, Frances Goodrich, and an uncredited Michael Wilson. Filming began on 15 April, the same day as Wyler's *The Best Years of Our Lives*. The production was lavishly budgeted, costing $3,780,000, an enormous sum for that era (McBride, *Frank Capra* 526). Capra shot the film at his usual leisurely pace, exposing 350,000 feet of film over an eighty-four-day schedule (527).

It's a Wonderful Life was not originally scheduled to open nationwide until 30 January 1947, when the Christmas holiday competition was less pronounced. But needing a last minute Christmas attraction, the film's distributor, RKO, opened it in New York on 21 December and, in order that it might qualify for the Academy Awards, on 25 December in Los Angeles. On national release, *It's a Wonderful Life* opened to weak reviews and poor box-office returns (McBride, *Frank Capra* 529). In the postwar atmosphere, the film was regarded as an anachronism. The *New York Times*'s Bosley Crowther called it a "quaint and engaging modern parable . . . [but] a little too sticky for our taste," though the ever-reliable industry booster *Hollywood Reporter* dutifully described it as "the greatest of all Capra pictures" (529). The *New Yorker* was considerably more dismissive, noting snidely that "Mr. Capra has seen to it that practically all the actors involved behave as cutely as pixies" (529–30).

Capra had argued with William Wyler that the story line of the latter's *The Best Years of Our Lives* was too downbeat (McBride, *Frank Capra* 515), but now he had to watch in disbelief as audiences decisively rejected *It's a Wonderful Life* and flocked to see *The Best Years of Our Lives*, which had opened a month earlier. Capra's film pulled in a weak $3.3 million in first-release domestic rentals, while Wyler's picture tallied $11.3 million. Because of the poor box-office receipts, cash flow problems piled up at Liberty and Capra was forced to sell it (to Paramount) shortly after. Capra subsequently lost all control over the film. Paramount vaulted the original nitrate negative, which rapidly began to deteriorate—it was not, after all, a Paramount production and so special precautions against heat and air damage were not taken. Eventually even the copyright for the film lapsed, leaving *It's a Wonderful Life* seemingly in the public domain.[1]

In the early 1990s, however, it was discovered that the underlying story rights for *It's a Wonderful Life* had never lapsed, and so, because the film was based on that story, it once again became eligible for copyright protection. The negative was restored by the American Film Institute to pristine perfection. Now secured by copyright and saved from nitrate destruction, *It's a Wonderful Life* lives on as Capra's most popular film. Perhaps it says something about our current era that we need to believe in such a film; audiences of the time were far more discerning and realistic (McBride, *Frank Capra* 534), closer on all fronts to the ravages of an expansive war and confronted more brutally with shortages and cultural despondency at home when the war was over.

Moral Yardsticks: *My Darling Clementine* and *The Postman Always Rings Twice*

John Ford had not lost his commercial footing in Hollywood. Though Ford, too, worked during the war on various propaganda films and documentaries, he reentered the Hollywood mainstream with one of his most enduring films, *My Darling Clementine*, for Twentieth Century Fox. Henry Fonda was the perfect Fordian personification of Wyatt Earp; strong, silent, and dependable. As the love interest Chihuahua, Linda Darnell came with the Twentieth Century Fox stock company and did acceptable work, and so did Victor Mature in one of his best performances, as the consumptive gunslinger Doc Holliday. Tim Holt and Ward Bond, as Wyatt's brothers Virgil and Morgan, provide acceptable background support, but the real star of the film, other than Fonda, is Walter Brennan. Playing the vicious head of the Clanton gang, Brennan is as convincing a mob leader as the American screen has ever portrayed. Ford, economical as always, filmed "to the cut," shooting only the coverage he needed and getting the maximum out of each camera setup. While no one can argue that *My Darling Clementine* is not a deeply sentimental project, the nemesis that Wyatt Earp faces at the O.K. Corral is real enough: it is unreasoning violence incarnate.

One of the last of Ford's great black and white westerns, *My Darling Clementine* is both a valentine to a lost age, as are many of the director's films, and a rousing tale of good versus evil. Indeed, the stark black-and-white cinematography of Joe McDonald lends the film the appearance of a high-contrast Daguerreotype of the Old West, in perfect keeping with the film's polarized moral stance. Wyatt Earp is portrayed as a man of unimpeachable honor and integrity, an approach that takes great liberties with the true historical record of the period. But Ford, as always, is not after accuracy; he wants the legend. In *My Darling Clementine*'s unequivocal moral universe, John Ford films just that.

The film is rapturously mythical, holding out a moral yardstick audiences could use not only for estimating the value of their daily postwar experience but also for aspiring to what everyone hoped would be sunnier days ahead. In Tay Garnett's *The Postman Always Rings Twice*, however, audiences found one of the truly great 1940s noirs, a deeply engaging critique of corrupt social relations, corrupt love, cynical exploitation, and heartless manipulation, done, ironically enough, for that least noir of studios, the all-American MGM. Based on James M. Cain's brutal novel, this film tells the story of a drifter, Frank Chambers (John Garfield), who takes a job at a cheap roadside lunch counter run by Nick Smith (Cecil Kellaway), an older man married (somewhat incongruously) to the lusciously overripe Cora (Lana Turner, incandescent in a series of white one-piece swimming suits and tight-fitting dresses). This is a taut morality tale, entirely in keeping with the cynicism of post-World War II American society. Frank falls for Cora, and the two soon plan to kill Nick and take over the lunch counter (small potatoes, indeed). Once the horrid deed is done, however, Cora and Frank start coming apart at the seams and eventually betray each other. Hume Cronyn has a delightfully slimy turn as Arthur Keats, the couple's defense attorney, who defends them at their murder trial knowing that they are guilty. "Blind man without a cane could see you're in a bad way," Keats tells Frank, before getting the pair off on a technicality that, of course, doesn't stick.

The main attraction of the film, however, other than its foredoomed plot line and hard-boiled dialogue, is the palpable sexual tension created between Frank and Cora, who can't seem to keep their hands off each other. And who can blame them? Grandfatherly Nick doesn't seem to be much of an attraction for Cora—she's fond of him, but that's all. Frank, on the other hand, is a muscular hero who can slap women around and make them like it. Short on brains, long on brawn, and always looking for an angle, Frank is the ideal man for Cora, and Cora is the ideal woman for him, unsatisfied, stuck in a boring job in a boring town with a boring husband, ready to turn any situation molten.

Brilliantly photographed by Sidney Wagner, with appropriately shabby art direction by the gifted Randall Duell and Cedric Gibbons, *The Postman Always Rings Twice* is a tale of lust run rampant, of common sense sacrificed for momentary ecstasies. As Ken Fox and Maitland McDonagh note,

> Except for two scenes in which Turner wears black (one when she contemplates suicide and the other when she goes to her mother's funeral), the alluring platinum blond actress wears nothing but white in the film, further propelling her haughty phosphorescent steaminess: this angelically venal little trollop begged to be dirtied up. Though she is a *femme fatale* here, Turner is a softer, more emotionally vulnerable Lucrezia Borgia than her sisterly counterparts in other Cain stories. Even at the end, she is seeking love, not revenge, telling Garfield after the murder that she wants "kisses that come from life, not death." So impressed was Cain with Turner's performance that he presented her with a leather-bound first edition of the novel, inscribing it, "For my dear Lana, thank you for giving a performance that was even finer than I expected." (636)

It is odd that MGM, surely the most prestigious of Hollywood studios during the Studio Era of the 1930s to the 1950s, should have tackled such a seamy project, but Garfield and Turner played their roles to perfection and the film was a major box-office and critical success. Once again, postwar audiences had voted with their feet to see a more realistic and violent depiction of American life. Gone were the devotees of the saccharine sweetness that pervaded the screen between 1934 and 1945, the years in which the Motion Picture Production Code was most strictly enforced, when Shirley Temple's musicals ruled at the box office, along with the perpetual misadventures of MGM's own Andy Hardy. There was a New Deal in Hollywood, and it offered the public something they hadn't seen in a very long time: direct situations, adult conflicts and passions, truly desperate needs played out against a background of stunning shadows and morbidly fascinating darkness.

■ ■ ■

These are just a few of the many films made this year in Hollywood, a year in which more Americans went to the movies each week than at any other point in cinema history. In discussing these key films, I have necessarily, for reasons of space, ignored a great deal. Not included here are the many Republic westerns and serials, such as *The El Paso Kid, Days of Buffalo Bill, The Phantom Rider, Red River Renegades, Santa Fe Uprising*, and *Stagecoach to Denver*; or the low-budget Producers Releasing Corporation (PRC) westerns, such as *Ambush Trail, Driftin' River, Ghost of Hidden Valley, Outlaws of the Plains, Thun-*

der Town, and *Tumbleweed Trail*. I have omitted horror films, such as Mono-gram's *The Face of Marble*, as well as the travelogues, newsreels, cartoons (*Daffy Doodles, Hair-Raising Hare, Mouse Menace, Racketeer Rabbit,* and Disney's elaborate *Song of the South*), documentaries (*Glimpses of California, Here Comes the Circus, Cradle of Liberty*), novelty shorts (such as *Atomic Power* and *Bored of Education*), and screen sing-alongs that made moviegoing, above all, a social experience. One went to the movies not only to see the stars, but also to be with one's friends. If the "A" picture didn't satisfy you, there was always the second feature on the bill. The movie house was a place where one saw the latest films, but also the newsreels and *March of Time* two-reel docudramas that helped to shape our collective public consciousness as a nation.

Thus entertainment commingled with news and information; you would see your friends and neighbors a few rows down and wave to them. You had gotten through the war, and if the postwar peace had not yet brought utopia, still you would be all right. The future seemed uncertain, fraught with betrayal from former wartime allies—the Red menace film was just on the horizon—but at least you were taking stock of your situation and could see clearly what society offered you, what guarantees it would and would not make. The films of the year were part of America's growing up process, as the influences of the war, leading to new and different ways of constructing one's public self, allowed men and women new options in their daily existence. There and then, with the painfully optimistic struggles of *The Best Years of Our Lives*, the traumatized, mute fear of *The Spiral Stair-case*, the desperate hungers of *The Big Sleep*, the cloyingly optimistic socia-bility of *It's a Wonderful Life*, the morally explicit antagonisms of *My Darling Clementine*, and the craven, clutching, catastrophic duplicities of *The Postman Always Rings Twice*, Hollywood was showing a picture of an America that clung to the hope of being able to move forward out of a time of lingering and insidious pain.

NOTE

1. The film began to appear widely on television and on videocassettes; anyone who wished to do so could make a copy and sell it. It was also during this period that *It's a Won-derful Life* attained the status of a "Christmas classic," precisely because it cost nothing to broadcast. Capra briefly toyed with the idea of colorizing the film to renew the copyright shortly before his death, but ultimately abandoned the project.

1947

[image: row of small squares]

Movies and the "Enemy" Within

TONY WILLIAMS

It is a year of postwar angst, when Harry Truman faces opposition to his legislative plans from both houses of Congress, controlled for the first time in eighteen years by Republicans who attempt to abolish New Deal programs. He articulates the Truman Doctrine, espousing greater involvement in world affairs and the containment of communism, on 12 March abandoning diplomacy as a means to deal with a new enemy outside the border of the United States, the Soviet Union. Nine days later, Truman invokes an "enemy" within, signing Executive Order 9835, establishing the federal Civilian Employee Loyalty Program, allowing for dismissal of employees deemed "disloyal" in executive departments and agencies on "reasonable grounds"; in June he proposes the Marshall Plan to aid the war-devastated economies of Western Europe (Offner 185–212). Chuck Yeager becomes the first person to fly faster than the speed of sound; Henry Ford, who never traveled that quickly, dies; and at an even slower speed, yet with inexorable progress, India declares independence from British rule. Jackie Robinson of the Brooklyn Dodgers becomes the first African American to play major league baseball. Jackson Pollock starts "action painting," throwing rather than brushing paint onto his canvas. The transistor is invented, and the Frisbee is introduced. B. F. Goodrich invents the first tubeless tire. The CIA is created. It is thus a time of explicit exertion, in the arts and in public affairs, in science, and in policing and intelligence.

The image of the communist infiltrator inside American borders is convoked early. In January, Ronald Reagan attempts to persuade Father George Dunne, a Jesuit professor of political science, that the recent studio strike was communist-led and -inspired, and that Herb Sorrell, president of the Conference of Studio Unions, and his associates are all communists. Sorrell is kidnapped, badly beaten by phony policemen, and left in the desert (Bruck 96–98). In March, Roy Brewer, of the International Alliance of the Theatrical and Stage Employees Union, urges HUAC to begin investigating Hollywood. The Screen Actors Guild selects Reagan, its former president, on 10 March to complete the term of Robert Montgomery, who had resigned; a month later Reagan (otherwise known as informant T-10) and his wife, Jane Wyman, give information about fellow members of SAG to the FBI. Mobsters and gangsters are on the move: Bugsy Siegel is murdered in his Beverly Hills home on 20 June, and Johnny Roselli returns to Hollywood after serving half of his six-year sentence for his involvement in the Bioff-Browne-Schenk extortion and racketeering scandal affecting the industry. Howard Hughes is preoccupied with his "spruce goose," the largest aircraft ever built, which flies one mile at an altitude of seventy feet. On 14 December, Reagan and Jane Wyman separate, a month after his election to a full term as president of the Screen Actors Guild. Wyman cites "extreme mental cruelty" in her divorce suit (Moldea 77).

It was a remarkable year for Hollywood cinema. As well as the international releases of The Archers's *Black Narcissus* and Carol Reed's *Odd Man Out*, the year saw a diverse mixture of thrillers and comedies. Edmund Gwenn won an Academy Award for his role in *Miracle on 34th Street*, while Cary Grant angelically solved the marital problems of Loretta Young and David Niven in *The Bishop's Wife* and Rex Harrison provided a spiritual presence in *The Ghost and Mrs. Muir*. Young brought country values to the forefront in *The Farmer's Daughter*, while Myrna Loy enlisted Grant's aid toward resolving the adolescent problems of younger sister Shirley Temple in *The Bachelor and the Bobby-Soxer*, and Hedy Lamarr played the title role in Bob Hope's *My Favorite Brunette*. *The Egg and I* introduced the hayseed humor of Ma and Pa Kettle to the screen for the first time. William Powell played the title role in *Life with Father*, and, with Myrna Loy, appeared in the final Thin Man film, *Song of the Thin Man*.

Social problem films were not absent from the screen. American audiences learned that it was bad to be antisemitic in *Gentleman's Agreement*, with Gregory Peck. Female adjustment to postwar society appeared in melodramas such as *Smash-Up—The Story of a Woman* and *Possessed*, as well as noirs such as *Lady in the Lake* and *The Two Mrs. Carrolls*. Male insecurity also appeared in Ronald Colman's performance in *A Double Life*, Edward G. Robinson's performance in *The Red House*, Lawrence Tierney's friendship with Elisha Cook Jr. in *Born to Kill*, and Anthony Mann's first film noir, *T-Men*. Charlie Chaplin offended postwar sensibilities with his black comedy *Monsieur Verdoux*, counterpointing more acceptable comedies such as *The Secret Life of Walter Mitty* and *The Road to Rio*. Adventure films such as *Captain from Castile, Sinbad the Sailor,* and *Unconquered* provided heroic opportunities for Tyrone Power, Douglas Fairbanks Jr., and Gary Cooper, while Enterprise Studios began releasing films such as *The Other Love*.

This was the year the House began investigating the Hollywood film industry, leading to the 24 November Waldorf-Astoria Declaration, the eventual imprisonment of the Hollywood Ten, and the collapse of liberal opposition to the blacklist that had been led by Humphrey Bogart and others. Two westerns—*Duel in the Sun* (King Vidor) and *Pursued* (Raoul Walsh)—employed the especially subversive aspects of film noir style in depicting the postwar crisis affecting American institutions. *Body and Soul* (Robert Rossen), *Brute Force* (Jules Dassin), *Crossfire* (Edward Dmytryk), *Dark Passage* (Delmer Daves), *Nightmare Alley* (Edmund Goulding), and *Out of the Past* (Jacques Tourneur) all represented the "dark side" of the American dream in both an international and national perspective. Indeed, there is an effulgence of darkness through many genres of Hollywood film, derived from the general influence of noir cinema in which the civilian world seems pervasively threatened by vague, looming forces, an "enemy" that somehow cannot be named or identified easily and that threatens to devour masculinity, security, and loyalty. In diverse ways these films all contradicted the encroaching official ideological optimism, which would become a dominant trend in a postwar American society reacting both to the Blacklist and the Cold War. The Blacklist—a secret producers' agreement to refrain from hiring persons who had been labeled communist—shook both liberal and conservative forces in American society, and in making the films discussed here Hollywood went beyond covering its own complicity in the nationwide witch hunt in order to blanket the nation with a cloak of progressiveness that promised a shinier tomorrow.

The Dark City I: *Crossfire*, *Out of the Past*, and *Body and Soul*

Crossfire tells the story of Finlay, a detective of Irish Catholic descent searching among a coterie of demobilized American servicemen after the war for the murderer of a Jewish civilian named Samuels (Sam Levene). His principal target is Mitchell (George Cooper), a sensitive artistic type homesick for his wife. Mitchell's roommate Keeley (Robert Mitchum) protects his friend by hiding him out in the balcony of a movie theater, and goes to the trouble of calling Mrs. Mitchell to convince her to come and comfort him. In her absence, and in a drunken stupor, Mitchell has a few tentative romantic moments with a prostitute, Ginny (Gloria Grahame), who, when he is finally apprehended by Finlay, cannot provide him with an alibi for the murder. Finally it becomes clear to Finlay, in discussions with Keeley, that Mitchell is in fact innocent, the true killer being a man who could

Robert Ryan (l.), Robert Mitchum (center), and Robert Young in *Crossfire* (Edward Dmytryk, RKO). Courtesy Jerry Ohlinger Archives.

murder a total stranger out of nothing but blind and generalized hatred, in this case antisemitism. This is Montgomery (Robert Ryan), Finlay's earliest source of evidence and a virulent hatemonger who "won't let no Jew tell me how much of his Scotch I can drink!"—especially not one of those shirkers who, in Montgomery's twisted view, will do anything to avoid having to go off to war. Montgomery is cornered and finally killed, after Finlay has an opportunity to make a long speech about the evils of blind racial and ethnic hatred to Keeley and a young, notably innocent soldier from Tennessee. As it turns out, the victimized Samuels had been a soldier himself, a fighter who had gone to war on Montgomery's side. The hate killing was therefore a form of crossfire.

The source for *Crossfire*, Richard Brooks's generally neglected novel *The Brick Foxhole*, is a crucial text for understanding the social malaise depicted in the film. Both works involve adaptation to postwar society, yet their "happy endings" differ. Although the Mitchells reunite at the end of the novel, it is at the cost of the deaths of both Montgomery and Keeley. As representative of the defunct New Deal, Keeley enlisted to put his "finger in the dike" and "save the nation" (Brooks 226). But the novel ends by suggesting that his sacrifice may be just as futile as Mary's attempt to prove that she was better than Ginny by erasing her rival from her husband's mind entirely. Nothing will ever be the same again for Mary Mitchell. Mitigating some of this killing and despondency, and despite censorship and cinematic changes, *Crossfire* reflects its source in depicting a mood of national weariness and rootlessness following the "good war."

Producer Adrian Scott and director Edward Dmytryk employed techniques of film noir to convey the general insecurities of culture that year. The film begins with a tour de force of noir filmmaking: we find ourselves in Samuels's apartment as he is being murdered, the action shown in shadowy reflections on the walls while offscreen a fight to the death transpires under the illumination of a table lamp. Throughout, *Crossfire*'s demobilized servicemen exist in a cultural limbo, either playing cards lazily, hanging out at bars, or getting drunk. The optimistic world of FDR is now a lost world: a portrait of the former president hangs in Captain Finlay's office a year after his death, often crisscrossed by ominous shadow bars. Accused soldier Jeff Mitchell cannot adjust to his imminent civilian status. Employed as an artist during the New Deal WPA scheme, he has been relegated to painting Army buildings during wartime and now faces an uncertain postwar future in which the economy could again crash. His marital problems and depressive insecurities echo those of the man (Paul Kelly) he meets in Ginny's apartment. Ginny embodies sexual fantasies of the wartime woman who became not a typical Rosie the Riveter but a prime example of the independent femme fatale of film noir. Although Ginny is much more vulnerable than Mary, she is a figure misunderstood and demeaned by Irish Catholic cop Finlay. The nonchalant Keeley embodies the "Baby, I don't care" attitude of actor Mitchum's other major appearance this year, in *Out of the Past*. Ryan's Montgomery exhibits the violent embodiment of family values when he compares those who don't respect their mothers with those who don't respect the service. His racism developed while he was a white cop in "the jungle" of East St. Louis, and his murder of Samuels represents the logical culmination of the antisemitic outbursts of certain members of the House Un-American Activities Committee—notably Mississippi congressman John Rankin, who sought to link Hollywood, communism, and Judaism, hysterically decried the "loathsome, lying, immoral, anti-Christian filth" perpetrated by "alien-minded Communistic enemies," and called Walter Winchell a "slime mongering kike."

Crossfire is more subversive than Elia Kazan's comparatively milquetoast *Gentleman's Agreement* in showing that hearts and minds cannot be easily won in a politically dangerous postwar world. It links film noir to a more radical social consciousness theme than any prewar Warner Bros. movie. As

Keeley comments: "The snakes are loose. Anybody can get them. But they're friends of mine." His remarks evoke the choking climate of postwar insecurity, where America, not knowing who else to attack—or how, or why—ate itself up.

Jacques Tourneur's *Out of the Past* tells the story of Jeff Bailey (Robert Mitchum), hired by gambler Whit Sterling (Kirk Douglas) to find his former girlfriend, Kathie Moffat (Jane Greer), who, he says, shot him and ran off with his money. Locating her in Mexico, Jeff instantly falls in love. Kathie deduces Jeff's reason for looking for her and assures him that Whit was a romantic tyrant, whose money she did not steal. As they are about to leave Mexico, Whit shows up. Jeff tells him he has not found Kathie, and sails to San Francisco with her that night. Soon, however, one of Whit's associates finds them. Kathie coolly shoots him dead, leaving Jeff to deal with the body. Now stunned, Jeff learns that she had in fact stolen Whit's money. He goes to Tahoe to meet Whit, where the double-crosser Kathie has already told Whit of their affair. Subsequently, she implicates him in a pair of murders, that of Whit's associate and that of a San Francisco lawyer named Eels, making him the target of a manhunt. After she shoots Whit, Jeff finally flees south with Kathie, driving deliberately into a stakeout where both are killed.

Credited to Geoffrey Homes (pseudonym of screenwriter Daniel Mainwaring) from his 1946 novel *Build My Gallows High, Out of the Past* was reworked by Frank Fenton using both Homes's original and a draft by James M. Cain. The film reflects postwar disillusionment and male insecurity, forming an excellent companion piece to *Crossfire* and highlighting a particular actor who was gaining prominence. It was truly the year of Robert Mitchum. He replaced Dick Powell as RKO's star attraction and gained the role of Jeff Bailey after Warner Bros. refused to loan out Humphrey Bogart. Although the war and its aftermath are never mentioned in *Out of the Past*, Mitchum's Bailey obviously represents another incarnation of those rootless *Crossfire* servicemen seeking a return to their former lives and finding things radically changed.

Like Mitchell in *Crossfire*, Bailey can never return to agrarian prewar values no matter how much he tries. He is not only contaminated by the urban jungle embodied in his trenchcoat and fedora, and Nicholas Musuraca's noir lighting, but suffers rejection by the good citizens of Bridgeport, California, who act less like idyllic Norman Rockwellesque folk than like a frenzied mob. Jeff is led back to his past by the machinations of femme fatale Kathie and jealous gambler Whit, whose Lake Tahoe residence suggests early intimations of mob involvement and political corruption in the state of Nevada. *Out of the Past* is more indebted to the soft-boiled tradition of pulp fiction than to its hard-boiled counterpart represented by Dashiell Hammett, Raymond Chandler, and James M. Cain. Embodied in the fiction of David Goodis and Cornell Woolrich, the soft-boiled tradition emphasized male insecurity and paranoia in the face of the powerful female. Jeff's failure of masculinity before Kathy's controlling figure parallels elements in Woolrich's *Waltz into Darkness,* which appeared at the same time as the film. Although Jeff nonchalantly says, "Baby, I don't care," before succumbing to Kathy's embraces, the spider woman has already set her trap, as visualized by the nets in the Mexican beach scene and her first appearance as an erotic maternal figure emerging from the Mar Azul significantly situated near the Cine Pico. In her final scene, the "good mother" becomes the "bad object" of Jeff's dream, hauling in her prey like an expert fisher of men and dressed in a severely tailored costume with hood covering her attractive hair. She kills Whit, the only person who could save Jeff. Whit's reasons for wanting Kathie's return are ambiguous, but they suggest both revenge and masochism. Soul brothers in a weak masculine homoerotic bonding, he and Jeff are powerless to counteract a figure deadlier than the male. At the climax, audiences will still remember Kathie as a threat to masculinity, civil order, and American values: the HUAC assault can be thought to be directed against feminists as well as Reds.

Originally intended as a biography of boxing champion and World War II hero Barney Ross, the subject's sudden arrest on charges of drug addiction resulted in last-minute changes that made *Body and Soul* an enduring legacy of postwar cinema. The production was not smooth. Enterprise Studios executive Charles Einfeld lost interest and the entire project seemed on the verge of collapse, but star John Garfield, producer Bob Roberts, and director Robert Rossen wanted to continue and prevailed upon Abraham Polonsky to come up with an idea at a time when the disillusioned Paramount scenarist was already planning to return to New York. Polonsky conceived the fundamental premises of *Body and Soul* while walking the two blocks separating Paramount from Enterprise Studios. He reworked Clifford Odets's play *Golden Boy* into a romantic story combining the boxing movie genre with thirties' Warner Bros. social consciousness. The changes were fortuitous. *Body and Soul* was an homage to the thirties influence of Odets as well as a film noir reflecting the postwar climate of betrayal and disillusionment. Despite Polonsky's offhand description of the film as "a fable," the project attracted many progressive talents, including not only Garfield but also the future Blacklist victim Anne Revere, Group Theatre veteran Art Smith, Lloyd Gough (whose wife, Karen Morley, would later be blacklisted), and the great African American actor Canada Lee.

John Garfield and Hazel Brooks in *Body and Soul* (Robert Rossen, Enterprise/United Artists). Courtesy Jerry Ohlinger Archives.

Roberts (Lloyd Goff), the New York fighting racket boss, fixes a fight between Charlie Davis (Garfield) and the black champ, Ben Chaplin (Lee), who suffers from a blood clot in the brain. Ben is told that the fight will go fifteen rounds and result in a decision, but Charlie is not told that Ben is ill and Roberts goads him to pummel Ben. Ben is so severely injured he must retire from the ring and eventually becomes Charlie's trainer. At the film's conclusion, Roberts sets up a big fight for Charlie with Jack Marlowe (Artie Dorrell), which will supposedly be fixed in Charlie's favor. Ben tries to persuade the boxer not to go along with the fix. Overhearing him, Roberts comes in and fires Ben. Ben is furious, and punches the air so forcefully he falls down dead. But during the match, after several rounds with neither fighter really engaged, Marlowe starts punching Charlie with greater force, and Charlie realizes that, just as Ben was once, now *he* is Roberts's set-up. Instead of giving in, he fights back and KOs Marlowe.

As John Schultheiss (188–89) points out, the opening image of a punching bag swinging in the wind evokes images of lynching. It is an appropriate metaphor for the death of Canada Lee's Ben. As the camera pans right and cranes into an overhead exterior shot of Charlie Davis lying on a bed, a close-up abruptly introduces us to what Paul Buhle and Dave Wagner appropriately describe as the "scarred and swollen face" of John Garfield, "shriven of its 1930s optimism and possessed now of a postwar familiarity with death" (113). These scenes offer us images of a tormented soul bereft of the community values and ideals that inspired him in his youth. He symbolizes the plight of progressive forces in America which had begun to face HUAC's vicious reaction, and would soon succumb.

Despite his success, Charlie Davis is morally contaminated by his various compromises, such as shunning his Jewish roots and betraying his friend Shorty (Joseph Pevney) and fiancée Peg (Lilli Palmer). As a Mephistopheles figure, underworld promoter Roberts articulates to Charlie the key line of *Body and Soul*, stressing his use-and-abuse philosophy: "Everybody dies. Ben, Shorty, even you." Discerning Charlie's scruples about throwing a fight, he adds, "You've got to be businesslike, Charlie, and businessmen have to keep their agreements." These business agreements involve not only betrayal of a community that trusts its hero but also the Judas figure who signed this devil's contract. However, Charlie counteracts his betrayal in the boxing ring by taking revenge on Roberts and following the moral advice offered earlier by Ben. Charlie responds to Roberts's ultimate threat by throwing his words back at him: "What are you going to do, kill me? Everybody dies." Indeed, his final line, "I never felt better in my life!" echoes Ben's defiant words to Roberts, "I don't scare anymore."

The Dark City II: *Nightmare Alley, Brute Force,* and *Dark Passage*

Like *Crossfire* and *Out of the Past, Nightmare Alley* reflects the contemporary postwar malaise that would soon turn in a reactionary direction, similarly reflecting the end of New Deal hopes and a world of limited masculine agency characterized by individual character flaws and powerful femmes fatales. Yet unlike those two films, *Nightmare Alley* was released by a major studio, Twentieth Century Fox, then headed by Darryl F. Zanuck, and produced by comedian George Jessel. Although these men appear unlikely travelers in the world of film noir, their involvement in this project reveals Hollywood's interest in marketable topics and reflects a time when dark pessimism was not regarded as un-American.

Nightmare Alley was written by Jules Furthman from a novel by William Lindsay Gresham, rights to which had been purchased in September 1946 for $50,000. As Charles Shapiro notes, Gresham was "bard of the carnivals and Homer of the freaks" (218). He had a fascination with the dark side of the entertainment industry from a very early age. As a veteran of the Spanish Civil War he conceived the plot of his novel from a medic who had worked in a carnival fighting Franco. "A man learns, from working in a carnival side show, that a geek is made by exploiting another person's desperate need. Taking this as his guiding principle in life, he rises higher and higher, finally meets someone who works the same process on him, and tumbles back literally into the pit—biting the heads of chickens for a bottle a day" (Shapiro, 219). Gresham's novel uses the carnival world to comment on an equally sick and degrading society outside the confines of the freaks.

Nightmare Alley is a film of betrayal. Carnival worker Stanton Carlisle (Tyrone Power) manipulates everyone around him and finally obtains the code to a mind-reading act. Thus equipped, he leaves the carnival and rises in high society. Ironically, his upper-class audiences are as gullible and easily seduced by tricks as the working-class fairground spectators. Carlisle preys upon individual desires using narratives from the common stock of collective human emotions to manipulate his spectators into a desired submissive effect—similarly to the operations of Hollywood's ideological machinery. A typical victim is Ezra Grindle (Taylor Homes), changed from a resentful, rich Chicago socialite into a pathetic, weak-kneed figure desiring to see his lost 1912 love once again. Paralleled with this is Carlisle's earlier manipulation of a tough town marshal (James Burke) out to close down the fairground. However, his fall comes when he meets a cold maternal psychoanalyst figure, Dr. Lilith Ritter (Helen Walker), a woman who strongly resembles Jane Greer in the final scenes of *Out of the Past.* Ritter embodies not only that dangerous female antithesis to Eve from Jewish lore but also the treacherous psychologist figure who often manipulated patients into confessing to HUAC in this dark time.

Zanuck assigned the project to director Edmund Goulding, who had guided one of Tyrone Power's most effective performances in the underrated *The Razor's Edge* (1946). Generally cast in romantic action roles, Power played an unscrupulous and devious character containing the seeds of his own destruction as seen by his fascination with the geek in the film's opening scene. That most expressionistic of Hollywood cinematographers, Lee Garmes, depicted dark noir lower depths and the high key-lit world of predatory capitalism that comes to ensnare the hero. Although the film visually expresses the postwar pessimism of a public that regards the New Deal as over, it omits several characters from the novel—including an African American who rides a boxcar north to help in the union movement and who saves Carlisle's life. In the novel, Carlisle responds by saying, "Listen, kid, you got everything figured out so close. What sense does it all make? What sort of God would put us here in this goddamned, stinking slaughterhouse of a world? . . . It's a nut house. And the biggest loonies are at the top" (Gresham 770–71).

Jules Dassin's violent prison drama *Brute Force* not only exemplifies the existentialist motifs of film noir recognized by many critics but also reflects the mood of its time in several striking ways. Reading the isolated prison as a metaphor for "Fortress America," *Brute Force* reflects an era torn between different alternatives and finding "no exit" in the Sartrean sense of the phrase. Confined in a prison constructed to house far fewer inmates than its current population, the convicts inhabit a world in which hell is not just other people but an environment dominated by the changing mood of the political world outside. A right-wing politician rides the tail of aged, world-weary, and liberal Warden Barnes (Roman Bohnen) about the number of violent incidents inside the "lock-up," while sadistic Captain Munsey (Hume Cronyn) waits to take control with his own form of "new order." Although Barnes receives the support of alcoholic Dr. Walters (played eloquently by Group Theatre veteran Art Smith, who would soon face the Blacklist), he is ineffective to combat the force of a new ideological hero. A portrait of Abraham Lincoln hangs hopelessly above his desk, paralleling the image of FDR in Captain Finlay's office in *Crossfire*.

In the "land of the free" (whose prison population is still higher than that of any country in the Western world), the ideals associated with the Great Emancipator are now as redundant as those recently associated with the New Deal. The warden is very much an embattled figure, similar to those politicians struggling against the Republican-dominated Congress eager to remove all traces of Roosevelt's "socialist" legacy from the thirties. Finally, the opposition wins by firing Barnes and placing the ruthless Munsey in his stead. A final cataclysm is provoked in which nobody really wins. Hume Cronyn's Munsey embodies not only characteristic Nazi features but gay attributes as well, which have often been depicted negatively in film. Espousing Nietzschean ideology, Munsey brutally rejects compassion as a weakness that denotes a follower rather than a leader. His quasi-Nazi sympathies logically lead to the Gestapo-like torture of Louie (Sam Levene). Nazi overtones in this scene are suggested by the music of Wagner, Hitler's favorite composer, playing in Munsey's office, and the portrait hanging there of Munsey himself dressed in something resembling an SS commandant's uniform. Interestingly, Louie's torture resembles the similar victimization of Samuels (also played by Levene) in *Crossfire*.

Munsey's significance in this film relates to a time when history was being hastily rewritten in America. A blind eye was turned to the slave labor practices used only a few years earlier by Nazi rocket scientists hastily recruited for Cold War rocket research; to war criminals like Dr. Josef Mengele who were aided in escaping to South America; and to the accusation of prewar anti-Nazi activists of being "premature anti-Fascists" during the McCarthy era. Those hearing the antisemitic outbursts of politicians such as Gerald K. Smith, John Rankin, and Jack Tenney could easily be excused for believing that a dark history was about to repeat itself and that wartime sacrifices were for nothing. Before fleeing into exile (eventually in Pacific Palisades), distinguished German author Thomas Mann noted similarities between Nazis and the Cold War warriors.

In *Brute Force,* middle-age convict Gallagher (Charles Bickford) tries to mediate between both sides until he finds himself a victim of the reactionary forces outside the prison when his parole is withdrawn. He then decides to join the prison break and later dies in front of the prison gates, receiving a tantalizing glimpse of the world outside. Such a view is also granted in the opening scenes to Joe Collins (Burt Lancaster), watching the body of a sixty-two-year-old inmate who has died while working in the hazardous, unhealthy climate of the "drainpipe" where Munsey assigned him. Although no proletarian hero, Collins finds himself spurred into revolt not only by Munsey's brutality but also by the outside world's denial of more positive relationships that could have turned these men in a different direction. With the exception of cynical gambler Spencer (John Hoyt), it is American capitalism that has forced these men into crime. Lister (Whit Bissell) embezzled money to preserve his marriage. Soldier (Howard Duff) committed his first crime by stealing food to aid starving Italians who suffered from American aerial bombardment. Joe turned to crime to find money for his ailing girlfriend (Ann Blyth). During the sequence when Munsey attempts to blackmail Lister into becoming a stool pigeon, the convicts watch a recent movie depicting the manufactured ideals of cozy domesticity and rural life—*The Egg and I*—obviously selected for its deliberate ironic undertones. This sequence ends with Lister's suicide after Munsey has lied to him about his wife filing for divorce.

Nobody wins in the climax of the film. Dr. Walters tends to one survivor of the prison riot, which has cost the deaths of all the leading characters. He asks, "Why do they do it? They never learn. They always fail. But they keep trying. Nobody escapes. Nobody ever escapes." The film ends with a close-up of his face as the camera tracks out to show him framed by the prison bars. It is a bleak ending for a work belonging to the genres of prison movie and political film noir. The audience is also trapped in its own prison and will face further confinement from the Cold War reaction of this year and beyond. Defeat may tilt the odds, but people will still "keep try-ing" if only to move further past that tantalizing glimpse of freedom seen by Joe Collins in the film's opening sequence and by Gallagher toward the end, as for a too-brief moment the gates open and the bright world beyond is made tangible.

Dark Passage is based on David Goodis's second novel, which was pur-chased by Warner Bros. producer Jerry Wald, leading to a six-year studio contract for the author. Like Cornell Woolrich, David Goodis embodies the underside of a noir literary tradition represented by "tough guy" writers such as Cain, Chandler, Hammett, and Spillane. Both Woolrich and Goodis depict un-American layers of male insecurity, masochism, and homosexual panic in works appreciated better in France than in America. This was Goodis's year. Wald's acquisition of *Dark Passage* obviously influenced RKO's *Out of the Past* with its passive hero and unhappy ending.

Dark Passage is decidedly unusual in its construction. It not only treats a rare Goodis novel with a happy ending, but also attempts to continue the radical point-of-view perspective begun by Robert Montgomery in *Lady in the Lake* (1947). However, although the audience shares the hero's camera eye during the first thirty minutes of the film, director Delmer Daves also inserts objective shots in a return to familiar narrative techniques. The star teaming of Bogart and Bacall results in a "happy ending" similar to their earlier excursion in the noir world of *The Big Sleep* (1946). Although many critics question *Dark Passage*'s credentials as a film noir, it does contain rel-evant noir features. The protagonist's first encounter with his ideal woman, her continuing support of him, and their final meeting in Peru have ele-ments common to a dream fantasy—so much so that French critics have drawn attention to the film's surrealist affinities.

Vincent Parry (Bogart) escapes from prison where he has been sen-tenced for murdering his wife. After overpowering the driver of a Stude-baker whose striped car seat comes from pieces of a carnival tent (substituting for the predominant orange color motif used in Goodis's novel), he encounters the fantasy figure of Irene Jansen (Bacall), who helps him through a police cordon. Suspicious of women after his unhappy mar-ital relationship and unpleasant experiences with his wife's jealous and shrewish friend Madge Rapf (Agnes Moorehead), Vincent feels more at home in the company of men such as his friend George (Rory Mallinson) (whose homosexual feelings for him in the novel do not appear in the film), friendly taxi driver Sam (Tom D'Andrea), and disbarred plastic surgeon Dr. Coley (Houseley Stevenson). After an operation to change his face, Vincent returns to find George dead.

Dark Passage is also a man-on-the-run film anticipating later HUAC-inspired works such as *Night and the City* (1950) and *He Ran All the Way* (1951). Apart from the latent homosexual overtones that derive from Goodis, Vincent's security in the company of men may represent the returning veteran's feeling of belonging to those who have shared his own experiences rather than to "women at home" who have often now changed in many ways. Agnes Moorehead's Madge represents a demonic noir incarnation of a femme fatale who chooses suicide rather than clearing the name of an unjustly accused man by admitting that she was the one who killed Vincent's wife (out of passion for him). Her position resembles those wives of blacklisted figures who divorced their spouses and later informed on them. Irene, by contrast, represents the faithful, supportive version of the girl at home. Irene and Madge also embody those split depictions of female characters seen in *Out of the Past*. *Dark Passage* is an allegory of postwar readjustment (see essays by Telotte for a fuller discussion of this intriguing film). But Bacall and Bogart's presence also makes this film another version of Hawks's experiments in both *To Have and Have Not* (1944) and *The Big Sleep* by contrasting the romantic couple with the alienating environment of film noir where the female is often "deadlier than the male."

The Dark Plains: *Duel in the Sun* and *Pursued*

Described on release as "Lust in the Dust" by those regarding this David O. Selznick production as little better than a vulgar exhibitionist attempt to recapture the success of his *Gone With the Wind* (1939), *Duel in the Sun* is actually a key text for understanding the contradictory moods of official optimism and underlying pessimism within this year. Like film noir, it depicts a world of "American ideals gone rotten" (Durgnat and Simmon 241), using the western genre to dramatize, in Robin Wood's words, "an ideological system that was rotten at its very foundations, and leaves it a heap of rubble" ("*Duel*" 195). The film has contacts with other western traditional noir counterparts such as *Pursued* and *Ramrod*. But, as Durgnat and Simmon also state, its "power comes from its hybrid nature, its Janus sense" (243) in collapsing many styles and themes to implode the ideological foundations of Western capitalism from within. *Duel in the Sun* has several claims to be regarded as the first western color film noir, its pessimism equaling the bleakest examples of the classical black and white tradition as well as anticipating the world of social chaos contained in the later neo-noirs of the 1970s. As Jerome Pryor shows, *Duel in the Sun* is a dark classical operatic symphony deliberately utilizing dissonant aural and visual

Gregory Peck and Joseph Cotten in *Duel in the Sun* (King Vidor, Selznick Pictures Corporation/Vanguard Films Production). Courtesy Jerry Ohlinger Archives.

expressionist devices "in order to expose a more pungently expressive emotional world" (15). In a work involving the hybrid authorship of King Vidor, David O. Selznick, Josef von Sternberg, and William Dieterle (and probably countless others, as in *Gone With the Wind*), *Duel in the Sun* uses that most traditional of American genres to depict ideological breakdown. It also suggests that the origins of noir are deeply embedded in the western.

Duel in the Sun is the only western of its generation to deal seriously with the problem of miscegenation. It depicts a heroine who represents an incarnation of a libido feared by society and at the same time draws parallels with the female horror film monster. Pearl (Jennifer Jones) is a "stranger in a strange land," having the creative potentials embodied by a solitary wild flower seen in the prologue. But as the opening voiceover informs the audience that the flower is "quick to blossom, early to die," so are Pearl's chances for survival doomed, in a western environment as hostile to human potential as film noir's urban jungle. As the half-caste daughter of a sexually free mother, Pearl is already stereotyped as a traditional femme fatale. She finds herself torn between two ideological paths that eventually destroy her. Pearl may either submit to the repressive civilized norms represented by her deceased dissolute father, Chavez (Herbert Marshall), and his former genteel sweetheart Laura Belle (Lilian Gish), or she may become the sexually loose stereotype desired by Laura Belle's son Lewt McCanles (Gregory Peck), who takes after his racist, land baron father, Senator McCanles (Lionel Barrymore).

The film depicts two unsatisfactory worlds, neither of which offers a safe haven for the heroine. While the range environment of corruption, violence, racism, and capitalist acquisitiveness—typified by the railroad attempting to encroach upon the million-acre McCanles ranch—offers no sanctuary for Pearl, neither does the genteel world of Laura Belle. Finding herself faced with unsatisfactory patriarchal alternatives—her true father, who was hanged for murdering his Indian wife and her paramour, or the crippled, resentful McCanles—Pearl sets off on a fatal mission to save the good son, Jesse (Joseph Cotten)—who takes after his mother—by killing his dark fraternal alter ego. Lewt and Pearl die in a climactic operatic *liebestod* at Squaw's Head Rock. However, as several critics note, their exit parallels an earlier deathbed sequence between old McCanles and Laura Belle in which she confesses that she once ran away from him when she found her oppressive domestic situation too hard to bear. McCanles tells her of his jealously toward Chavez that turned his love to hate. However, he breaks down as his dying wife crawls to him (anticipating Pearl's motions in the climax) to confess that he had always been her husband. If there is an embrace, it occurs offscreen. All we see in the final shot is a rocking wheel chair symbolizing the crippling of human potential, represented by an aggressive ideological system destroying everyone physically and emotionally.

Like that of *Duel in the Sun*, *Pursued*'s narrative derives from a screenplay by Niven Busch, revealing tensions within the American family stylistically depicted within a hybrid combination of western and film noir. The plot involves the attempts of Jeb Rand (Robert Mitchum) to uncover the events leading to the massacre of his family and his victimization by the mysterious Grant Callum (Dean Jagger), brother-in-law of Ma Callum (Judith Anderson) who rescued Jeb from the massacre many years before. Until the climax, all Jeb can remember is a series of episodic flashbacks often characterized by images of spurs worn by his father in the last moments of his life. Eventually, Jeb finds that he is a victim of family vengeance and is saved from hanging only by the last-minute intervention of his sweetheart, Thorley Callum (Teresa Wright), who has decided to make a break with the past. *Pursued* thus has associations with Jacobean revenge melodrama as well as being another of the year's entry in the catalog of the "running man" theme. It is not accidental that Dean Jagger was a rabid McCarthyite in real life and was ideally cast in his role as paranoid avenger of the American way of life as defined in this film.

Andrew Britton has suggested that the film is an example of Hollywood's social determination of neurosis, which occurs in many genres dealing "in the form of symbolic drama with sexual repression in the bourgeois American family" (196). However, *Pursued* can also be read as an allegorical foreshadowing of the paranoid Blacklist era. Jeb Rand finds himself a blacklisted outcast in this particular western society, a man as obsessed with the purity of country and family as Robert Ryan's Montgomery is in *Crossfire*: "He don't respect the service, he don't respect his mother." Britton also notes the film's relationship to film noir "in which, again and again, the villain is there to suggest that American ideology gives birth to monsters" (199). Like *Duel in the Sun*, *Pursued* treats the theme of the family in a very different way from John Ford in emphasizing the darker underside of its effects on the individual. James Wong Howe's cinematography contributes as much to this western's noir associations as it does to *Body and Soul*, adding psychological depth not only to the internal tensions surrounding the main characters but also to depictions of the threatening external landscapes, dark alleys, and narrow streets within the film. Jeb's memories occur in the form of flashbacks, one noted feature of film noir as seen in *Body and Soul*, *Brute Force*, *Crossfire*, and *Out of the Past*. Memory is an escape from the unbearable disappointment of the present.

While *Duel in the Sun*'s western society unjustly sees miscegenation as the threat to the status quo, *Pursued* visits the sins of a deceased father's adultery onto the son whom it demonizes. The malevolent Grant explains the reasons for Jeb's success as a Spanish-American War hero to his jealous brother: "Jeb comes by his instincts naturally. He inherits them." Doubted by others, Jeb begins to doubt himself. One night, for example, Thorley attends a dance with the mild-mannered Prentice McComber (Harry Carey Jr.), and Jeb pressures her to dance with him. Grant convinces Prentice that she has been insulted and urges him to avenge her, with the result that he steps into a gunfight with Jeb and is killed. Speaking offscreen during Prentice's burial, Jeb suggests that perhaps "some badness locked up in me" is the cause of "the mystery of people hating me." He also remarks that "I had the feeling of some lost and awful thing over me again," in words very similar to his final words to Thor: "There was a black dog riding my back, and yours, too."

Pursued is a "scapegoat" film. Although having little direct references to what David Caute has described as a "climate of fear" infecting American society, it does contain certain indirect reverberations that would reveal themselves a year later. Dean Jagger's Grant Callum emerges as a psychotic representative of the rabid religious fundamentalism that would emerge with the blacklist, a zealous intention to visit "the iniquity of the fathers upon the children." Although others attempt to reject his authority, Grant is, like *Brute Force*'s Captain Munsey, an uncontrollable force until one person's final intervention. In this case, it is Ma who finally takes responsibility for her past "sins" and kills this logical culmination of the American family's punitive patriarchy, in the same way that in *Brute Force* Joe Collins destroys the deadly symbol of contemporary American fascination with Nazi methods of law and order. However, although Jeb and Thor ride away from society with Ma's blessing, their contemporaries in real life will soon not be so fortunate.

■ ▨ ■

The year ended with the strong tide of McCarthyite reaction ready to overwhelm what it held to be the dissonant voices of an unpatriotic "disloyal opposition" that was vainly struggling to continue the cultural legacy of the New Deal movements of the 1930s. In Washington, Harry Truman began to construct the National Security State apparatus that would dominate the national budget for future decades. The success of that apparatus would depend upon demonizing convenient internal and external scapegoats, and Hollywood would be one particular target. The various films of the year selected here exhibit conflicting tendencies toward tentative optimism and bleak pessimism, reflecting the lack of alternative clear-cut social directions in the immediate postwar era. Some films would bluntly reflect pessimism. But others such as *Brute Force* and Henry Hathaway's *Kiss of Death* intuitively and touchingly reflected the grim mood of a national state that would both physically and psychologically destroy talent and hope: they were thus optimistic at heart, and extraordinarily depressing. It was a year lacking the cohesive ideology of the war years and of a New Deal era in which alternative directions appeared possible. Although they all variously reflect a breakdown of national ideology, these films also suggest nothing to put in its place. Instead, they depict a dark mood stylistically represented by the appropriate representation of film noir. With little oppositional alternatives to counter a reactionary mood that would reach its culmination in the 1950s and reawaken again in the early years of the new millennium, in 1947 a nightmare had begun.

1948

Movies and the Family

JOANNA RAPF

In *State of the Union*, presidential candidate Grant Matthews (Spencer Tracy) finally comes to the realization that ambition at the expense of family is not worth it: "I'm neither happy nor successful, not as a man, husband, or a father." The horror of a world war over, postwar America turned its focus homeward, as Muriel Blandings (Myrna Loy) bluntly states in another film, *Mr. Blandings Builds His Dream House*: "It isn't a house we're building, it's a home, for ourselves and our children and maybe our children's children." The films of the year largely embody a quest for a new optimism. This quest can be seen in the three models for alternative ways of life that, according to William Graebner, Americans turned to after World War II (58–60). All three, as will be discussed below, found cinematic expression this year, and all three are reflected in what is sometimes called the postwar "cult of domesticity." The first is the flight to the suburbs, exemplified by Levittown in the East and on the other coast by the fact that in San Bernardino, California, McDonald's opened its first drive-in restaurant—the chain was to proliferate like the so-called "rabbit hutches" of Levittown so that its golden arches would spread across the country as symbols of the safe and the predictable in family food and fun. The second model, as seen in the popularity of the ranch house, looks back at the historical West. The year's most symbolic manifestation of this glorification of westward expansion was Eero Saarinen's design for another arch, that commemorating Thomas Jefferson and the Louisiana Purchase to be constructed in St. Louis, "The Gateway to the West." Finally, the third model also looks ahistorically at the American past, a nostalgic revisioning of the turn of the century, before the age of the automobile and the telephone. This was Norman Rockwell's America, where life was slower and people felt connected to each other and their roots in small towns.

These three "alternatives" represent a yearning for something better, more secure, less frightening than a world threatened by atomic destruction, the communist menace, labor unrest, human conditioning and manipulation—B. F. Skinner's *Walden Two* was published this year—and overbearing women no longer content with the patriarchal structure of society. *Life* sponsored a roundtable on "Happiness" in order to explore "the failure in America to achieve genuine happiness" (Davenport 98). Just as Grant Matthews in *State of the Union* honestly confesses to his wife, Mary (Katharine Hepburn), about not being happy or successful as a man, husband, or father, so the *Life* roundtable concluded: "Today it is becoming apparent to millions that economics does not itself hold the answers to the underlying problems of a democratic society. The war and its aftermath have shaken us from that position. People are searching themselves and their societies for deeper answers than the outer world alone is able to reveal" (Davenport 113). Those "deeper answers" seemed to be found by turning inward, to the family, to the home, to psychiatry and psychoanalysis. The year witnessed a profusion of self-help books, such as Dale Carnegie's best seller, *How to Stop Worrying and Start Living;* studies of the American character, such as David Riesman's *The Lonely Crowd*, and similar works by Nathan Glazer and Reuel Denny; and books on male and female behavior, such as Margaret Mead's *Male and Female* and the Kinsey Report, *Sexual Behavior in the Human Male,* both of which raised questions of what is normal, abnormal, right, or wrong. The family was the place where men and women learned answers to these questions and found "private and personal solutions" to social issues (May, *Homeward* 14). Muriel Blandings's "home" becomes a place for Grant Matthews to find his happiness and success.

The danger in turning inward is that domesticity can become an escape from confronting social problems, a retreat from the kind of political activism that characterized the 1930s. Now there was a recognition—unconscious, or perhaps even conscious—of the failure of Marxism and a fear of facing realities both home and abroad: the assassination of Gandhi in India, continued segregation and lynching in the South, the airlift in Berlin, the establishment of the State of Israel, the witch hunts that were ferreting out alleged communists in all areas of American life. Americans seemed to look away from world and national events, and their taste in entertainment reflected this. They watched Ed Sullivan and Ted Mack's "Original Amateur Hour" on television and listened to Arthur Godfrey on the radio. An MGM survey showed that the kinds of films they most wanted were musicals (Sklar, *Movie* 282–83). Westerns, although not one of the more popular genres in the survey, made a resurgence in part for reasons discussed above, and in part just because they were, as McDonald's was soon to become, familiar, predictable, safe. Americans wanted to escape to the prewar past.

The year featured the first full season of television in the United States. The result was not only that families began to stay home to watch "the box," but that they were bombarded with entertainment that asked them to consume, and consume they did. Advertising became a growing and successful business. In the four years after the end of the war, "Americans purchased 21.4 millions cars, 20 million refrigerators, 5.5 million stoves, and 11.6 million televisions and moved into over 1 million new housing units each year" (May, *Homeward* 165). The smooth, white, bowling pin–shaped Shmoo, introduced by *Lil Abner* cartoonist Al Capp, epitomized consumerism by skipping the production process. It could, or so it was said, lay eggs already in their cartons, give milk already in its bottles, and, depending on how it was cooked, taste like pork, chicken, or steak. Versions of the delightful creature were sold to children everywhere, and a popular song reiterated that "a Shmoo can do most anything." The home no longer had to do with producing—the farmer, the craftsperson, the home*maker*—but it had everything to do with consuming. Americans seemed to be more interested in buying than saving, in surviving rather than in social progress, and in themselves rather than the world outside their doors. Homes and families came to represent "a source of meaning and security in a world run amok. Marrying young and having lots of babies were ways for Americans to thumb their noses at doomsday predictions" (May, *Homeward* 24).

Popular films included *Johnny Belinda*, about a deaf-mute who is an unwed mother, *Treasure of the Sierra Madre*, which looks at the human propensity for greed and concludes that the real "treasure" is home, and *Red River*, a western that is really about a "father" and "son" coming to terms with each other. In a year that produced H. C. Potter's *Mr. Blandings Builds His Dream House* and Frank Capra's *State of the Union*, the films with which this essay began, the idea of family was central to what people were seeing on the motion picture screen, as in Abraham Polonsky's *Force of Evil*, a noir film about two brothers, and the nostalgic *I Remember Mama* and *Summer Holiday*, although the latter may be parody.

This essay first looks at family within the context of the fears that permeated American society, what Graebner describes as "the age of doubt." The films discussed include *Force of Evil*, *Treasure of the Sierra Madra*, *Johnny Belinda*, and *State of the Union*. Although these may have happy Hollywood endings, their narratives explore a dark side of life that the films discussed in the second part of this essay seek to gloss over. Using Graebner's three models for "alternative" visions, the flight to the suburbs will be exemplified in *Mr. Blandings Builds His Dream House*, the glorification of the West in *Red River*, and a simpler life at the turn of the century in *I Remember Mama* and (though perhaps as parody) in *Summer Holiday*.

■ Films in the "Age of Doubt"

David Cook reminds us that postwar America gave us "a cinema of disillusionment and searching which rejected the epic heroes and callow idealism of World War II films" (452). The style most associated with this disillusionment is film noir, a term coined by French critics who noticed a new cynicism, a nihilism growing out of unrelieved despair in the shadowy urban world of the American detective film. Films such as Billy Wilder's *Double Indemnity* (1944), Edward Dymtryk's *Murder, My Sweet* (1945), Robert Siodmak's *The Killers* (1946), and Delmer Daves's *Dark Passage* (1947) "held up a dark mirror to postwar America and reflected its moral anarchy" (Cook 452–53). Male fears of the castrating woman in the figure of the femme fatale, the spider lady of noir, as well as anxiety about the future and a horror of the recent past, serve to color narratives of crime, violence, and corruption, of human beings trapped by fear and paranoia, and of a society coming apart at the seams. In describing this genre that he used so well in later decades, Paul Schrader has written: "Film noir's techniques emphasize loss, nostalgia, lack of clear priorities, and insecurity, then submerge these doubts into mannerism and style" (58).

Force of Evil, based on Ira Wolfert's novel *Tucker's People*, is a good example of the noir style. Written for the screen by Abraham Polonsky and starring John Garfield, both left-wingers, and both soon to be blacklisted by the House Un-American Activities Committee (HUAC), the film looks at people caught up in the New York numbers racket. It opens with Garfield's voiceover narration, as we look down Wall Street at Trinity Church, a resonant juxtaposition of money and spiritual values: "This is Wall Street, and today was important, because tomorrow, July 4, I intended to make my first million dollars. An important day in any man's life." This voiceover thus undercuts any easy optimism about postwar America by mentioning that Joe Morse (Garfield) intends to make his first million precisely on July Fourth. American Independence Day will, ironically, mark his fall through his responsibility for the bankruptcy of hundreds of innocent numbers players and the death of his brother, Leo (Thomas Gomez). Innocent American workers, believing in luck, will play "the old Liberty number," 776, and Morse, a lawyer working for mobster Ben Tucker (Roy Roberts), will arrange for it to come in and bankrupt all the small numbers banks, including his brother's. It is a complicated scheme whereby Tucker will consolidate the whole numbers racket into his empire.

The bonds of family in *Force of Evil* are not well developed. Joe and Leo have not seen each other for years. It is hinted that Leo, the older brother, sacrificed a lot so that younger brother Joe could go to college and become a lawyer. Leo may work in the small-time numbers racket, but he has a good heart and he treats his employees kindly. Although we never find out much about the brothers' background, their bond of blood, their family tie, is what gives the film a redeeming moral center. Leo dies, a victim of his brother's July Fourth scheme, and Joe, who has tried to save him by bringing him in on the deal, is ravaged by guilt and the contrast between Leo's goodness and his own callous greed. Like Fred Dobbs (played by the ultimate noir antihero, Humphrey Bogart) in *Treasure of the Sierra Madre*, Joe Morse's conscience torments him. Dobbs, after thinking he has killed his partner, Bob Curtin (Tim Holt), wanders in a daze, mumbling, "Conscience, it will pester you to death." Joe, driven by his conscience, finds his brother's body under the George Washington Bridge. The location is visually meaningful, for George Washington, the symbolic father of America, on America's birthday, shadows the muddy grave of this victim of inescapable corruption. The dark ending was too much for the Breen Office, the motion picture industry's official censorship bureau. Polonsky had to add a coda where Joe gives himself up to the authorities for his role in the scheme. His final voiceover tells us: "I turned back to give myself up, because if a man's life could be lived so long and come out this way—like rubbish—then something was horrible, and had to be ended one way or another, and I decided to help" (Buhle and Wagner 121).

The similarities between *Force of Evil* and *Treasure of the Sierra Madre* not only have to do with a man corrupted by greed and stricken by conscience. Both films also posit family as a refuge from a society contaminated by "rubbish." The family bonds fail in *Force of Evil*, but in *Treasure*, after the death of Dobbs, and after the other partner, Howard (Walter Huston), rides off with Mexican Indians to join their idyllic community and become their medicine man, Bob Curtin (Holt), the third and youngest man in the initial trio of prospectors, heads to Texas to find the widow of James Cody, the material-driven wanderer who forced himself on them as a fourth partner and died as a result. The original novel by B. Traven, first published in 1935, contains an epigraph that Huston incorporated into his story as a letter from Cody's widow. After his death, the three prospectors read it together:

> Little Jimmy is fine, but he misses his daddy almost as much as I do. . . . I've never thought any material treasure, no matter how great, is worth the pain of these long separations. . . . The country is especially lovely this year. . . . I do hope you are back for the harvest. . . . Remember we've already found life's real treasure.
>
> Forever yours, Helen

Earlier in the film, Howard had asked Curtin what he was going to do with his share of the riches earned from the gold they had prospected. Howard, the old man, is going to retire somewhere, buy a hardware or grocery store and read comic books and adventure stories. His ideal is a leisurely but still productive life. Dobbs's ideal, in a negative comment on postwar America, is all about consuming. He wants to take a Turkish bath, buy clothes, and eat in fancy restaurants. Only Curtin talks about producing rather than leisure and consuming. He remembers picking fruit one time, "Hundreds of people, old and young, whole families workin' together." And he decides he would like to have a peach orchard where he can watch his own trees "blossom and bear," watch "the fruit get big and ripe on the boughs, ready for pickin'."

Lesley Brill has argued that most of Huston's protagonists "spend themselves, sometimes deviously or unconsciously, looking for a home" (17–18). In *Treasure of the Sierra Madre* Humphrey Bogart's Fred Dobbs never learns what the real treasure is and is killed by Mexican bandits. But both Howard and Curtin do. Howard unselfishly saves the life of an Indian boy and is welcomed into a community unspoiled by western "civilization," dripping with lush vegetation, and free of the trappings of twentieth-century commercialism. It is Howard, an early environmentalist, who had insisted the prospectors leave their mountain, Sierra Madre, the "mother," the way they found her after they took their gold. Curtin, as Brill states, "experiences the corruption of the world and his fallible character, but he eventually returns to his childhood dream of family and fruit-growing" (30). He, too, finds life's "real treasure" is not gold, not buying and spending, but caring, giving, producing together, and maybe even loving each other. It is no accident that the first shot of the film is a date, "Feb. 14, 1924," and that shortly thereafter we see, unobtrusively in the distance, two commercial mannequins of a bride and groom in a storefront window. Love is presented as a consumer product and Valentine's Day is never acknowledged. Without ever stating it, this film is about finding what love and family really mean.

The same can be said of *Johnny Belinda*, based on a play by Elmer Harris. The voiceover that begins this film identifies its locale as a quaint fishing village on Cape Breton Island. Although it was shot in California, the art direction makes its bucolic scenery look like landscape paintings by Constable, with idyllic pastures and streams, quaint barns and mills, and rolling hills down to the sea. But the pastoral beauty hides gossipy old ladies and townspeople who resent such outsiders as the new doctor in town, Robert Richardson (Lew Ayres), and the McDonald family, who make their living

Deaf and mute, Belinda (Jane Wyman) finds out she is pregnant after being examined by Dr. Horace M. Gray (Jonathan Hale) as Dr. Richardson (Lew Ayres) looks on, in *Johnny Belinda* (Jean Negulesco, Warner Bros.). Collection Joanna Rapf.

from their mill: Black (Charles Bickford), his sister Aggie (Agnes Moorehead), and Black's deaf-mute daughter, Belinda (Jane Wyman), whose mother died in childbirth.

In the course of the film, Dr. Richardson teaches Belinda sign language, and Black and Aggie learn she is not dumb, but a living, feeling person with whom they can communicate. In a touching moment, Belinda's first signed word to Black is "Father," as slowly, with the intervention of Richardson, three people become a family. But, as in *Treasure of the Sierra Madre*, the discovery of the meaning of love and family comes only after suffering and loss. Belinda is raped by the callous fisherman, Locky McCormick (Stephen McNally), who is engaged to Stella (Jan Sterling), the girl who works for the good doctor. When the doctor takes Belinda to a specialist about her hearing, he finds out she is pregnant, although he does not know the identity of the father and because of the trauma she does not remember. Richardson understands this, because he had seen such trauma in the war. He is the disillusioned returning veteran of postwar America. He tells Belinda that the war made him lose faith in everything, including himself.

But in caring for her, and bringing her happiness, he has found happiness. Black's sister, Aggie, who had never liked Belinda, is horrified to hear she is pregnant and appalled by the shame it brings on the family. But her icy demeanor is broken as Richardson explains to her that there is only one shame, and that is the shame of "failing a human being who needs you." And so Aggie is transformed as she, too, experiences what it means to care for someone, to connect with your roots, first as she recognizes the importance of a family "sticking together" when in need and then when she helps Belinda with her baby. Black for the first time connects with his daughter as a human being and experiences the joy of being a grandfather, and finally dies defending the family honor.

The McDonalds, ostracized by the town because of the illegitimacy, are in debt, without credit or customers for their mill. Many think the doctor is the father and he loses his patients. When he offers to marry Belinda to make her respectable, her father, before he is killed by Locky, rejects the offer because he believes Richardson does not love her the way a man should love a woman. When Dr. Richardson has to leave to make a living in Toronto, the good townspeople decide a deaf-mute is an unfit mother and arrange for Stella and Locky, now married, to take baby Johnny from Belinda. Defending her baby, Belinda kills Locky and is tried for murder. But the film holds up the legal system as a staunch and generously lenient advocate of family when it comes to the rights of parents. Belinda is acquitted because she was only protecting her "home," and with Canadian Mounties flanking the doorway, mother, baby, doctor, and aunt exit the court and drive off as a firm family unit. Dr. Richardson's last line to Belinda, who has not uttered a sound for the whole film, even during childbirth, is simply, "You don't have to say anything."

And indeed, she doesn't. Jane Wyman, who in private life was Mrs. Ronald Reagan, had herself just lost an infant daughter; she acts from the depths of her heart and soul. As Bosley Crowther said in his review of the film in the *New York Times*: "Her face is the mirror of her thoughts." Max Steiner's Oscar-nominated music only adds to the emotional impact of this family drama that no doubt had a little extra resonance for audiences, not just because of the awakening from disillusion on the part of a returning veteran, the theme of finding happiness in the love and care of making a family, but also in the reassuring response to the fear of sex crimes that dominated the headlines of the time, such as "Ex-Marine Held in Rape Murder" or "Veteran Beheads Wife with Jungle Machete" (Goulden 37–40).

Of the three films exemplifying the "age of doubt" in this essay, Frank Capra's *State of the Union* is the most explicit evocation of the conflicts embodied in the fragility of family structures in these postwar years. Based on a 1945 Pulitzer Prize–winning play by Howard Lindsay and Russel Crouse, it follows Capra's 1946 *It's a Wonderful Life* in exalting the virtues of homespun honesty, the wisdom of the "people," and the central value of family. Capra's most famous films are instantly recognizable for a term that has become associated with him, "Capracorn," signifying their populist ideology, sentimental optimism, and cloyingly sweet conclusions. But recent studies of the director have begun to question the wholesomely simplistic outlook that he himself encouraged in his autobiography, *The Name above the Title*. Vito Zagarrio argues that Capra, in spite of himself, "ends up pointing out some of America's social problems" (67). In his films we often have a "sense of a society in danger, of a family charged with tensions, of individuals brimming with fear, as well as the pursuit of happiness" (68).

The title of *State of the Union* refers not only to the state of the country but also to the state of a marriage. Grant Matthews is a self-made man who has run a successful aeronautics business, is married to a beautiful woman, has two perfect children, a ten-year old daughter, Joyce, and an eight year-old son, Grant Jr., and lives in an elegant Long Island suburb. He embodies the American dream in every respect, except that his marriage is falling apart because of his affair with an ambitious and ruthless newspaper tycoon, Kay Thorndyke, skillfully played by twenty-two-year-old Angela Lansbury. He forgets his son's birthday, and later his own anniversary, as he becomes swept up in a scheme to become president of the United States. He is initially reluctant—"I can be interested in the country without being interested in politics"—but the hold Thorndyke has on him, which is as powerfully sexual as it can be under the watchful eye of the Breen Office, sways him to betray his better instincts.

Kay, who has inherited her newspaper empire from her father, might be viewed as another version of the femme fatale or spider woman from film noir. She is manipulative, cold-hearted, selfish, and ambitious, wielding the kind of female power that it is said men feared when they returned from the war. Women, who had found a new sense of self in the workplace during the war, were now encouraged to give up working positions to the returning veterans and again make their homes the center of their lives. Older studies of this period in American history have documented how women decided against acquiring a higher education and pursuing a career, how they married at younger ages, and "concentrated on rearing their children and keeping house" (Mintz and Kellog 174–75). Women who did not follow this path were considered threatening, and on film at least they needed to be put in their place (in noir this usually meant being killed). But recent studies of social attitudes toward women in the postwar period have found in the literature of the time, along with stories that glorified domesticity, others that "expressed ambivalence about domesticity, endorsed women's nondomestic activity, and celebrated women's public success" (Meyerowitz 252). But such ambivalence rarely, if ever, showed up on film.

In *State of the Union*, Kay is clearly portrayed as a sinister, castrating woman while the moral center of the film is the populist wisdom and influence the good wife, Mary, has on her wayward husband. The first hint of his transformation comes in a typically Capraesque encounter when Grant stands outside the White House and talks with another visitor, a common man, who inspires him to recall the great men who have lived there, those "martyrs, saints and poets" who fought and died for human liberty. It is an epiphany of mythic proportions. Only after this encounter at the White House does Grant confess to Mary, in a self-aware moment, how he is neither happy nor successful as a man, husband, or father. The great Americans before him had a "cause" they could die for. "I have no cause, Mary. . . . It's always me first and everyone else second."

The rest of the film is about finding that cause. As a potential presidential candidate, Grant begins to make speeches that convey ideas he takes from Mary rather than his handlers, Thorndyke and Jim Conover (Adolphe Menjou). Some of these ideas sound a lot like Garry Davis and his world citizenship movement:

> "The American dream is not making money; it's the well-being and freedom of every individual throughout the world."
> "We can't be an island of plenty in a world of starvation."
> "The brotherhood of man is not just an idealistic dream, but a practical necessity."

But Grant also says he knows what is driving the country in this election year, namely, fear: "fear of the future, fear of the world, fear of communism, fear of going broke." He articulates concisely the underpinnings of "the age of doubt," and it is a fear to which he again succumbs as he is persuaded by Kay, for pragmatic reasons (and his never overtly expressed, misdirected sexual desire), to follow her political course and abandon the emotional ideals of his wife.

Mary practices what she preaches. In her comfortable, suburban Long Island home she and her children are involved with "operation breadbasket," sending care packages of American goods, including chewing gum and comic books, to the less fortunate children in Europe. When her husband's

In *State of the Union* (Frank Capra, Liberty Films), Spencer Tracy as Grant Matthews and Katharine Hepburn as his loyal wife, Mary, save their "union." Collection Joanna Rapf.

handlers plan to use her, her house, and her children for an elaborately staged televised version of what Roosevelt coined a "fireside chat," in order to promote Grant's candidacy as a family man, she is horrified. "This may be a stable to the dark horse, but it is still home to me." However, as a loyal wife, she finally agrees. *State of the Union*, in the first full year of television, presciently acknowledges the powerful role this new medium will come to play in politics and the powerful role advertising will play in shaping how ideas and products are consumed.

It is here, in the domestic sphere made public, that Grant has his second awakening. This time he learns the truth of one of Mary's earlier statements, that the "real wealth of the world is in honesty." Here is another redefinition of wealth, similar to what emerges in the conclusion to *Treasure of the Sierra Madre*. And like that film, this one too ends with a reaffirmation that the bedrock of American values is in forms of family. Grant admits that he "sold out." All along, his wife had known the truth: like the American people, he was scared, and when people are scared, "they will be led by communists and fascists." But through the unwavering support and love of Mary and his children, he has found the courage to withdraw as a candidate for president, "not because I'm honest, but because I'm dishonest." The paradox, of course, is that in recognizing his dishonesty he has become honest again and discovered the "real wealth of the world." The film suggests that if people like Grant find courage, out of that courage our young country can find "greatness greater than we ever dreamed."

It's a hopeful ending, but a conditional one. The structure of the family is fragile and an oppressed and poverty-filled world needs to be cared for. The new medium of television has emerged as a potent propaganda weapon, making is easier than ever for communists and fascists to lead people who are easily scared, an idea that will help usher in the McCarthy era. "The age of doubt" is conducive to fear. Happiness is elusive. Alternative visions of better times are quite alluring.

Alternative Visions

Graebner's "cult of domesticity" highlights the flight to the suburbs. *Mr. Blandings Builds His Dream House* typifies the ideal of a safe, secure, happy family life in suburbia. It begins with a comforting voiceover by Bill Cole (Melvyn Douglas), Jim Blandings's lawyer, who tells us his client was born and raised in New York City, is a college graduate and an advertising executive who makes $15,000 a year, and has a lovely wife and two fine kids. We also learn the family has a loyal black maid, Gussie (Louise Beavers). It all seems perfect, another fulfillment of the American dream, except that Blandings is a "modern cliff dweller," living in a cramped two-bedroom New York apartment with only one bathroom and very little closet space. As we go into a flashback that reveals the Blandings's frustration with their living quarters, Cole tells us that "it all started one September morning. . . ."

During a hasty breakfast-table conversation, Jim Blandings (Cary Grant) makes a snide remark about his daughters' expensive private schools. "Progressive education" and permissive child rearing were increasingly coming under attack that year for "having contributed to a confused and spiritually adrift culture" (Graebner 27). Blandings's remark is triggered by a homework assignment that consists of finding a classified ad typical of the "disintegration of our present society" and writing a human-interest story from it. One daughter has found an ad for the sale of an old farmhouse, and she tells her father that she will write about how the times have forced someone to "stoop to crass commercialism" by putting an ad in the paper in order to sell their home. Her teacher has told her that middle-class people like the Blandings cannot understand the hard times, and also that advertising is "a parasitic profession."

Although the film makes fun of the flourishing postwar field of advertising—to the point where, at the end, it is Gussie who unwittingly saves Blandings's job by coming up with the advertising slogan for his Wham ham account, "If you ain't eatin' Wham, you ain't eatin' ham"—the comedy is accepting rather than satiric. Satire aims at reform. *Mr. Blandings Builds His Dream House,* however, allows its audience to enjoy the foolishness of its characters without condemning them. As a harried urban dweller, hassled in his Madison Avenue job, Blandings speaks in advertising clichés and makes an aside to his secretary about a private joke "between me and whoever is going to be my analyst." The increasing popularity of psychiatry and psychoanalysis reflects one way anxious Americans, especially in the cities, tried to deal with postwar anxiety.

To escape some of his frustrations, Blandings is himself victimized by exactly the same kind of "crass commercialism" that his daughter had condemned. He sees an ad for an old farmhouse in Connecticut and buys it. Rather than remodel their New York apartment, he and his wife decide to remodel this "piece of American history," a place that dates back to the American Revolution, where a general no one has ever heard of once stopped (patriotism then, as now, was often linked to rural life). As Blandings's own ads may "bamboozle the American public," he in turn is "bamboozled" into buying a house and land for much more than they are worth. The house is not salvageable and must be torn down; the Blandings are left with "the nicest vacant lot in the State of Connecticut."

The rest of the film tells the story of building the "dream house," the "home for ourselves and our children, and maybe our children's children," cited at the beginning of this essay. Rather than satire, the film employs parody, a technique of exaggeration, to create its comedy. Working with their architect, the Blandings ask for only the "barest necessities," four bedrooms, each with its own bath and two closets, a sewing room, a basement play-room, a backyard barbecue, all the expansive and expensive new ideas of home ownership that were being sold to the American public after World War II, only doubled and tripled. Mrs. Blandings discusses with the head painter the subtleties of the colors she wants in the house, using tiny samples of red thread, minuscule dots of green on a floral fabric, and sub-tle distinctions of white and yellow. When the painter asks his boss what colors to paint the rooms, he says simply, "Red, green, white, and yellow."

Both Mr. and Mrs. Blandings are the butt of this parody of middle-class (really upper-class) consumers, hoodwinked into building a house they can-not afford, cheated by contractors, confronted by one disaster after another. But they are not criticized for their dream. Although they are foolish and extravagant, in following their hearts rather than their heads they live out an idea that is first stated defensively at the beginning of the film: "You can't measure the things you love in dollars and cents." As in *Treasure of the Sierra Madre* and *State of the Union*, money is finally rejected as a source of wealth. Indeed, building the dream house, like Curtin's orchard in *Trea-sure of the Sierra Madre* and Dunson's ranch in *Red River*, can be seen as a metaphor for America, overcoming natural adversity along with the cheats and the scoundrels who populate the landscape, in order to create a home of peace and prosperity for our children and "our children's children."

The realization that this dream matters more than money or a job comes near the end of the film when the inarticulate "well man," whom we suspect has been digging unnecessarily to overcharge the Blandings, shows up at the house with $12.56. Jim thinks this local, money-grubbing water specialist has come to bilk him one last time and is stunned to find that instead he has come to return $12.56 that he has overcharged. This revela-tion of unassuming honesty is one of those little moments that can trans-form a man's life, like Grant's discovery of the truth of his wife's statement that the "real wealth of the world is in honesty" in *State of the Union*. The fairy-tale ending to *Mr. Blandings Builds His Dream House* shows us the com-pleted country home, landscaped and peaceful, with Jim still employed (thanks to Gussie's inadvertent creativity in giving him the needed adver-tising slogan), and the congenial family group, including the narrator/lawyer Bill Cole, who has been a source of jealous suspicion on the part of Mr. Blandings, gathered round each other as they read a book, *Mr. Blandings Builds His Dream House*, presumably the very novel by Eric Hodgins on which the film is based. Cole, with his voiceover, takes us out of the narrative, inviting the audience to "drop in and see us sometime."

There is no illusion of realism here. The dream house is an American dream, and audiences wanted to visit the Blandings, if not move in with them.

The suburban world of *Mr. Blandings Builds His Dream House*, along with *State of the Union*, illustrate how, after the war, fatherhood became crucial to a man's identity, perhaps even more important than a job. Citing researcher Ruth Tasch, Robert Griswold, in his study of American fatherhood, writes that at the time, "fathers recorded not merely the fun they had with their offspring, but their happiness 'in being appreciated, the new sense of values, the new purpose which life has, and their stake in perpetuating the species'" (191). The nurturing father, perhaps also emblematic of the guiding, protective hand of a nurturing nation, appears in westerns of the year such as John Ford's *Three Godfathers* or Howard Hawks's *Red River*.

An idealized look at American expansion into the West is the second of Graebner's three "alternatives" to the darker vision seen in the postwar flourishing of film noir, and *Red River* is a good example. In this film, Thomas Dunson (John Wayne) unofficially adopts a young boy, Matt (Mickey Kuhn), orphaned in an Indian attack on the wagon train Dunson has just left. The attack also kills the only woman Dunson has ever truly loved. When Matt grows up (now played by Montgomery Clift), Tom and Matt form a family unit as they head to Texas to build a cattle ranch. It is made clear from the outset that the plot is going to involve Matt earning the right to add his initial to the Dunson brand. As a father figure, Dunson is stern and unyielding, but he raises a strong "son" with human values, along with the ability to shoot as well, if not better, than he. And because he has had an involved "father," Matt has someone against whom he can measure himself. Classically, *Red River* is about the necessity of a son killing off his father, literally or symbolically, in order to grow into manhood.

The aspect of fatherhood that involves perpetuating the species has driven Dunson from the beginning of the film. He describes the significance of his cattle ranch in terms of nurturing the whole country with "good beef for hungry people, beef to make 'em strong, to make 'em grow." When, during the cattle drive, Matt takes the cattle away from his increasingly dictatorial surrogate father, Dunson turns to Tess Millay (Joanne Dru), whom he has just met after another Indian raid on a wagon train, and tells her the story of losing the only woman he had ever loved, of losing Matt ("I thought I had a son"), and asks her to bear him a son. She understands what he is asking, and instead convinces him to take her along on the last leg of the revenge quest to kill the rebellious son. When at the end of the film Matt beats Dunson in a fistfight, and finally "earns" the initial "M" on the "D" brand, he has earned not only the right to ownership, but also the right to be a man and start his own family. Dunson tells him, "You'd better marry that girl, Matt," referring to Tess, who has brought their father/son clash to an abrupt halt.

The link between generations that helps tie a family together is visually presented in this film through a bracelet that Dunson's mother gave him, that he, in turn, gave to his love who was killed on the first wagon train (he learns this by finding the bracelet on an Indian he kills), that he then gives to Matt, who finally gives it to Tess. The circle has come around; a new generation will begin. The thrashing of John Wayne, the invincible western hero, at the end of *Red River* signifies the traditional movie hero of the past giving way to the more tortured, anguished, and fallible hero of late forties films, exemplified by Montgomery Clift as Matt. In the settling of the West, the progress of the railroad (an important factor for the cattle drive), and the creation of a new family to assure generation, *Red River* presents an optimistic vision for America's future.

A less complicated past also served as an "alternative vision" for postwar audiences. The most famous of these films that centered on what seemed to be simpler family life at the turn of the century is *I Remember Mama,* directed by George Stevens. Based on Kathryn Forbes's autobiographical book, *Mama's Bank Account,* and a play from that book by John Van Druten, the film tells the story of a Norwegian family in San Francisco circa 1910. As a story, very little really happens beyond the everyday, the quotidian mirror of the minor crises of domesticity—a sick child, a sick cat, a boarder who owes rent, a high school graduation, the death of an uncle—but the framing story, in which the oldest daughter, Katrin (Barbara Bel Geddes), learns to follow her dream and become a writer is, like *Mr. Blandings Builds His Dream House,* an affirmation that dreams are worth pursuing. Katrin's voiceover opens and closes the film: "I remember Mama and the house where I was born. . . ." A successful writer, a poised young woman, she looks back on how she became that way, at the family that taught her not only what death looks like, but what love looks like.

The film begins with the counting of money. Each week, when Papa (Philip Dorn) brings home his wages, Mama (Irene Dunne) carefully divides up the small sum for family necessities. Usually there is barely enough, and when they are short, members of the family generously volunteer to do extra or go without, so that they "do not have to go to the bank" and draw on what they believe to be the money they have saved. At the end of the film, when Katrin gets a $500.00 check for the sale of her story, "Mama's Bank Account," and eagerly says she will put the money in the bank, she finds out, as does the audience, that there has never been any money there. When Mama is asked by her daughter why she has kept up the illusion of the bank account all these years, she says, in her lilting Norwegian accent, "Is not good for little ones to be afraid, not to feel secure." Perhaps, as Mama thinks, the thought of having money is security, but metaphorically, the audience realizes that Mama's real bank account is the love and caring between the members of her family and the values she has instilled in them. Like so many films of this period, the "treasure" is found to be not money but the values of home. Even the ending of *Red River* underlines this theme. Matt has had the $50,000 check for the cattle he "stole" from his "father" made out to "Thomas Dunson." The man who bought the herd remarks that the money ought to make things right; Matt knows it won't. He tucks the check under his hat; we never see it again. Love, respect, the bonds of family have nothing to do with literal "bank accounts."

I Remember Mama, as a quintessential family story, embodies in its genuine and moving domestic incidents all the ideals of home that have been explored in various ways in other films of the year. Mama tells Katrin, when asked why they came to this country from Norway, "It's good for families to be together." Her greedy sisters, hopeful of getting some of Uncle Chris's money when he dies, are disappointed, but ultimately moved, to find out that he has given all his money away to lame people so that they can learn to walk. The boarder, Mr. Hyde (Sir Cedric Hardwicke), when he cannot pay the rent, goes off and leaves a worthless check, along with all his books. When she learns the check has no value, Mama tells her sisters and family that they have been paid with "far better things than money." During his stay, Hyde has read to them (in heart-warming scenes of a family gathered together around a table listening to Dickens's *A Tale of Two Cities*). Mama even remarks on the value of staying home and reading together when she points out that because of this her son, Nels (Steve Brown), has not gotten involved with the neighborhood gangs.

But the most explicit rejection of consumer culture and affirmation of the roots of family is in the story of Mama's broach. Like the bracelet Dunson was given by his mother in *Red River*, Mama's broach was from her mother. As Dunson passed his bracelet on to his "son," so Mama had always planned to give the broach to Katrin as a present for her graduation from high school, a welcome to adulthood, a sign of passing on to a new generation. Katrin, on the other hand, has her heart set on a fancy new "dresser set" that she has seen displayed in a storefront window. She tells her sister, Dagmar (June Hedin), that Mama's old broach is ugly. So deep is Mama's love for her daughter that she trades her broach, the only tangible item she has from her mother, for the dresser set. Katrin's excitement at getting this gaudy consumer product is short-lived. When her sister tells her how her mother obtained it, Katrin is heartbroken, and stumbles through her role of Portia in the school play, *The Merchant of Venice,* a tale that itself centers on greed. Ultimately Katrin trades back the dresser set for the broach. We see her wearing it, a part of her identity now as it was her mother's, in the final shot of the film as she narrates the conclusion of the narrative. Katrin has discovered the meaning of family.

Summer Holiday, directed by Rouben Mamoulian, is set four years earlier than *I Remember Mama,* in 1906. It is based on Eugene O'Neill's only comedy, *Ah! Wilderness,* which he wrote in one month in 1932. Almost all of O'Neill's plays are tortured examinations of aspects of his own family, but this one consists of nostalgic and idealized recollections; its subtitle is "A Comedy of Recollection in Three Acts." Shortly after the premiere in 1933, O'Neill explained the play this way:

> My purpose was to write a play true to the spirit of the American large small-town at the turn of the century. Its quality depended upon atmosphere, sentiment, and exact evocation of the mood of a dead past. To me, the America which was (and is) the real America found its unique expression in such middle-class families as the Millers, among whom so many of my own generation passed from adolescence into manhood.
>
> (qtd. in Gelb and Gelb 762)

As Katrin passes from adolescence to adulthood in *I Remember Mama,* so does Richard Miller, the sixteen-year-old son in *Ah! Wilderness.* As the play ends, Richard is no longer embarrassed to kiss his father, which he does impulsively as he hurries out. Both the play and the film come to a close with Nat Miller, the father, saying to his wife:

> First time he's done that in years. I don't believe in kissing between fathers and sons after a certain age—seems mushy and silly—but that meant something! And I don't think we'll ever have to worry about his being safe!—from himself—again. And I guess no matter what life will do to him, he can take care of it now.

Then, in a rare sentimental appreciation of romance between older people, the play concludes not just with Richard's newly found romance with his girl, Muriel, but with a statement of the enduring value of the parents' love. Nat Miller quotes from *The Rubaiyat of Omar Khayyám,* the source of the play's title:

> .   Yet Ah, that Spring should vanish with the Rose!
>   That Youth's sweet-scented manuscript should close!

In a family gathering in *Summer Holiday* (Rouben Mamoulian, MGM), Mickey Rooney (l.) outlines his idea of a perfect democracy to his father (Walter Huston) as his mother (Selena Royle) looks on. Collection Joanna Rapf.

And echoing John Keats, he adds: "Well, Spring isn't everything, is it Essie? There's a lot to be said for Autumn, Autumn's got beauty too, And Winter— if you're together!"

Richard, of course, is based on O'Neill himself, and is a prototype for Edmund in O'Neill's darkest play, *Long Day's Journey Into Night*. *Ah! Wilderness* is filled with literary references—to Ibsen, Shaw, Carlyle, Oscar Wilde, Swinburne, "the greatest poet since Shelley! He tells the truth about real love." O'Neill's description of Richard's character notes his "extreme sensitiveness," "a restless apprehensive, defiant, shy, dreamy, self-conscious intelligence about him." John Orlandello sees in Richard "a delicate balance of the would-be-poet, the would-be anarchist, and the would-be romantic" (70). Both these descriptions, however, are a far cry from Mickey Rooney, who plays Richard in *Summer Holiday*. Having already done seven Andy Hardy films, it was hard to see him as anything but the brash and charming boy next door.

Summer Holiday is, in fact, based on the 1935 film *Ah! Wilderness*, which also featured Mickey Rooney. That film was adapted from O'Neill's play by the writing team of Frances Goodrich and Albert Hackett, and retained some semblance of fidelity to the source material. Although the writers toned down some of Richard's bitterness, political radicalism, and anti-social inclinations, both Goodrich and Hackett believed that the "picture was entirely O'Neill" in spite of the fact that Wallace Beery, who played Uncle Sid, refused to say O'Neill's lines (McGilligan 201). But *Summer Holiday* is another story, a typically lush Arthur Freed Technicolor production based on the Goodrich and Hackett screenplay, rather than the original play, and has little to do with O'Neill's small-town vision. The musical numbers are lavish. In the opening song, "It's Our Home Town," Nat Miller (Walter Huston) gives us a singing tour of the town he calls "our home," with its perfectly fenced homes, happy families, and happy children who mind their mothers and drink their milk. Everyone is singing, everything rhymes. This can easily be seen as parody, whether intended or not, a trivialization of the romantic nostalgia O'Neill worked so hard to achieve. Although *Ah! Wilderness* was for O'Neill "the way I would have liked my childhood to have been," the film is nothing like the New London of O'Neill's childhood. Orlandello comments that in *Summer Holiday,* the "delicacy of tone, much of which is retained in the 1935 adaptation, is now replaced with the broadness and caricature quality of comic strips" (87).

Also undercutting the nostalgia of O'Neill's visions is Mamoulian's use of tableaux vivants from famous American paintings. For example, as we make a transition from the Miller home to Richard's high school graduation, we hear the singing of "dear old Danville High," look at the stern faces of elderly women in the audience, and then are given a re-creation of Grant Wood's painting *Daughters of the American Revolution.* Mamoulian follows this with Wood's *Woman with Plant,* his famous *American Gothic,* and finally Thomas Benton's *Reaper.* Obviously, it is anachronistic to be looking at famous paintings from 1930s America in a film set in 1906, but the ironic similarities between art and life seem to suggest that "large small-town" America is not what it seems. We see this again in the men's section of an elaborately staged triple picnic sequence that is not in the 1935 film. It starts with a close-up of a motionless trumpeter, then the camera pulls back to reveal a tableau vivant of A. M. Willard's *The Spirit of '76.* The drunken men at this picnic, however, are the antithesis of "the spirit of '76."

Founding fathers, such as Washington and even Abraham Lincoln, so inspirational to Frank Capra, are used in this film to suggest that Americans may have lost their original spirit. Toward the end of *Summer Holiday,* while having his heart-to-heart talk with his son after Richard's escapade with a prostitute, Nat Miller is so nervous that unconsciously he squishes a clay image of Abraham Lincoln on his son's desk. At the graduation, Richard is introduced as valedictorian by Mr. Peabody, the president of the local bank who boasts it has assets of "three and one-half millions of dollars." As he wishes the same successful future to Richard, we can see in the background a framed portrait of George Washington. The first part of Richard's graduation speech is unbearably corny, and his father cuts him off before he can give its main part, condemning the capitalist system. In O'Neill's play, we hear Richard's rhetoric at home, and Nat Miller affectionately chides him, "Son, if I didn't know it was you talking, I'd think we had Emma Goldman with us." Not in *Summer Holiday*. Instead, any socialist idealism that may have inspired Richard is abruptly dispersed when he gets the opportunity to drive a new Stanley Steamer: consumerism triumphs over Marxism and we have another lavish musical number, this time celebrating the joys of riding in an automobile.

One of the biggest musical numbers in the film is on the Fourth of July, a day used with great irony for the dark vision of *Force of Evil*. In *Summer Holiday* the celebration is so extreme, so over the top, with its American flags and roosters and firecrackers, that it causes a picture of George Washington hanging over the Millers' bed to tumble down, representing not only a logical cause and effect, but also a symbolic comment. The conclusion of *Force of Evil* also ironically comments on the heritage of America's founding father, as Joe finds his brother's body under the George Washington Bridge. *Force of Evil*, a film that confronted some of the dark realities of the American family, and *Summer Holiday*, a film that professed to escape from those realities, are thus strangely linked through their peculiar, if superficially dissimilar perspectives on the American dream.

※　※　※

The year was permeated with ambivalence: an exuberant enthusiasm for America, its heritage, and its future—the building of McDonald's golden arches—and a tremendous fear and anxiety about deracination and a loss of security, control, and spiritual "treasure." It was a year when Grant Matthews's unhappiness as a man, husband, and father and Muriel Blandings's optimism collided and produced a series of films that explored the family as an answer to their conflict, as a community, in various forms, that would allow its members, in the words of Dale Carnegie's bestseller, to "stop worrying and start living."

But as a number of prescient observers realized at the time, in many ways America as a nation had failed its people. It had won the war but lost on the home front, as returning veterans found that postwar dream and reality were not the same thing. An emphasis on consuming rather than producing, on economic rather than spiritual wealth, and the ever-present external threat of atomic annihilation, led people to turn inward, to their homes and families, not just for a sense of security in a perilous world but for an understanding of those ideals that shaped America and made it a land where dreams can come true. The key films of the year look back nostalgically at a past that existed, if it ever did, for the most part in the paintings of Norman Rockwell, and simultaneously gesture toward the future and the cold war with a combination of fear and trepidation. We knew what the past of America had been, or we thought we knew. But what would the future hold?

1949

Movies and the Fate of Genre

MARCIA LANDY

After winning election to a full term in November of 1948, President Truman began the new year by dubbing his domestic program the Fair Deal, an extension of the New Deal that promised expansion of social welfare legislation, civil rights, and "a bold new program for making the benefits of our scientific advances and industrial progress available for the improvement and growth of underdeveloped areas" (Goldman 93). Race was a timely topic, given Truman's executive order declaring "equality of treatment for all persons in the armed services" (Goldman 83).

The "war" on communism also intensified in the first trial of Alger Hiss, the formation of the Blacklist, and the institution of loyalty oaths. Among the international events that were to shape the future were the birth of the North Atlantic Treaty Organization, the creation of the two Germanys, and the advent of the People's Republic of China. Equally significant for the future was the appearance of two books—George Orwell's *Nineteen Eighty-four*, dramatizing the dangers of totalitarianism, and Simone De Beauvoir's *The Second Sex*, a harbinger of the feminist movement. In short, the year was a forecast of things to come involving economic, racial, gender, and international issues.

Hollywood Anticipates the Future

The year was also exemplary for attempts to reestablish continuity with social and cultural institutions after the effects of wartime. No site is perhaps more revealing of this struggle for continuity and against rupture, for containment and renovation, crisis and recuperation, than the Hollywood film industry. The beginning of the decade revealed the steadily declining hegemony of the studio system. Box office returns had hit their lowest point of the decade by 1947 and 1948 (see Schatz *Boom, Genius*). The fate of Hollywood appeared precarious thanks to competition from new forms of entertainment: television and drive-in theaters (itself owed to the increased ownership of automobiles). The waning fortunes of the studio system were further aggravated by governmental anti-trust legislation and its implementation, the loss of European film markets, and the influx into the United States of European films, especially Italian Neorealist films, such as Roberto Rossellini's *Open City* (1945), Vittorio De Sica's *Bicycle Thieves* (1948), and Rossellini's *Paisan* (1946). Hollywood had to contend with the disappearance of homogeneous audiences (Ray 138) and develop new strategies to restore its profits and prestige.

As a consequence, major studios took measures to stem the financial bloodletting through the radical cutting of production and personnel costs, the termination of star and producer contracts, and the farming out of productions to independent companies. These were often formed by underemployed directors and stars, for example Frank Capra's Liberty Films and Humphrey Bogart's Santana Productions. "Economic necessity," wrote John Russell Taylor, "pointed the way towards smaller films, depending on stronger ideas rather than high production values, and so provided an opportunity for younger writers and directors with things to say" (92). To a greater or lesser degree, the economic and cultural crisis produced signs of amelioration in the quality of films, and in rising box office returns. MGM saw a turnaround in profits rising from $4.2 million in 1948 to $6 million in 1949, and Universal reduced its losses from $3.1 million in 1948 to $1 million in 1949 (Schatz, *Boom* 353).

According to Schatz, "perhaps the single most remarkable aspect of the postwar American cinema was the overall quality and vitality of the movies themselves. Despite the declining market and mounting outside pressures, Hollywood's output in the late 1940s was by any standard, as strong as any period in industry history. The war and the war-related flood of new talent brought a spirit of innovation and even a certain progressivism to Hollywood" (*Boom* 353). The films of this year are a testimonial to this "overall quality and vitality." They are further evidence of a union of the old and the new, in relation to the production of genre films and in the connection of conventional narratives to innovative styles.

In treating the problematic issue of continuity and rupture in his study of American cinema of the 1940s, Dana Polan has argued for an understanding of these films that rethinks the oft-held notion of a radical break between the war years and the postwar era. In Polan's view, "the war period already represents certain challenges to a classic narrativity and its ties to specific representations of wartime power and ideology and . . . the postwar period continues many of the drives toward narrative classicism apparent in the wartime narrative of authority" (17). While there is no dramatic break with the narrativity of prewar films, there are more obvious signs of a further unraveling of the industry's power and authority in the treatment of genres and their styles.

A striking characteristic of the films produced this year was the eclectic quality of many of the genres, revealing the fluid boundaries between them, combined with a fusion of documentary and feature forms, on-location and studio shooting, professional and nonprofessional actors, and realism and fantasy. Diverse films such as George Cukor's comedy *Adam's Rib*, Joseph L. Mankiewicz's comedy-drama *A Letter to Three Wives*, George Marshall's comedy *My Friend Irma*, Stanley Donen and Gene Kelly's landmark musical *On the Town*, Max Ophüls's melodrama *Caught*, Raoul Walsh's gangster film *White Heat*, Robert Wise's taut fight film *The Set Up*, Robert Rossen's political exposé *All the King's Men*, and Cecil B. DeMille's spectacular biblical epic *Samson and Delilah* not only reveal indebtedness to other genres, but also display a high degree of self-consciousness about the status and effects of the cinematic medium, as well as a high degree of ambivalence, uncertainty, and ambiguity about romance, marriage, the family, politics, and social institutions.

A noteworthy intermingling of genres and styles occurred in the social problem film, in its blend of location and studio shooting with European and Hollywood filmmaking, resulting in a mix of "social consciousness with old-fashioned storytelling" (Ray 144). The year is also distinctive for its introduction of films that highlight the issue of race in the context of this kind of storytelling. An examination of films produced and released during the year challenges conventional assessments of the Hollywood cinema of the postwar years. The films are not a direct reflection of a society in transition. Whether intentionally or by osmosis, the films reveal instead a more oblique and indirect relation to the cultural, political, and industrial challenges confronted by Hollywood and, more broadly, by America in its negotiation of continuity and change.

■ The Musical

The musicals included such varied films as *On the Town*, Charles Walters's *The Barkleys of Broadway*, Henry Levin's *Jolson Sings Again*, Robert Z. Leonard's *In the Good Old Summertime*, and Busby Berkeley's *Take Me Out to the Ball Game*. These films exemplified what Rick Altman has described as a key element in the postwar musical form: reflexivity. In *The Barkleys of Broadway*, *Words and Music*, and *Jolson Sings Again*, reflexivity functions by "foregrounding and undercutting the conventions of show musical syntax, only in order to reaffirm them all the more convincingly (if in a slightly more limited and better defined fashion)" (Altman 252). *In the Good Old Summertime*'s self-referentiality resides largely in its being a musical remake of Ernst Lubitsch's *The Shop around the Corner* (1940), and in its reaffirmation of the folk musical's emphasis on community. *Take Me Out to the Ball Game* focuses on a typical American form of entertainment, and in so doing ultimately reaffirms traditional American cultural values. However, to identify the musical as merely instrumental in promoting national ideology is to misrepresent its form of address and its popularity. In fact, "The musical is always about Hollywood. . . . Constantly reminding the viewer that he/she is watching a film, the musical regularly transforms itself into an experimental discourse on the status of film viewing—and hearing" (Altman 7).

With the musical *On the Town*, the Freed Unit at MGM "came of age" (Schatz, *Boom* 449). The Unit's success can be attributed to its reliance on a group of artists, writers, dancers, technicians, and directors (including Gene Kelly, Stanley Donen, Betty Comden, and Adolph Green). Its style, its technical expertise, and its uses of narrative reveal the ways in which the film introduces, yet recasts, past forms of the musical and its ideological predilections. Starring Kelly (Gabey), Vera-Ellen (Ivy Smith), Frank Sinatra (Chip), Betty Garrett (Brunhilde Esterhazy, better known as Hildy), Jules Munshin (Ozzie), and Ann Miller (Claire Huddesen), *On the Town* was shot in New York City. While it is tempting to link location shooting to the tendency toward greater realism in the films of the postwar era, *On the Town*'s treatment of the city is not as clear-cut as it might seem to be.

New York, the "wonderful town," is not "a site of geographic certainty," but a "space for the representation of environment as a potentially or inherently ambivalent site" (Polan 234–35). While *On the Town*'s images of New York—the subway, Brooklyn Bridge, Wall Street, China Town, Rockefeller Center, and Grant's Tomb—invoke tourism as a sign of increasing mobility and cosmopolitanism in the postwar era, the camera and the editing transform these actual places into a zone of fantasy (Telotte, "Ideology" 38). Rick Altman indicates how "the camera counters the realism of location photography by freeing the camera from its spectator's eye view of the city. Throughout *On the Town* the camera dances, making New York obey its rhythm rather than vice versa" (281).

The camerawork in *On The Town* recalls such films as Dziga Vertov's *Man with a Movie Camera* (1929), Walter Ruttmann's *Berlin: Symphony of a Great City* (1927), and Jean Vigo's *À propos de Nice* (1930) in its emphasis on dynamism, movement, and especially in conveying what Kelly described as his desire "to capture on screen the frenetic energy of live performance"

(Parkinson 32). According to Richard Dyer, "this energy runs throughout the whole film, *including the narrative*. In most musicals, the narrative represents things as they are, to be escaped from. But most of the narrative of *On the Town* is about the transformation of New York into utopia" (Dyer 188, original emphasis).

The utopian elements are not to be confused with "traditional" portraits of literary utopias. They provide images through the medium of popular entertainment of "what utopia would feel like rather than how it would be organized" (Dyer 177). Through music, dance, and romance, the musical creates images of a world removed, but not too far removed, from daily existence that holds out hope of a different world in the future. *On the Town* is not silent about the war or about the trials of city life, but in its views of the city, its romantic coupling, and its musical numbers, the film creates imaginary bridges between past, present, and future and between everyday and ideal worlds. There is only one scene that takes place within a home, namely in Hildy's crowded apartment, but the space appears cramped and constraining in contrast to the expansiveness of and potential for movement in the external milieu of the city. Most of the action happens in public spaces—at the pier, the street, the subway, museums, the Empire State building, and Coney Island.

The number entitled "Prehistoric Man," set in the "Museum of Anthropological History," transforms a familiar and static location into a dynamic space. The episode features exhibits including a dinosaur, an African figure, and a statue of *Homo erectus*. The statue is created to look like Ozzie, and Claire, overwhelmed by the similarity, photographs Ozzie standing beside it. Very quickly Claire overcomes her "scientific curiosity" as she praises "Pithecanthropus's" freedom from repression, grabbing Ozzie and kissing him. Gabey, Chip, and Hildy join the pair in song and dance, seizing various artifacts, drums, and headdresses and dancing to the beat of tomtoms, until Ozzie upsets the dinosaur and it comes crashing down, thus disturbing their play. For a brief moment the objects had mutated to accommodate a utopian landscape, but then the characters are returned to the ordinary world of duty and responsibility.

The observation deck of the Empire State Building is another dominant setting for the couples. Through song and dance, they transform the vast and anonymous space into a theater, a place of energy, integration, play, and freedom from constraints. In the background the image of the New York skyline merges with the characters to create a utopian world. Gabey's fantasies about Ivy, after her disappearance from Club Sambacabana, are also enacted in this dream world. In keeping with the musical's predilection

"Countering realism." Gene Kelly (l.), Frank Sinatra (center), and Jules Munshin in *On the Town* (Stanley Donen and Gene Kelly, MGM). Collection Marcia Landy.

for reimagining actual places and refashioning commonplace objects, Gabey invokes her poster image as Miss Turnstiles that had earlier captured his imagination in the subway, and dances with it, turning loss into wish fulfillment. Thus, places and objects are "given a new meaning by their use within the number" (Sutton 193), highlighting the characters' immersion in the space of creativity.

With its three sailor protagonists, the film looks backward to the war and forward to assimilation into the postwar milieu. While in Hildy's words, "things have changed," the narrative "energy" reconciles continuity with even the most conspicuous changes. Gabey's discovery that he and Ivy are both from Meadowville, Indiana (the "backbone of American civilization"), as exemplified in their rustic dance number, evokes American pastoral mythology. At the same time, the New York metropolitan landscape in which they perform is also a reminder of the dislocations linked to the war and to increasing urbanity. New York functions as a character: as an obstacle that separates the protagonists, and as a means to unite them. Though the film ends with the promise of reunion, this "utopian" resolution is fraught with uncertainty. The film's narrative concludes with the men returning to their ship, thus invoking yet another separation similar to those so common to wartime films.

On the Town's narrative depends on the tenuousness and pressure of time—one day—in which the sailors seek to gratify their different desires for pleasure. Time poses constraints on the characters. The film is a consummate example of the seductive power of the musical, conveying its intertextuality in its many allusions to cinema (*The Lost Weekend*) and even to theater ("I'm just a streetcar named impulsive," says Lucy) and in its timely references to the Kinsey Report and to other forms of entertainment. *On the Town's* introduction of time, physical movement, and energy contaminates a "happy ending, exposing [the sense that] as no more than a representation, home is grounded in nothing that assures its permanence or its invulnerability" (Polan 254).

▰▰▰▰▰▰■ Comedy

The year also saw the appearance of a number of mainstream comedies, the most commercially successful being Charles Lamont's *Ma and Pa Kettle*, with Marjorie Main and Percy Kilbride in the title roles. The film was a spin-off from the 1947 comedy *The Egg and I*. *Ma and Pa Kettle* took in $2.5 million at the box office, and spawned a number of film and television situation comedies set in the rural landscape (Schatz, *Genius* 467). These films, ostensible celebrations of domesticity, were also crucial "not only to restabilizing the social and political structure, but also to promoting postwar consumer culture" (Schatz, *Boom* 373).

In contrast to comic films such as *Ma and Pa Kettle* and other exemplars of the "cult of domesticity," *Adam's Rib* is a romantic comedy that offers a darker and more complex portrait of femininity and marriage. The film reveals continuity with certain studio values in the choice of director, two stars, and expensive-looking production values. *Adam's Rib* is exemplary for its fusion of the old and new. The film's brittle artifice and its attempts to please all sides of the gender divide do not finally produce the utopian pleasures of *On the Town* or of other Hepburn/Tracy films. Instead, the film leaves the spectator suspended between past and present. Its theatricality situates it, like *On the Town,* in an indeterminate or ambivalent place, the space of entertainment, but without celebrating the power of theatricality to transform mundane reality.

Another critically acclaimed and commercially successful comedy with a satiric edge, *A Letter to Three Wives* was made at Twentieth Century Fox, a studio described by Schatz as having a "split personality" (Schatz, *Boom* 335). It produced on the one hand formulaic musicals starring Betty Grable and costume dramas starring Tyrone Power, and on the other, social problem and women's films. Despite dire predictions by Darryl F. Zanuck, the dictatorial chief of production at Fox, *A Letter to Three Wives* was ultimately both popular and critically esteemed. Capitalizing on the talents of newcomers, the film is a blend of romantic comedy, melodrama, woman's film, mystery thriller, and social problem film.

In sharp contrast to the sophisticated MGM studio look of *Adam's Rib* and Fox's glossy *A Letter to Three Wives,* Paramount, a studio noted for its pursuit of an "inexpensively made product with lesser-known but popular actors" (Dick, *Engulfed* 33), contributed to the year's comedies with the commercially successful *My Friend Irma.* Created by veteran producer Hal B. Wallis and the adept comedy director George Marshall, *My Friend Irma* is a show business musical with an emphasis on entertainment, courtship, romance, and transformations of the common or ordinary into the exceptional. Earlier in the 1940s, Paramount had produced the Bob Hope and Bing Crosby "road" films; now, they introduced another comedy duo, Dean Martin and Jerry Lewis, who went on together to create a series of hits lasting well into the 1950s.

My Friend Irma focuses on the struggles of singer Steve Laird (Martin) and his zany sidekick, Seymour (Lewis), to escape from their humdrum occupation at "Orange Delicious," a hole-in-the-wall juice stand where Steve works at the counter and Seymour squeezes the fruit. They are "discovered" by a down-and-out Damon Runyonesque character, Al (John Lund), who unashamedly exploits everyone. As the romantic interest, the film stars Marie Wilson as Irma Peterson, the increasingly popular incarnation of the "dumb blonde," and Diana Lynn as Jane Stacy, Irma's roommate. After several setbacks, Steve and Seymour escape from their dreary lives as citrus fruit "jerks" and find romance and success.

While the outline of this scenario seemingly situates *My Friend Irma* in the prewar film era by dramatizing upward mobility through success in show business, it also highlights differences in its treatment of comedy. The film is based on a popular radio show of the same name that later became a TV series. Eschewing established stars, and introducing new comic talents such as Martin and Lewis, the film relies for its effects on doubling and splitting—Steve and his alter ego, Seymour, Jane and her zany opposite, Irma. Lewis's portrayal of Seymour introduces the motif of the split personality that the team was to recreate in their subsequent films and on television. Lewis demonstrates his signature spastic gestures, his obsessive attachment to and competitiveness with Martin, and his hysterical responses to situations that are further exaggerated when placed alongside his partner's restrained and indifferent reactions.

Martin and Lewis are exemplary of the increasingly problematic character of masculinity in the postwar era. Lewis's onscreen persona, often described as "the sissy," is an amalgam of childishness, seemingly undifferentiated sexuality, and inchoate hysteria. Similarly, the figure of Irma the wacky blonde is Seymour's female counterpart. Also childlike, physically uncoordinated, unaware of her surroundings, and forgetful, Irma stands in stark contrast to earlier blonde heroines. If she is a screwball, her zaniness emblematizes a disordered mental state, which produces laughter by its flouting of any expectation of rational and motivated behavior. Several times in *My Friend Irma*, the issue of normality and abnormality (or "difference") is introduced, a further sign of the infiltration of psychology into popular culture, and of comedy's increased turn toward paranoia in the climate of the Cold War.

Melodrama

Melodrama continued to be a major Hollywood form, focusing on perturbations of the social and moral order: the trials and discontents of maternity, threatened and disintegrating familial relations, the abuses of patriarchal power, marriage fatigue, class misalliance, and physical and psychic illness. The style of these films depended on a heightened theatricality, visual and verbal excess, and an emphasis on the inadequacy of verbal language to express desire and suffering. *The Heiress,* for example, starring Olivia De Havilland, is based on the stage play of Henry James's story *Washington Square* and focuses on a life and death struggle between an upper-class father and daughter. In King Vidor's melodrama *Beyond the Forest,* a family melodrama, Bette Davis was cast as one of many frustrated, ambitious, if not mad, women of the postwar era. But while many of the themes of melodrama were evident in these films, there were signs of a different stylistic treatment that looked toward the future of the form in the coming decade.

Max Ophüls (in the United States, he signed himself Max Opuls), an esteemed European filmmaker, directed two such significant melodramas, *The Reckless Moment* and *Caught,* both films featuring tortured female protagonists. Christian Viviani describes *Caught* as a combination of the "woman's picture," film noir, and auteur filmmaking (Viviani 88). The film, made by an "independent" company of the 1940s, Enterprise Productions, was released by MGM.

Indeed, of all the films discussed thus far in this chapter, this was the most problematic upon initial release. Hostile critics and sparse audiences greeted its opening in New York (Turner 195). *Variety* described it as "an out-and-out soap opera on film" with "top notch performances" but having "a certain triteness about the original plot" ("*Caught*" 10). It is now considered to be a key work of the forties both for its stylistic innovation and because it is a primary example of the female gothic film genre, along with Alfred Hitchcock's *Rebecca* (1940), George Cukor's *Gaslight* (1944), and Joseph L. Mankiewicz's *Dragonwyck* (1946) (Doane, "*Caught*" 76). The movie is yet another showcase for the talents of actors new to Hollywood: Barbara Bel Geddes as Leonora Eames, Robert Ryan as Smith Ohlrig, British actor James Mason as Larry Quinada, and Viennese actor Curt Bois as Franzi.

Paranoia is the term that best describes the dark and sinister world of *Caught,* an affect that connects it to other films released in the same year, such as *The Set-Up* and *White Heat.* Both productions focus on the technology of vision, calling attention to film spectatorship, but *Caught* specifically explores how the woman is captured through the cinematic image and implicated in becoming what she sees. The camera, projector, and screen reduce her to an object of the male gaze, the position of a viewer, and not an agent of the narrative (Doane, "*Caught*" 76). The film is a critique not only of commercial uses of the cinematic image but of narratives that assign conventional positions to male and female characters. In its explorations of power, *Caught* focuses only on the troubled state of femininity but also on the problematic character of masculinity.

Leonora is a young woman imbued with the desire for money and marriage to the right man. This country-bred Cinderella achieves her dream, reinforced by images from women's magazines and fashion advertisements, and marries Smith Ohlrig, a superficially charming millionaire who turns out to be a psychotic tyrant. A disillusioned Leonora leaves Ohlrig's mansion and finds employment in the city with a dedicated pediatrician, Larry Quinada. Ohlrig, unable to bear his wife's rejection, seduces her once again, but Leonora discovers that nothing has changed and returns to her job. Quinada, unaware of Leonora's marital status, reveals his love and proposes. Discovering that she is pregnant, Leonora once again returns to her domestic prison, however, and the film climaxes with a confrontation between the two men, Leonora's aborted pregnancy, and possibly the death of the millionaire.

This description of the narrative does not begin to capture the film's manipulation of narrative conventions or audience expectations, however. The reflexive aspects of the film's cinematic structure, a hallmark of Ophüls's work, make evident *how* the female is caught within the narrative. The film's emphasis is shifted from her story to an exploration of visual images of commodities exemplified in fashion advertising and in the cinema, revealing of Leonora's position in the film as a spectator, yet as a "spectator who refuses to see" (Doane, *"Caught"* 78). Her romance with images of wealth and luxury is emblematized in the fur coat that she craves. Her graduation from "car hop" to model is not the conventional narrative of aspiring to success in the world of entertainment but a fantasy derived from media (fashion magazines and movies), namely, of capturing and marrying a "handsome young millionaire." The commodity serves as a sign of her immersion in the fantasy of becoming that which she desires, of living a life of wealth and luxury. However, her marriage to Ohlrig reveals the illusory and dangerous character of this desire.

The most striking scene depicting the dissolution of the visual display of wealth and power occurs as Leonora is forced to sit through Ohlrig's showing of an "industrial film" selling one of his products, a self-serving advertisement that Ohlrig describes hyperbolically as a masterpiece of cinematic art. Her unintentional laugh during the screening undermines his illusion of mastery by interrupting the "masterpiece" and calling attention both to herself and to the act of viewing. His rage is provoked. The filming of this night scene, characteristic of film noir with its dark and uncertain, even desperate, view of the world, relies mainly on a ray of light emanating from the projector behind Ohlrig. Leonora's hapless position as viewer is underscored as Ohlrig castigates her for being inattentive to the film—"Perhaps if you watch the picture you would not be bored"—admonishing her that she "is no longer in a movie theater." When the lights go on, she announces that she is leaving him. Ohlrig, alone, his face twisted in anger, reaches for pills, staggers to a chair, then tosses a ball onto his pool table, the first indication that a psychiatrist's diagnosis had been correct: although "there is nothing wrong with your heart," according to the doctor, Ohlrig persists in showing symptoms that say, "I'm not all powerful. I'm weak. Take pity." By contrast to Leonora's immersion in fantasies of romantic love, Ohlrig manifests his own immersion in fantasies of power that ultimately reveal his feelings of impotence.

More than a conventional equation of cinema and advertising, this scene conveys how relations between husband and wife are deeply implicated in who controls the power to name, define, and hence determine "reality" in relation to cinematic spectatorship. However, morally upright Dr. Quinada is not a stark contrast to Ohlrig. He presents another version of masculinity, one attuned to expectations of correct social behavior and one that belongs to another cinematic context attuned to social realism. If for Ohlrig Leonora is another commodity that can be appropriated, displayed, and destroyed according to his whim, Quinada's relationship to Leonora is based on an authority consonant with his conceptions of moral responsibility. Nonetheless, for him, too, she is just an image, but one that he seeks to remake. Leonora submits to his critical interrogation of her behavior and frivolous appearance. In response to his criticism of her clothing, hairstyle, and treatment of patients, she sheds her furs and jewels, changes her hairdo, and adopts a proper posture to suit the situation. The film's depiction of the elusive and unstable character of femininity is starkly dramatized by visually identifying her (in her absence) with an empty desk: the camera circles it and moves between the two doctors Hoffman and Quinada, who argue her character and fate. Here the film conveys a parallel between Quinada and Ohlrig in their common attachment to reigning representations of femininity. Yet now Leonora is not a hapless victim but complicit in the drama of appearances. All the characters are "caught" in the drama of visibility and invisibility.

The familiar melodrama of marital conflict is transformed into an investigation of the commodification and power of the visual image in general and of the importance of soliciting the attention of the female spectator in particular. Although *Rebecca* and *Adam's Rib* contain home movies that tellingly comment on the instabilities in, and conflicts of, the couples' relationships, *Caught* dramatizes here a naked contest for power that overwhelms and eludes narrative resolution. It undermines predictable and transparent conceptions of storytelling in favor of examining the viewer's relation to cinema. Rather than glamorizing and celebrating the world of entertainment, Ophüls's film dares to explore cinema's dangerous hold on the spectator.

▪ The Boxing Film

In the panoply of genre features released this year, the boxing film plays an important role. Mark Robson's *Champion*, starring Kirk Douglas, turned many of the conventions of the fight film on their heads, presenting Douglas as Michael "Midge" Kelly, a ruthless competitor who will stop at nothing to get to the top of the racket. A popular genre from the silent era, the fight film is a narrative that has addressed aspirations of wealth, the struggle of immigrants to assimilate, conceptions of masculinity, and conflicts between "body and soul," success and morality. A far less well known and less publicized film than *Champion*, *The Set-Up*, starring Robert Ryan, exemplifies many of the eclectic characteristics of late 1940s cinematic practice, combining characteristics of the gangster film, film noir, and the social problem film. Once again, the actors are not established stars, although Ryan's career was on the rise.

Stoker Thompson (Robert Ryan) is an aging boxer who refuses to retire. Stoker's dilemma is a pretext for *The Set-Up*'s exploration of the underside of American popular culture, of "losers" rather than winners, and of corruption in sport. Audrey Totter plays the role of Thompson's wife, Julie, who tries to convince him to abandon the brutal world of boxing and settle for an ordinary (and respectable) occupation as the owner of a small business. The mainly male characters in the film are fighters, young men and old, African Americans and Latinos, driven either by their desire for success or by gangsters who exploit the fighters until they die. Stoker is a proud man, with only one aim in the fight game: he refuses to be beaten. During a fixed fight, he refuses to "lie down" and throw the match. He is rewarded for winning by being so brutally beaten that he will never be able to fight again.

The fixed fight takes place in an arena ironically called "Paradise City," which is situated in the middle of rough streets, tenements, cafes, and run-down hotels inhabited by unemployed workers, gamblers, gangsters, and marginal figures like Stoker. The jazz soundtrack echoes the contemporary isolation of the characters. While the film centers on the sport of boxing and its connections to gangsterism, its style is different than that of earlier crime films. The lighting, closer to that of film noir, is critical to the film, and the treatment of character more enigmatic. The scenes take place at night, often on dark, lonely, and slick streets, and the actors are filmed in shadow. In the framing there is an emphasis on intersecting diagonal and vertical lines, and the overarching tone of the film is one of claustrophobia and hopelessness. The characters move through space in dreamlike or somnambulistic states.

As in film noir, dominant images involve windows that frame the characters, clocks that are a reminder of the pressures of time and its irreversibility, and mirror shots that reveal the divisions in and internal conflicts among the characters, especially Julie and Stoker. *The Set-Up* also highlights spectatorship, in the extensive close-up shots of the crowd as they display fascination, disgust, and a lust for blood during the fight sequence. In particular, the women are singled out by Wise's camera, as they gesticulate and scream for more violent action ("Let's have some action!" and "Let him have it, baby!"), in contrast to Julie, who refuses to attend the fight, afraid of seeing the brutality. Not only does *The Set-Up* relentlessly visualize the exploitation and cruelty endemic to boxing, but the reflexivity of the fight scenes suggests that more is involved in the film than viewing prizefighting; namely, the character of popular "entertainment" as an incitement to violence and power.

Politicians and Gangsters

Aside from anti-communist films such as R. G. Springsteen's *The Red Menace*, which focused on international political intrigue, few movies addressed contemporary American politics in ways reminiscent of Frank Capra's earlier populist dramas of political corruption. *All the King's Men*, however, was a film that explored the American political system and the drama of demagoguery in a different manner. Directed and produced by Robert Rossen for Columbia, the film was shot on location in Louisiana. The character of Willie Stark (Broderick Crawford) is based on the notorious Louisiana politician Huey P. Long. Stark's rise to power, narrated by newspaperman Jack Burden (John Ireland), is more than a melodramatic exposé of a crazed and evil figure. Stark begins his career as a rebel against entrenched privilege, retreats from the political stage, and studies law with the support of his idealistic schoolteacher wife, Lucy (Anne Seymour). After a local tragedy, Stark returns to the public arena but cannot fight the politicians. With the coaching of Burden and Sadie Burke (Mercedes McCambridge), however, he learns to "make 'em cry, laugh, mad at you." In his next (and successful) bid for elected office, aided by alcohol, he throws away his speech and becomes theatrical, sentimental, and anecdotal. If the crowd is aroused and Stark reaps the political rewards of playing on the emotions of his audience ("I'm on my own. I'm out for blood")—if, in short, he now succeeds with the political machine—he simultaneously becomes increasingly autocratic, threatening, and bullying, buying off opponents and having them murdered until he is himself betrayed, exposed, and finally assassinated.

All the King's Men eschews binary distinctions between villains and saviors. Like many other films of the year, it draws attention to the union of media and politics, especially through the role of newspapers and newsreels in the creation of Willie Stark. The film narrative, far from restricting its focus to the corrupting role of wealth and privilege, implicates the masses (and the film's viewers) as voyeuristic and impressionable spectators upon the drama of political corruption.

White Heat, also dramatizing the seedy side of social relations, capitalizes on James Cagney's most famous gangster films, such as William Wellman's *Public Enemy* (1931), but then takes everything one step further. After almost two years out of work, Cagney signed a contract with Warner Bros. to work on three films, of which *White Heat* was the first. According to Robert Sklar, the film "was not exactly a conventional gangster picture" (*City* 253), which is putting it mildly. In keeping with the times, the genre had now to contend with the psychological and stylistic complexities of film noir, an increased psychologizing of character, Cagney's aging image, and new conceptions of criminality and law enforcement (Sklar, *City* 254–55). *White Heat* combines elements of different genres—the gangster film, prison drama, and melodrama—in the context of incest and with a highlighted concern for media and technology in telling the story of Cody Jarrett (Cagney), a psychotic gangster with a pronounced Oedipal fixation. *White Heat*'s spectacular treatment of violence foreshadows the urban dramas of the next decades. Moving swiftly from first frame to last, *White Heat* begins with a violent train robbery gone wrong, and ends with a cataclysmic explosion and Cody's death.

Central to the development of Cagney's character is his incestuous relationship to his mother (Margaret Wycherly). She is his nurturer, his comrade, and, ironically, his undoing. Ambitious for him and overprotective, she tells him, "I don't know what I'd do without you." His symptoms of dependency and dysfunctionality are expressed in his habitual loss of motor capacity, which experience he describes as "having a red buzz saw in my head." Cody's relationship to "Ma" has been characterized as gender reversal (Fischer, *Cinematernity* 96), since he exhibits symptoms of feminine hysteria and dependency while Ma exhibits behavior identified with masculinity.

Popular psychology plays a critical role in the film, as one of Cody's gang, Big Ed Somers (Steve Cochran), calls him "crazy," and the FBI agent who goes undercover to catch him, Hank Fallon (Edmond O'Brien), alludes to "insanity in the family" and to Cody's "psychopathic devotion" to his mother. This image of Cody and Ma is excessive and prompts the question

Virginia Mayo (l.), Margaret Wycherly, and James Cagney in *White Heat* (Raoul Walsh, Warner Bros.). Collection Marcia Landy.

of whether the screenplay (by Ivan Goff and Ben Roberts) has a serious investment in such a portrait, or whether it has a different design on the viewer. While popular literature and government documentaries of the postwar era had their version of "healthy mothering," the narrative does not seem to be primarily interested in a sociological or psychoanalytic treatment of Cody's relationship to his mother. Rather, *White Heat* intersects with scientific discourses of crime detection (Clark, "*White Heat*"). Cody is a relic from an earlier era, a primitive force that requires control in scientific terms. The police's mobilization of the arsenal of technology to capture Jarrett involves "a new technique of radio directed pursuit (elaborately explained in the film) that can follow the criminals and help them foil the crime" (Sklar, *City* 255).

Dana Polan, commenting on the role of science and technology in the plot, writes, "Just as the wartime narrative suggested a certain need for a society of scrutiny that would carefully examine and work to control all aberration, so the narratives of crime investigation come to suggest that crime is a force that must be met through a cold, calculating rationalism"

(165). Cody's relation to Ma is not so much a nod to the "science" of psychoanalysis as a means, through hyperbole and excess, to escalate the irrational dimensions of his antisocial behavior and its equally violent "treatment." The film highlights instead the growing role of the FBI as undercover specialists, infiltrators, and informers, perhaps a link to the atmosphere of containment generated by World War II and the Cold War.

While anti-communist films such as George Sidney's *The Red Danube* did not do well at the box office or with critics (Higham and Greenberg 75), *White Heat*, invoking parallel scenarios without invoking communists, was highly successful with audiences. The ending of the film deploys a dramatic explosion of energy, with Cody shouting, "On top of the world, Ma!" just moments before an explosion in a petroleum refinery blows him to bits, fusing the excessiveness of his relationship to Ma with the end of the world. Although *White Heat* makes no pretense of overtly politicizing its motifs and visual displays, it is saturated with allusions to World War II, the war against maniacal power-hungry "dictators," and the elevation and legitimization of technology (for example, the technology of the bomb) to destroy enemies of order, if not civilization. In Tom Conley's words, the film, in an apocalyptic explosion, "burns the history of genres," announcing "the tidal force of a new wave" (Conley 138, 145).

The Social Problem Film and Issues of Race

Like other genres in transition, the social problem film was not a new genre either. The designation "social problem" characterizes films that feature poverty and crime, juvenile "delinquency," alcoholism, drug abuse, the effects of familial neglect or abuse, and, to a lesser degree, racism. The films give prominence to the social and economic causes of the "problems," involving the pivotal role of lawyers, social workers, physicians, or psychiatrists in the determination, analysis, and outcome of the conflicts. The year saw the release of Maxwell Shane's *City Across the River* and Nicholas Ray's *Knock on Any Door*, both of which focused on the plight of the juvenile offender. *Knock on Any Door* stars Humphrey Bogart as Andrew Morton, an attorney who rises out of the squalid and oppressive environment that dooms young "Pretty Boy" Nick Romano (John Derek). In real life, Bogart's career was at a crossroads. He had left Warner Bros., phased out along with Errol Flynn, Edward G. Robinson, and Bette Davis. To revive his screen image and find roles that he respected, Bogart joined with producer Mark Hellinger to form his own independent production company, Santana Productions. *Knock on Any Door* was their first property.

Bogart had earlier declared his support for the "unfriendly witnesses" identified by the House Un-American Activities Committee (HUAC). Now, with *Knock on Any Door,* he was tackling the contentious subject of juvenile crime.

Knock on Any Door opens with the shooting of a policeman and the escape of a gunman on a darkened street. Romano is accused of the crime, but insists on his innocence. He convinces Morton to take the case and, while at first reluctant, Morton finally acquiesces. The film becomes a narrative of investigation, as the attorney tracks down witnesses for the defense. Through flashbacks, the film investigates Romano's history, his unfortunate family life, his father's death, his initiation into the life of the streets, his time in the reformatory, his marriage, his attempts to establish a normal life, and finally his return to crime. District Attorney Kerman's (George Macready) relentless examination and badgering of Nick finally breaks through the young man's tough exterior and produces the confession, "I killed him! I hate cops!" Shocked, Morton is left to plead for the boy's life: "If Romano is guilty, so are we." *Knock on Any Door* is another instance of the increased emphasis in American postwar culture and its cinematic texts on the instability of social relations. Thus, while the film might seem to be a continuation of earlier cinema, it provides signs of a shift in the old Hollywood formulas—an increasing uncertainty, if not anxiety, about narrative trustworthiness.

In the critical literature on the films of the year, the trend toward social realism is associated with films featuring racial issues, especially those that were successful critically and/or commercially—Mark Robson's *Home of the Brave,* Alfred L. Werker's *Lost Boundaries,* Elia Kazan's *Pinky,* and Clarence Brown's *Intruder in the Dust.* What is particularly striking about these films is how they negotiated genre production, since they too manifest the eclecticism characteristic of nearly all the films discussed in this chapter. While war films, according to critics and producers, were not of particular interest to audiences, several of the popular films of the year were indeed war films—but with a difference (Schatz, *Boom* 308). For example, William Wellman's *Battleground* was considered one of the best pictures of the year, as was Allan Dwan's *The Sands of Iwo Jima;* both films were praised for their critical treatment of war and their supposed realism.

Home of the Brave, produced by Stanley Kramer, was distinguished by its treatment of racism in the armed services. In situating a "postwar good sensitive Negro" (Bogle 145) at the center of the narrative, *Home of the Brave* appears to counteract prewar cinematic treatments of race. At the same time, the film reduces the question of race to a diagnosable medical problem that can be "treated" in the interests of conformity, eradicating complexity and difference. What seems apparent is that black characters generally have become cinematic objects of surveillance, if not of discipline. It dramatizes the dilemma of race passing, with Patricia "Pinky" Johnson (Jeanne Crain) returning to her home in the South after having been educated to be a nurse in the North. She is surprised to find that she has to confront the racism of both the white and black community. Escaping from a love affair with a white man in the North, who does not know her family background, Pinky tries to adapt to life with her Aunt Dicey (Waters) only to be harassed, arrested, and almost raped by whites, and rejected by her fellow African Americans. "I'm a Negro. I can't forget it. I can't be anything else," Pinky finally states, embracing her own culture and rejecting the notion of race passing. "You can't live without pride." Thus, while the film returns Pinky to her "kind," it also anticipates the issue of black pride.

But perhaps the most complex treatment of race during this year was *Intruder in the Dust*, based on William Faulkner's novel. A less commercially successful film than *Pinky*, it was more ambitious in many respects (Crowther, "Intruder" 19). *Intruder in the Dust* stars actor Juano Fernandez in the role of Lucas Beauchamp, an image of the "maddening Negro" (Kael, *Kiss* 284) in contrast to that of the "good Negro," and the film is "different in directorial style to the bulk of [Clarence] Brown's star-ridden productions" (Kael, *Kiss* 265). The success of *Intruder in the Dust* lies in its amalgamation of realism through the use of location shooting (it was shot in Oxford, Mississippi, and used the local townspeople as extras [Degenfelder 138]) with fictive narratives involving rites of initiation, crime detection, and social realism. Most significant, this film presents the "black man as an actual protagonist in white society" (Lead 164).

Intruder in the Dust focuses on the wrongful arrest of a black man (Fernandez) for the murder of a white man, and its effect on a young boy, Chick Mallison (Claude Jarman Jr.), and the community. For Chick, Lucas is an enigma, a proud black man who refuses to behave in subservient fashion. The young boy's initiation into adulthood involves his rejecting conceptions of blackness that he has acquired from his family and from the townspeople. But it is Lucas who ultimately demonstrates that resolution of social injustice resides with the community itself. Through the combined efforts of Chick, Lucas's lawyer John Galvin Stevens (David Brian), and Miss Habersham (Elizabeth Patterson), the "mystery" of the dead white man is unraveled. Lucas escapes lynching and is acquitted of the murder charge against him.

A description of narrative events—Lucas's arrest, his imprisonment, the discovery of the real culprit, and his acquittal—does an injustice to the

film's philosophic and stylistic investigation of race. Lucas's character is presented in distant and enigmatic terms, undermining a conventional psychological approach to account for his arrogance and aloofness. The
presentation of the other characters and the community eschews a sociological analysis, and the film deromanticizes small-town life and rosily nostalgic portraits of the South. The crowd scenes emphasize distinctions
between insiders and outsiders, highlighting the threatening character of
the mob (reminiscent of another lynch mob, in Fritz Lang's 1936 film *Fury*).
Since the issue of racism involves "color," the film incriminates members of
the community in seeking to "erase" the sight of blackness. But *Intruder in
the Dust* insists on the visibility of Lucas's body, and ties seeing to touch,
through repeated images of hands. Lucas's unjust arrest without evidence
underscores the fact that his "crime" is not murder but polluting the community with his presence, and making that presence visible and tangible.
Repeatedly, *Intruder in the Dust* focuses on the characters' perceptions of
Lucas and his perceptions of others, posing the question of the disjunctive
and problematic relation between seeing, knowing, and acting. The film,
like *Knock on Any Door*, is a key instance of the increased attention to political connections between race and the politics of vision.

Back to Basics

        While forces both outside and inside the movie industry sub-
dued Hollywood's progressive impulse after the late burst of race dramas and
social problem films, perhaps the most significant development in the year's
conservative swing was the release of a biblical spectacle that earned over $5
million and became "the biggest box office hit of the decade." Cecil B.
DeMille's *Samson and Delilah* "was not only a throwback to an earlier era but
an augur of things to come" (Schatz, *Boom* 393), and easily dispels the view
that the most successful films of the year were as socially conscious as *Intruder
in the Dust* or *All the King's Men* or *The Set-Up*. While the genre of the biblical
costume drama was hardly new to Hollywood and certainly not to DeMille,
this end-of-the-decade extravaganza, according to Bosley Crowther, "out
Babels anything he's done. There are more flowing garments in this picture
(the most sensational being Lamarr's peacock gown), more chariots, more
temples (the most dramatic being the destruction of Dagon's temple), more
peacocks, more plumes, more animals, more pillows, more beards, and
more sex than before" ("*Samson*" 29).

        Audiences were clearly not clamoring for more realism. By contrast,
what needed reinforcing was the ongoing fascination with Hollywood

Surpassing spectacle: stars, sex, and Cecil B. DeMille. Hedy Lamarr in *Samson and Delilah* (Cecil B. DeMille, Paramount). Collection Marcia Landy.

spectacle as entertainment, adding more by way of sexual innuendo, popular psychology, and erotic images of the body to meet changing perceptions about cultural and social life (Harcourt-Smith 410). The end of the decade casts a backward look at Hollywood's golden age in a style geared toward contemporary audiences, and gazes forward to the 1950s and 1960s with their spate of biblical super-spectacles.

■ ■ ■

The range of films discussed in this chapter does not reveal an industry in ruins, nor does it, by the same token, reveal a radical quest for innovation. The idea of conservatism with profit seemed to be a guiding motive of most film production. While a number of the films draw on genres and motifs identified with the heyday of Hollywood cinema in the studio years, they are infected to a greater or lesser degree by the changing cultural and political environment in the industry and in the nation. The films' eclecticism appears to be a strategy to woo audiences. These films do not merely recycle old forms, but they alter them to address changing cultural conditions, and in the process shed light on the tensions and anxieties, if not hysteria and paranoia, of post–World War II America. The self-conscious emphasis on entertainment and theatricality reveals an ambivalence and uncertainty about the postwar world. The portraits of marriage, family, the urban and rural milieux, race, technological change, and the status of entertainment are sufficiently diplomatic and restrained in style to avoid censure, but the films are not mute about their plundering of the past to accommodate to the present. The films of 1949 are portents, in the final analysis, of commercial filmmaking practices in the coming decades that will continue to wed the old and the new.

1940 – 1949

Select Academy Awards

1940

Best Picture: *Rebecca*, Selznick, United Artists

Best Actor: James Stewart in *The Philadelphia Story*, MGM

Best Actress: Ginger Rogers in *Kitty Foyle*, RKO Radio

Supporting Actor: Walter Brennan in *The Westerner*, Goldwyn, United Artists

Supporting Actress: Jane Darwell in *The Grapes of Wrath*, Twentieth Century Fox

Direction: John Ford, *The Grapes of Wrath*

Writing (original story): Benjamin Glazer, John S. Toldy, *Arise, My Love*, Paramount

Writing (original screenplay): Preston Sturges, *The Great McGinty*, Paramount

Writing (best written screenplay): Donald Ogden Stewart, *The Philadelphia Story*

Cinematography (black-and-white): George Barnes, *Rebecca*

Cinematography (color): Georges Périnal, *The Thief of Bagdad*, Korda, United Artists

Music (best score): Alfred Newman, *Tin Pan Alley*, Twentieth Century Fox

Music (original score): Leigh Harline, Paul J. Smith, Ned Washington, *Pinocchio*; Disney, RKO Radio

Music (song): Ned Washington (lyrics), Leigh Harline (music), "When You Wish upon a Star," from *Pinocchio*

1941

Best Picture: *How Green Was My Valley*, Twentieth Century Fox

Best Actor: Gary Cooper in *Sergeant York*, Warner Bros.

Best Actress: Joan Fontaine in *Suspicion*, RKO Radio

Supporting Actor: Donald Crisp in *How Green Was My Valley*

Supporting Actress: Mary Astor in *The Great Lie*, Warner Bros.

Direction: John Ford, *How Green Was My Valley*

Writing (original story): Harry Segall, *Here Comes Mr. Jordan*, Columbia

Writing (original screenplay): Herman J. Mankiewicz, Orson Welles, *Citizen Kane*, Mercury, RKO Radio

Writing (best written screenplay): Sidney Buchman, Seton I. Miller, *Here Comes Mr. Jordan*

Cinematography (black-and-white): Arthur Miller, *How Green Was My Valley*

Cinematography (color): Ernest Palmer, Ray Rennahan, *Blood and Sand,* Twentieth Century Fox

Music (scoring dramatic picture): Bernard Herrmann, *All That Money Can Buy,* RKO Radio

Music (scoring musical picture): Frank Churchill, Oliver Wallace, *Dumbo,* Disney, RKO Radio

Music (song): Oscar Hammerstein II (lyrics), Jerome Kern (music), "The Last Time I Saw Paris" from *Lady Be Good,* MGM

■ 1942

Best Picture: *Mrs. Miniver,* MGM

Best Actor: James Cagney in *Yankee Doodle Dandy,* Warner Bros.

Best Actress: Greer Garson in *Mrs. Miniver*

Supporting Actor: Van Heflin in *Johnny Eager,* MGM

Supporting Actress: Teresa Wright in *Mrs. Miniver*

Direction: William Wyler, *Mrs. Miniver*

Writing (original story): Emeric Pressburger, *The Invaders* (a k a *The 49th Parallel*), Ortus, Columbia

Writing (original screenplay): Ring Lardner Jr., Michael Kanin, *Woman of the Year,* MGM

Writing (best written screenplay): Arthur Wimperis, George Froeschel, James Hilton, Claudine West, *Mrs. Miniver*

Cinematography (black-and-white): Joseph Ruttenberg, *Mrs. Miniver*

Cinematography (color): Leon Shamroy, *The Black Swan,* Twentieth Century Fox

Music (scoring dramatic or comedy picture): Max Steiner, *Now Voyager,* Warner Bros.

Music (scoring musical picture): Ray Heindorf, Heinz Roemheld, *Yankee Doodle Dandy*

Music (song): Irving Berlin (lyrics and music), "White Christmas" from *Holiday Inn,* Paramount

■ 1943

Best Picture: *Casablanca,* Warner Bros.

Best Actor: Paul Lukas in *Watch on the Rhine,* Warner Bros.

Best Actress: Jennifer Jones in *The Song of Bernadette,* Twentieth Century Fox

Supporting Actor: Charles Coburn in *The More the Merrier,* Columbia

Supporting Actress: Katina Paxinou in *For Whom the Bell Tolls*, Paramount

Direction: Michael Curtiz, *Casablanca*

Writing (original story): William Saroyan, *The Human Comedy*, MGM

Writing (original screenplay): Norman Krasna, *Princess O'Rourke*, Warner Bros.

Writing (best written screenplay): Julius J. Epstein, Philip G. Epstein, Howard Koch, *Casablanca*

Cinematography (black-and-white): Arthur Miller, *The Song of Bernadette*

Cinematography (color): Hal Mohr, W. Howard Greene, *The Phantom of the Opera*, Universal

Music (scoring dramatic or comedy picture): Alfred Newman, *The Song of Bernadette*

Music (scoring musical picture): Ray Heindorf, *This Is the Army*, Warner Bros.

Music (song): Mack Gordon (lyrics), Harry Warren (music), "You'll Never Know" from *Hello, Frisco, Hello*, Twentieth Century Fox

▓▓▓▬ 1944

Best Picture: *Going My Way*, Paramount

Best Actor: Bing Crosby in *Going My Way*

Best Actress: Ingrid Bergman in *Gaslight*, MGM

Supporting Actor: Barry Fitzgerald in *Going My Way*

Supporting Actress: Ethel Barrymore in *None But the Lonely Heart*, RKO Radio

Direction: Leo McCarey, *Going My Way*

Writing (original story): Leo McCarey, *Going My Way*

Writing (original screenplay): Lamar Trotti, *Wilson*, Twentieth Century Fox

Writing (best written screenplay): Frank Butler, Frank Cavett, *Going My Way*

Cinematography (black-and-white): Joseph La Shelle, *Laura*, Twentieth Century Fox

Cinematography (color): Leon Shamroy, *Wilson*

Music (scoring dramatic or comedy picture): Max Steiner, *Since You Went Away*, Selznick, United Artists

Music (scoring musical picture): Morris Stoloff, Carmen Dragon, *Cover Girl*, Columbia

Music (song): Johnny Burke (lyrics), James Van Heusen (music), "Swinging on a Star" from *Going My Way*

▓▓▓▬ 1945

Best Picture: *The Lost Weekend*, Paramount

Best Actor: Ray Milland in *The Lost Weekend*

Best Actress: Joan Crawford in *Mildred Pierce,* Warner Bros.

Supporting Actor: James Dunn in *A Tree Grows in Brooklyn,* Twentieth Century Fox

Supporting Actress: Anne Revere in *National Velvet,* MGM

Direction: Billy Wilder, *The Lost Weekend*

Writing (original story): Charles G. Booth, *The House on 92nd Street,* Twentieth Century Fox

Writing (original screenplay): Richard Schweizer, *Marie-Louise,* Praesens Films

Writing (best written screenplay): Charles Brackett, Billy Wilder, *The Lost Weekend*

Cinematography (black-and-white): Harry Stradling, *The Picture of Dorian Gray,* MGM

Cinematography (color): Leon Shamroy, *Leave Her to Heaven,* Twentieth Century Fox

Music (scoring dramatic or comedy picture): Miklos Rozsa, *Spellbound,* Selznick, United Artists

Music (scoring musical picture): Georgie Stoll, *Anchors Aweigh,* MGM

Music (song): Oscar Hammerstein II (lyrics), Richard Rodgers (music), "It Might As Well Be Spring" from *State Fair,* Twentieth Century Fox

■ 1946

Best Picture: *The Best Years of Our Lives,* Goldwyn, RKO Radio

Best Actor: Fredric March in *The Best Years of Our Lives*

Best Actress: Olivia de Havilland in *To Each His Own,* Paramount

Supporting Actor: Harold Russell in *The Best Years of Our Lives*

Supporting Actress: Anne Baxter in *The Razor's Edge,* Twentieth Century Fox

Direction: William Wyler, *The Best Years of Our Lives*

Writing (original story): Clemence Dane, *Vacation from Marriage,* London Films, MGM

Writing (original screenplay): Muriel Box, Sydney Box, *The Seventh Veil,* J. Arthur Rank, Sydney Box, Ortus, Universal

Writing (best written screenplay): Robert E. Sherwood, *The Best Years of Our Lives*

Cinematography (black-and-white): Arthur Miller, *Anna and the King of Siam,* Twentieth Century Fox

Cinematography (color): Charles Rosher, Leonard Smith, Arthur Arling, *The Yearling,* MGM

Music (scoring dramatic or comedy picture): Hugo Friedhofer, *The Best Years of Our Lives*

Music (scoring musical picture): Morris Stoloff, *The Jolson Story*

Music (song): Johnny Mercer (lyrics), Harry Warren (music), "On The Atchison, Topeka and Santa Fe" from *The Harvey Girls*, MGM

1947

Best Picture: *Gentleman's Agreement*, Twentieth Century Fox

Best Actor: Ronald Colman in *A Double Life*, Kanin Productions, Universal-International

Best Actress: Loretta Young in *The Farmer's Daughter*, RKO Radio

Supporting Actor: Edmund Gwenn in *Miracle on 34th Street*, Twentieth Century Fox

Supporting Actress: Celeste Holm in *Gentleman's Agreement*

Direction: Elia Kazan, *Gentleman's Agreement*

Writing (original story): Valentine Davies, *Miracle on 34th Street*

Writing (original screenplay): Sidney Sheldon, *The Bachelor and the Bobby-Soxer*, RKO Radio

Writing (best written screenplay): George Seaton, *Miracle on 34th Street*

Cinematography (black-and-white): Guy Green, *Great Expectations*, J. Arthur Rank, Universal-International

Cinematography (color): Jack Cardiff, *Black Narcissus*, J. Arthur Rank, Universal-International

Music (scoring dramatic or comedy picture): Miklos Rozsa, *A Double Life*

Music (scoring musical picture): Alfred Newman, *Mother Wore Tights*, Twentieth Century Fox

Music (song): Ray Gilbert (lyrics), Allie Wrubel (music), "Zip-A-Dee-Doo-Dah" from *Song of the South*, Disney, RKO Radio

1948

Best Picture: *Hamlet*, J. Arthur Rank, Two Cities, Universal-International

Best Actor: Laurence Olivier in *Hamlet*

Best Actress: Jane Wyman in *Johnny Belinda*, Warner Bros.

Supporting Actor: Walter Huston in *The Treasure of the Sierra Madre*, Warner Bros.

Supporting Actress: Claire Trevor in *Key Largo*, Warner Bros.

Direction: John Huston, *The Treasure of the Sierra Madre*

Writing (motion picture story): Richard Schweizer, David Wechsler, *The Search*, Praesens Film, MGM

Writing (best written screenplay): John Huston, *The Treasure of the Sierra Madre*

Cinematography (black-and-white): William Daniels, *The Naked City*, Mark Hellinger Productions, Universal-International

Cinematography (color): Joseph Valentine, William V. Skall, Winton Hoch, *Joan of Arc*, Sierra Pictures, RKO Radio

Music (scoring dramatic or comedy picture): Brian Easdale, *The Red Shoes*

Music (scoring musical picture): Johnny Green, Roger Edens, *Easter Parade*, MGM

Music (song): Jay Livingston, Ray Evans (lyrics and music), "Buttons and Bows" from *The Paleface*, Paramount

■■■■■■■ **1949**

Best Picture: *All the King's Men*, A Robert Rossen Production, Columbia

Best Actor: Broderick Crawford in *All the King's Men*

Best Actress: Olivia de Havilland in *The Heiress*, Paramount

Supporting Actor: Dean Jagger in *Twelve O'Clock High*, Twentieth Century Fox

Supporting Actress: Mercedes McCambridge in *All the King's Men*

Direction: Joseph L. Mankiewicz, *A Letter to Three Wives*, Twentieth Century Fox

Writing (motion picture story): Douglas Morrow, *The Stratton Story*, MGM

Writing (best written screenplay): Joseph L. Mankiewicz, *A Letter to Three Wives*

Writing (story and screenplay): Robert Pirosh, *Battleground*, MGM

Cinematography (black-and-white): Paul C. Vogel, *Battleground*

Cinematography (color): Winton Hoch, *She Wore a Yellow Ribbon*, Argosy Pictures Corporation, RKO Radio

Music (scoring dramatic or comedy picture): Aaron Copland, *The Heiress*

Music (scoring musical picture): Roger Edens, Lennie Hayton, *On the Town*, MGM

Music (song): Frank Loesser (lyrics and music), "Baby, It's Cold Outside" from *Neptune's Daughter*, MGM

WORKS CITED
AND CONSULTED

Ackerman, Robert J. *Perfect Daughters: Adult Daughters of Alcoholics.* Deerfield Beach, Fla.: Health Communications, Inc., 1989.

Altman, Rick. *The American Film Musical.* Bloomington: Indiana UP, 1989.

The American Film Institute. "Citizen Kane." *The American Film Institute Catalog of Motion Pictures Produced in the United States: Feature Films, 1941–1950.* Ed. Patricia King Hanson. Berkeley: U of California P, 1999. 431–35.

Anderson, Benedict. *Imagined Communities: Reflections on the Origin and Spread of Nationalism.* New York: Verso, 1991.

Balio, Tino. *The American Film Industry.* Madison: U of Wisconsin P, 1976.

Barbour, Alan G. *The Thrill of It All.* New York: Collier Books, 1971.

Barson, Michael, and Steven Heller. *Red Scared: The Commie Menace in Propaganda and Popular Culture.* San Francisco: Chronicle Books, 2001.

Basinger, Jeanine. *A Woman's View: How Hollywood Spoke to Women, 1930–1960.* New York: Knopf, 1993.

———. *The World War II Combat Film: Anatomy of a Genre.* New York: Columbia UP, 1986.

Beevor, Antony. *Berlin: The Downfall 1945.* London: Viking, 2002.

Behlmer, Rudy, ed. *Inside Warner Brothers 1935–1951.* New York: Viking, 1985.

———. *Memo from David O. Selznick.* New York: Viking, 1972.

Bernstein, Matthew. *Walter Wanger, Hollywood Independent.* Minneapolis: U of Minnesota P, 2000.

Birdwell, Michael E. *Celluloid Soldiers: The Warner Bros. Campaign Against Nazism.* New York: New York UP, 1999.

Bogdanovich, Peter. *Who the Devil Made It.* New York: Knopf, 1997.

Bogle, Donald. *Toms, Coons, Mulattoes, Mammies, and Bucks: An Interpretive History of Blacks in American Film.* New York: Continuum, 2001.

Bookbinder, Robert. *The Films of Bing Crosby.* Secaucus, N.J.: Citadel, 1977.

Bordwell, David, and Kristen Thompson. *Film Art.* 4th ed. New York: McGraw-Hill, 2000.

"Boy Meets Facts." *Time* 21 July 1941: 73–74.

Brick, Howard. *Daniel Bell and the Decline of Intellectual Radicalism: Social Theory and Political Reconciliation in the 1940s.* Madison: U of Wisconsin P, 1986.

Brill, Lesley. *John Huston's Filmmaking.* Edinburgh: Cambridge UP, 1997.

Britton, Andrew. "Notes on *Pursued.*" *The Book of Westerns.* Ed. Ian Cameron and Douglas Pye. New York: Continuum, 1996. 196–207.

Brooks, Richard. *The Brick Foxhole.* New York: Sun Dial, 1946.

Brown, Gene. *Movie Time: A Chronology of Hollywood and the Movie Industry from Its Beginnings to the Present.* New York: Hungry Minds, 1995.

Brownlow, Kevin, and Michael Kloft, dirs. *The Tramp and the Dictator.* Photoplay Productions, TCM. BBC and Spiegel TV, 2002.

Bruck, Connie. *When Hollywood Had a King.* New York: Random House, 2003.

Buhle, Paul, and Dave Wagner. *A Very Dangerous Citizen: Abraham Lincoln Polonsky and the Hollywood Left.* Berkeley: U of California P, 2001.

Burgoyne, Robert. *Film Nation: Hollywood Looks at U.S. History*. Minneapolis: U of Minnesota P, 1997.

Burrows, Terry, ed. *A Visual History of the Twentieth Century*. London: Carlton, 1999.

Cameron, Ian, and Elisabeth Cameron. *Dames*. New York: Praeger, 1969.

——. *Heavies*. New York: Praeger, 1967.

Campbell, Russell. "Tramping Out the Vintage: Sour Grapes." *The Modern American Novel and the Movies*. Ed. Gerald Peary and Roger Shatzkin. New York: Frederick Ungar, 1978. 107–18.

Capra, Frank. *The Name above the Title: An Autobiography*. New York: Macmillan, 1971.

Carney, Raymond. *American Vision*. Cambridge: Cambridge UP, 1986.

Carringer, Robert L. *The Making of Citizen Kane*. Berkeley: U of California P, 1985.

"*Caught*." *Variety* 23 Feb. 1949: 10.

Cavell, Stanley. *Pursuits of Happiness: The Hollywood Comedy of Remarriage*. Cambridge: Harvard UP, 1981.

Churchill, Winston, and Randolph S. Churchill. *Blood, Sweat, and Tears*. New York: G. P. Putnam's Sons, 1941.

"*Citizen Kane*." *Time* 31 March 1941: 68.

Clark, Danae. *Negotiating Hollywood: The Cultural Politics of Actors' Labor*. Minneapolis: U of Minnesota P, 1995.

Clark, Thomas. "*White Heat*: The Old and the New." *Wide Angle* 1.1 (Spring 1979): 60–66.

Cobo, James. "The Magnificent Ambersons." <http://www.metalasylum.com/ragingbull/movies/ambersons.html>.

Conley, Tom. "Apocalypse Yesterday." *Enclitic* 5.2 (Winter/Spring 1981–82): 137–46.

Cook, David. *A History of Narrative Film*. 3rd ed. New York: Norton, 1981.

Cook, Pam. "Approaching the Work of Dorothy Arzner." *Feminism and Film Theory*. Ed. Constance Penley. New York: Routledge, 1981. 46–56.

"Coop." *Time* 3 March 1941: 78–82.

Corber, Robert J. *In the Name of National Security: Hitchcock, Homophobia, and the Political Construction of Gender in Postwar America*. Durham: Duke UP, 1993.

Costello, John. *Virtue under Fire: How World War II Changed Our Social and Sexual Attitudes*. Boston: Little, Brown, 1985.

Cross, Robin. *The Big Book of B Movies, or, How Low Was My Budget*. New York: St. Martin's, 1981.

Crowther, Bosley. "Afterthoughts on *Madame Curie* and Two Other Current Films." *New York Times* 9 Jan. 1944: Sec. 2, 3.

——. "All for the Best." *New York Times* 2 Jan. 1944: 3X.

——. "*Destination Tokyo*, a Highly Eventful Submarine Drama, With Cary Grant and John Garfield, Opens at the Strand." *New York Times* 1 Jan. 1944: 9.

——. "*Intruder in the Dust*: MGM's Drama of Lynching in the South." *New York Times* 23 Nov. 1949: 10.

——. "Rev. of *The Lady Eve*." *New York Times* 26 Feb. 1941: 17.

——. "Rev. of *Meet John Doe*." *New York Times* 13 March 1941: 25.

——. "On Soldiers in Films." *New York Times* 21 Nov. 1943: X3.

——. "*Samson and Delilah* Has Its Premiere at Two Theatres, Rivoli and Paramount." *New York Times* 22 Dec. 1949: 29.

Custen, George. *Twentieth Century's Fox: Darryl Zanuck and the Culture of Hollywood*. New York: Basic Books, 1997.

Daniell, Tina. "Philip Dunne: Fine Cabinetmaker." *Backstory: Interviews with Screenwriters of Hollywood's Golden Age*. Ed. Patrick McGilligan. Berkeley: U of California P, 1986. 151–69.

Davenport, Russell W. "The Pursuit of Happiness." *Life* 12 July 1948: 97–113.

Debord, Guy. *The Society of the Spectacle*. New York: Zone Books, 1994.

Degenfelder, E. Pauline. "The Film Adaptation of Faulkner's *Intruder in the Dust*." *Literature Film Quarterly* 1.2 (April 1973): 138–48.

Denzin, Norman K. *Hollywood Shot by Shot: Alcoholism in America Cinema*. New York: Aldine de Gruyter, 1991.

Dick, Bernard F. *Engulfed: The Death of Paramount Pictures and the Birth of Corporate Hollywood*. Lexington: UP of Kentucky, 2001.

———. *Joseph L. Mankiewicz*. Boston: Twayne, 1983.

———. *The Star-Spangled Screen: The American World War II Film*. Lexington: UP of Kentucky, 1985.

Dickson, Paul. *From Elvis to E-Mail: Trends, Events, and Trivia from the Postwar Era to the End of the Century*. Springfield, Mass.: Federal Street Press, 1999.

Dixon, Wheeler Winston. *Visions of the Apocalypse: Spectacles of Destruction in American Cinema*. London: Wallflower Press, 2003.

Doane, Mary Ann. "*Caught* and *Rebecca*: The Inscription of Femininity as Absence." *Enclitic* 5.2 (Winter/Spring 1981–82): 75–89.

———. *The Desire to Desire: The Woman's Film of the 1940s*. Bloomington: Indiana UP, 1987.

Doherty, Thomas P. *Projections of War: Hollywood, American Culture, and World War II*. New York: Columbia UP, 1993.

Durgnat, Raymond. *Jean Renoir*. Berkeley: U of California P, 1974.

Durgnat, Raymond, and Scott Simmon. *King Vidor—American*. Berkeley: U of California P, 1988.

Dyer, Richard. "Entertainment and Utopia." *Genre: The Musical*. Ed. Rick Altman. London: Routledge & Kegan Paul, 1981. 175–90.

Ebert, Roger. "The Great Movies: Yankee Doodle Dandy." *Chicago Sun-Times Online*. <http://www.suntimes.com/ebert/greatmovies/yankee_doodle.html>. 18 Dec. 2003.

Edwards, Anne. *Katharine Hepburn*. New York: St. Martin's, 2000.

Eliot, Marc. *Walt Disney: Hollywood's Dark Prince*. New York: Birch Lane, 1993.

Epstein, Dan. *20th Century Pop Culture*. London: Carlton, 1999.

Evans, Jessica. *Representing the Nation*. London: Routledge, 1996.

Feuer, Jane. *The Hollywood Musical*. 2nd ed. Bloomington: Indiana UP, 1993.

Fischer, Lucy. *Cinematernity: Film, Motherhood, Genre*. Princeton: Princeton UP, 1996.

———. *Shot/Countershot: Film Traditions and Women's Cinema*. Princeton: Princeton UP, 1989.

Fox, Ken, and Maitland McDonagh, eds. *The Virgin Film Guide*. 9th ed. London: Virgin, 2000.

French, Philip. *Westerns: Aspects of a Movie Genre*. New York: Oxford UP, 1977.

Friedrich, Otto. *City of Nets: A Portrait of Hollywood in the 1940s*. New York: Harper & Row, 1980.

Gabler, Neal. *An Empire of Their Own: How the Jews Invented Hollywood*. New York: Anchor Books, 1988.

Gallagher, Tag. *John Ford: The Man and His Films*. Berkeley: U of California P, 1986.

Gelb, Barbara, and Arthur Gelb. *O'Neill*. New York: Harper, 1960.

Goldman, Eric F. *The Crucial Decade—and After: 1945–1960*. New York: Vintage Books, 1956.

Goulden, Joseph C. *The Best Years: 1945–1950*. New York: Atheneum, 1976.

Graebner, William. *The Age of Doubt: American Thought and Culture in the 1940s.* Boston: Twayne, 1991.

Gresham, William Lindsay. "*Nightmare Alley.*" *Crime Novels: American Noir of the 1930s and 40s.* Ed. Robert Polito. New York: Viking, 1997. 517–796.

Griffith, Richard, and Arthur Mayer. *The Movies.* New York: Bonanza Books, 1957.

Griswold, Robert L. *Fatherhood in America: A History.* New York: Basic Books, 1993.

Gussow, Mel. *Don't Say Yes Until I Finish Talking: A Biography of Darryl F. Zanuck.* Garden City, N.Y.: Doubleday, 1971.

Harcourt-Smith, Simon. "'The Siegfried of Sex': Thoughts Inspired by Cecil B. De Mille's *Samson and Delilah.*" *Sight and Sound* 19.10 (Feb. 1951): 412, 424.

Hartmann, Susan M. *The Home Front and Beyond: American Women in the 1940s.* Boston: Twayne, 1982.

Harvey, James. *Romantic Comedy in Hollywood from Lubitsch to Sturges.* New York: Knopf, 1987.

Hawks, Howard. *Hawks on Hawks.* Ed. Joseph McBride. Berkeley: U of California P, 1982.

Henderson, Brian, ed. *Five Screenplays by Preston Sturges.* Berkeley: U of California P, 1986.

Herman, Jan. *A Talent for Trouble: The Life of Hollywood's Most Acclaimed Director, William Wyler.* New York: G. P. Putnam's Sons, 1995.

Higham, Charles. *Cecil B. De Mille.* New York: Charles Scribner's Sons, 1973.

———. *The Films of Orson Welles.* Berkeley: U of California P, 1970.

Higham, Charles, and Joel Greenberg. *Hollywood in the Forties.* London: Zwemmer, 1968.

Hirschhorn, Clive. *The Universal Story: The Complete History of the Studio and Its 2,641 Films.* New York: Crown, 1983.

Holmes, Richard. *World War II in Photographs.* London: Carlton, 2000.

Horne, Gerald. *Class Struggle in Hollywood 1930–1950.* Austin: U of Texas P, 2001.

Houseman, John. "Lost Fortnight: A Memoir." *The Blue Dahlia: A Screenplay by Raymond Chandler.* Ed. Matthew R. Bruccoli. New York: Popular Library, 1976. 7–23.

Hurst, Richard Maurice. *Republic Studios: Between Poverty Row and the Majors.* Metuchen, N.J.: Scarecrow, 1979.

Izod, John. *Hollywood and the Box Office, 1895–1986.* New York: Columbia UP, 1988.

Jackson, Charles. *The Lost Weekend.* New York: Farrar and Rinehart, 1944.

Jacobs, Lea. *The Wages of Sin: Censorship and the Fallen Woman Film, 1928–1942.* Berkeley: U of California P, 1997.

Jeffries, John W. *Wartime America: The World War II Home Front.* Chicago: Ivan R. Dee, 1996.

Johnston, Claire. "Dorothy Arzner: Critical Strategies." *Feminism and Film Theory.* Ed. Constance Penley. New York: Routledge, 1988. 36–45.

Kael, Pauline. *Kiss Kiss Bang Bang.* Boston: Little, Brown, 1968.

———. "Raising Kane." *The Citizen Kane Book.* New York: Limelight, 1984. 1–86.

Katz, Ephraim. *The Film Encyclopedia.* 4th ed. New York: HarperResource. 2001.

Kearns, Audrey, ed. *Motion Picture Production Encyclopedia 1948.* Hollywood: Hollywood Reporter, 1948.

Keyssar, Helene, and Vladimir Pozner. *Remembering War: A U.S.-Soviet Dialogue.* New York: Oxford UP, 1990.

Koppes, Clayton R. "Hollywood and the Politics of Representation: Women, Workers, and African Americans in World War II Movies." *The Homefront War: World War II and American Society.* Ed. Kenneth Paul O'Brien and Lynn Hudson Parsons. Westport, Conn.: Greenwood, 1995. 25–40.

———. "Regulating the Screen: The Office of War Information and the Production Code Administration." *Boom and Bust: American Cinema in the 1940s.* Ed. Thomas Schatz. History of the American Cinema 6. Berkeley: U of California P, 1997. 262–81.

Koppes, Clayton R., and Gregory D. Black. *Hollywood Goes to War, How Politics, Profits and Propaganda Shaped World War II Movies.* Berkeley: U of California P, 1987.

———. "What to Show the World: The Office of War Information and Hollywood, 1942–1945." *Hollywood's America: United States History Through Its Films.* Ed. Steven Mintz and Randy Roberts. St. James, N.Y.: Brandywine , 1993. 157–68.

Kozloff, Sarah. *Invisible Storytellers: Voice-Over Narration in American Fiction Film.* Berkeley: U of California P, 1998.

———. *Overhearing Film Dialogue.* Berkeley: U of California P, 2000.

Kozlovic, Anton Karl. "The Whore of Babylon: Suggestibility and the Art of Sexless Sex in Cecil B. De Mille's *Samson and Delilah." Sex, Religion, Media.* Ed. Dane S. Claussen. New York: Rowman & Littlefield, 2002. 21–33.

Lambert, Gavin. *On Cukor.* New York: G. P. Putnam's and Sons, 1971.

Lead, Daniel J. *From Sambo to Superspade: The Black Experience in Motion Pictures.* Boston: Houghton Mifflin, 1975.

Leaming, Barbara. *Orson Welles: A Biography.* New York: Viking, 1985.

Leeman, Sergio. *Robert Wise on His Films.* Los Angeles: Silman-James, 1995.

Leff, Leonard J., and Jerold L. Simmons. "Film into Story: The Narrative Scheme of *Crossfire." Literature/Film Quarterly* 12.3 (Fall 1984): 171–79.

Levy, Emanuel. *George Cukor, Master of Elegance: Hollywood's Legendary Director and His Stars.* New York: Morrow, 1994.

Lewis, Mark, with Leonard Matthews and Ken Sephton. *The Movie Book: The 1940s.* New York: Crescent, 1988.

Lucas, Blake. *"Shadow of a Doubt." Film Noir: An Encyclopedic Reference to the American Style.* Ed. Alain Silver and Elizabeth Ward. Woodstock, N.Y.: Overlook, 1992.

Lyons, Arthur. *Death on the Cheap: The Lost B Movies of Film Noir.* New York: Da Capo, 2000.

Maddox, Robert James. *The United States and World War II.* Boulder: Westview, 1992.

Maland, Charles J. *Chaplin and American Culture.* Princeton: Princeton UP, 1989.

Marill, Alvin H. *Katharine Hepburn.* New York: Pyramid, 1973.

Martin, Len D. *The Columbia Checklist: The Feature Films, Serials, Cartoons and Short Subjects of Columbia Pictures Corporation, 1922–1988.* Jefferson, N.C.: McFarland, 1991.

———. *The Republic Pictures Checklist: Features, Serials, Cartoons, Short Subjects and Training Films of Republic Pictures Corporation, 1931–1999.* Jefferson, N.C.: McFarland, 1998.

Matthews, Leonard. *History of Western Movies.* New York: Crescent, 1984.

May, Elaine Tyler. *Homeward Bound: American Families in the Cold War Era.* New York: Basic, 1988.

May, Lary. *The Big Tomorrow: Hollywood and the Politics of the American Way.* Chicago: U of Chicago P, 2000.

Mayne, Judith. *Directed by Dorothy Arzner.* Bloomington: Indiana UP, 1994.

McBride, Joseph. *Frank Capra: The Catastrophe of Success.* New York: Simon & Schuster, 1992.

———. *Hawks on Hawks.* Berkeley: U of California P, 1982.

———. *Searching for John Ford: A Life.* New York: St. Martin's, 2001.

McClelland, Doug. *The Golden Age of B Movies.* New York: Bonanza, 1981.

McGilligan, Pat. *Backstory: Interviews with Screenwriters of Hollywood's Golden Age.* Berkeley: U of California P, 1986.

"*Meet John Doe.*" *Time* 3 March 1941: 78.

Meyerowitz, Joanne, ed. *Not June Cleaver: Women and Gender in Postwar America, 1945–1960.* Philadelphia: Temple UP, 1994.

Mintz, Steven, and Susan Kellogg. *Domestic Revolutions: A Social History of American Family Life.* New York: Macmillan, 1988.

Modleski, Tania. *The Women Who Knew Too Much: Hitchcock and Feminist Theory.* New York: Methuen, 1988.

Moldea, Dan. *Dark Victory: Ronald Reagan, MCA, and the Mob.* New York: Viking, 1986.

Mosher, John. "*Meet John Doe.*" *New Yorker* 22 March 1941: 80–81.

Mosley, Leonard. *Zanuck: The Rise and Fall of Hollywood's Last Tycoon.* Boston: Little, Brown, 1984.

Muller, Eddie. *Dark City: The Lost World of Film Noir.* New York: St. Martin's Griffin, 1998.

———. *Dark City Dames: The Wicked Women of Film Noir.* New York: HarperCollins, 2001.

Neibaur, James L. *The RKO Features: A Complete Filmography of the Feature Films Released or Produced by RKO Radio Pictures, 1929–1960.* Jefferson, N.C.: McFarland, 1994.

Neve, Brian. *Film and Politics in America: A Social Tradition.* New York: Routledge, 1992.

"The New Pictures." *Time* 10 Oct. 1949: 96–102.

O'Brien, Geoffrey. *The Phantom Empire.* New York: Norton, 1993.

Offner, Arnold A. *Another Such Victory: President Truman and the Cold War, 1945–1953.* Stanford: Stanford UP, 2002.

Ohmer, Susan. "Female Spectatorship and Women's Magazines: Hollywood, *Good Housekeeping* , and World War II" *The Velvet Light Trap* 25 (Spring 1990): 53–68.

O'Neill, William L. *A Democracy at War: America's Fight at Home and Abroad in World War II.* New York: Free Press, 1993.

Orlandello, John. *O'Neill on Film.* Rutherford, N.J.: Fairleigh Dickinson UP, 1982.

Parkinson, David. "Dancing in the Streets." *Sight and Sound* 1.1 (Jan. 1993): 31–33.

Patton, Cindy. "White Fascism/Black Signs: Censorship and Images of Race." *Journal of Communication* 45.2 (Spring 1995): 65–77.

Pizzitola, Louis. *Hearst over Hollywood: Power, Passion, and Propaganda in the Movies.* New York: Columbia UP, 2002.

Place, Janey A. *The Non-Western Films of John Ford.* Secaucus, N.J.: Citadel, 1979.

Plunkett, Robert. "Classic War Films, Contemporary Echoes." *New York Times* 21 March, 1993: H13.

Polan, Dana. *Power and Paranoia: History, Narrative, and the American Cinema, 1940–1950.* New York: Columbia UP. 1986.

Pomerance, Murray. "Yankee Doodle Dandy." *1001 Movies You Must See Before You Die.* Ed. Steven Jay Schneider. New York: Barrons, 2004. 190.

"The Production Code." *Movies and Mass Culture.* Ed. John Belton. New Brunswick, N.J.: Rutgers UP, 1996. 135–49.

Pryor, Jerome. "*Duel in the Sun*: A Classical Symphony." *New Orleans Review* 17.4 (Winter 1990): 8–19.

Pryor, Thomas M. "By Way of Report: War Pictures Popular With Soldiers in Camps Here— Some Items from London." *New York Times* 16 Jan. 1944: X4.

———. "News and Comment on Various Film Matters." *New York Times* 2 May 1943: X4.

Putnam, Robert D. *Bowling Alone: The Collapse and Revival of American Community.* New York: Simon & Schuster, 2000.

Quart, Leonard, and Albert Auster. *American Film and Society Since 1945*. Westport, Conn.: Praeger, 2002.

Rabinowitz, Paula. *Black & White & Noir: America's Pulp Modernism*. New York: Columbia UP, 2002.

Ray, Robert B. *A Certain Tendency of the Hollywood Cinema, 1930–1980*. Princeton: Princeton UP, 1985.

Robertson, Patrick. *Film Facts*. New York: Watson-Guptill, 2001.

Roosevelt, Franklin Delano. "Message to Congress: January 6, 1941." *My Friends: Twenty-Eight History-Making Speeches*. Ed. Edward H. Kavinoky and Julian Park. Buffalo: Foster and Stewart, 1945. 76–83.

Rosenbaum, Jonathan. "*The Palm Beach Story*." *Chicago Reader Online* <http://spacefinder. chicagoreader.com/movies/capsules/06869_PALM_BEACH_STORY.html>. 19 Dec. 2003.

Rosten, Leo C. "The Movie Colony." *Movies in Our Midst: Documents in the Cultural History of Film in America*. Ed. Gerald Mast. Chicago: U of Chicago P, 1982. 403–19.

Sarris, Andrew. *The John Ford Movie Mystery*. Bloomington: Indiana UP, 1975.

Schatz, Thomas. *Boom and Bust: The American Cinema in the 1940s*. New York: Charles Scribner's Sons, 1997.

———. *The Genius of the System: Hollywood Filmmaking in the Studio Era*. New York: Pantheon, 1988.

Schickel, Richard. *The Men Who Made the Movies*. New York: Atheneum, 1975.

Schrader, Paul. "Notes on *Film Noir*." *Film Noir Reader*. Ed. Alain Silver and James Ursini. New York: Limelight, 1996. 53–64.

Schultheiss, John, ed. *Body and Soul: The Critical Edition*. Northridge: Center for Telecommunication Studies, California State University, 2002.

Sennett, Ted. *Hollywood Musicals*. New York: Harry N. Abrams, 1987.

"*Sergeant York*." *Time* 4 Aug. 1941: 71.

Shale, Richard. *The Academy Awards Index*. Westport, Conn.: Greenwood, 1993.

Shapiro, Charles. "*Nightmare Alley*: Geeks, Cons, Tips, and Marks." *Tough Guy Writers of the Thirties*. Ed. David Madden. Carbondale: Southern Illinois UP, 1968. 218–24.

Shohat, Ella, and Robert Stam. "The Imperial Imaginary." *The Film Cultures Reader*. Ed. Graeme Turner. London: Routledge, 2002. 366–78.

Shumway, David R. "Disciplinary Identities: Or, Why Is Walter Neff Telling This Story?" *Symploke* 7.1–2 (1999): 97–107.

Siegel, Joel E. *Val Lewton: The Reality of Terror*. New York: Viking, 1973.

Sikov, Ed. *Laughing Hysterically: American Screen Comedy in the 1950s*. New York: Columbia UP, 1994.

Silver, Alain, and Elizabeth Ward, eds. *Film Noir: An Encyclopedic Reference to the American Style*. Rev. and expanded ed. Woodstock, N.Y.: Overlook, 1988.

Sklar, Robert. *City Boys: Cagney, Bogart, Garfield*. Princeton: Princeton UP, 1992.

———. *Film: An International History of the Medium*. 2nd ed. New York: Prentice-Hall, 2002.

———. *Movie-Made America. A Cultural History of American Movies*. New York: Vintage, 1994.

Smith, Betty. *A Tree Grows in Brooklyn*. New York: Harper & Row, 1943.

Spicer, Andrew. *Film Noir*. Harlow, Eng.: Pearson, 2002.

Spoto, Donald. *The Dark Side of Genius: The Life of Alfred Hitchcock*. Boston: Little, Brown, 1983.

Stanley, Fred. "Don't Show It—The Enemy Is Looking." *New York Times* 14 Nov. 1943: X5.

———. "Hollywood Bulletins." *New York Times* 1 Aug. 1943: X3.

Stowell, Peter. *John Ford.* Boston: Twayne, 1986.

Sutton, Marin. "Patterns of Meaning in the Musical." *Genre: The Musical: A Reader.* Ed. Rick Altman. London: Routledge & Kegan Paul, 1981. 190–97.

Tasch, Ruth. "The Role of the Father in the Family." *Journal of Experimental Education* 20 (June 1952): 339–46.

Taylor, John Russell. *Hollywood 1940s.* New York: Gallery, 1985.

Telotte, J. P. "Ideology and the Kelly-Donen Musicals." *Film Criticism* 8.3 (Spring 1984): 36–46.

———. "Seeing in a *Dark Passage.*" *Film Criticism* 9.2 (Winter/Spring 1985): 15–28.

Thomas, Bob. *King Cohn: The Life and Times of Harry Cohn.* New York: Bantam, 1968.

Thomas, Tony. *The Films of the 1940s.* New York: Citadel, 1990.

Thompson, Peggy, and Saeko Usukawa. *Hard Boiled: Great Lines from Classic Noir Films.* San Francisco: Chronicle, 1996.

Thompson, Rick. "Andre de Toth, Luke Short, *Ramrod*: Style, Source, Genre." *Senses of Cinema Online.* <http://www.sensesofcinema.com>. 23 Oct. 2003.

Turner, George. "*Caught*: A Lost Classic." *American Cinematographer* (May 1998): 100–06.

U.S. Government Printing Office. *16th Census of the United States: 1940 Population, Volume III. The Labor Force.* 1943. 75–83.

Vaughn, Robert. *Only Victims: A Study of Show Business Blacklisting.* New York: G. P. Putnam's Sons, 1972.

Viviani, Christian. "*Caught*: Sans Objet: Max Ophuls en Amérique." *Positif* Sept. 2001: 88–89.

Wager, Jans B. *Dangerous Dames: Women and Representation in Weimar Street Film and Film Noir.* Athens: Ohio UP, 1999.

"War and Peace." *Time* 6 Jan. 1941: 12–13.

Ware, Susan. *Holding Their Own: American Women in the 1930s.* Boston: Twayne, 1982.

Warshow, Robert. *The Immediate Experience.* New York: Atheneum, 1971.

Weis, Elisabeth. *The National Society of Film Critics on the Movie Star.* New York: Viking, 1981.

Weiss, Nathan Norman. "Spiders in His Mind." *Hollywood Quarterly* 3.2 (Winter–Spring 1947–48): 189–91.

Wilder, Billy, and Charles Brackett. *The Lost Weekend.* Berkeley: U of California P, 2000.

Williams, Linda. "Feminist Film Theory: *Mildred Pierce* and the Second World War." *Female Spectators: Looking at Film and Television.* Ed. Diedra Pribram. New York: Verso, 1988. 12–30.

Willis, Donald C. *The Films of Frank Capra.* Metuchen, N.J.: Scarecrow, 1974.

Wills, Nadine. "'110 Per Cent Woman': The Crotch Shot in the Hollywood Musical." *Screen* 42.2 (Summer 2001): 121–41.

Witney, William. *In a Door, into a Fight, out a Door, into a Chase: Moviemaking Remembered by the Guy at the Door.* Jefferson, N.C.: McFarland, 1996.

Wolfe, Charles. "*Meet John Doe*: Authors, Audiences, and Endings." *Meet John Doe: Frank Capra, Director.* Rutgers Films in Print. 13. New Brunswick, N.J.: Rutgers UP, 1989. 3–29.

Wood, Robin. "*Duel in the Sun*: The Destruction of an Ideological System." *The Book of Westerns.* Ed. Ian Cameron and Douglas Pye. New York: Continuum, 1996. 189–95.

———. *Hitchcock's Films Revisited.* New York: Columbia UP, 1989.

———. "The Lady Eve." *International Dictionary of Films and Filmmakers 1: Films.* Ed. Nicholas Thomas and James Vinson. 2nd ed. Chicago: St. James, 1990. 487–88.

"A Yank in the RAF." *Newsweek* 6 Oct. 1941: 59–60.

Zagarrio, Vito. 1998. "It Is (Not) a Wonderful Life: For a Counter-reading of Frank Capra." *Frank Capra: Authorship and the Studio System*. Ed. Robert Sklar and Vita Zagarrio. Philadelphia: Temple UP. 64–94.

CONTRIBUTORS

MATTHEW BERNSTEIN teaches film studies at Emory University, specializing in the history of American film. He has written, edited, or co-edited several books, including *Walter Wanger, Hollywood Independent* (1994; 2000), *Controlling Hollywood: Censorship and Regulation in the Studio Era* (1999), *Visions of the East: Orientalism in Film* (1997), and *John Ford Made Westerns: Filming the Legend in the Sound Era* (2000). His essays have appeared in *Cinema Journal, Film Criticism, Film History, Film Quarterly, Griffithiana, Post Script, The Velvet Light Trap,* and *Wide Angle.*

WHEELER WINSTON DIXON is the James Ryan Endowed Professor of Film Studies and a professor of English at the University of Nebraska, Lincoln, and, with Gwendolyn Audrey Foster, editor-in-chief of the *Quarterly Review of Film and Video.* His newest books as author or editor include *Lost in the Fifties: Recovering Phantom Hollywood* (2005), *Film and Television after 9/11* (2004), *Visions of the Apocalypse: Spectacles of Destruction in American Cinema* (2003), *Straight: Constructions of Heterosexuality in the Cinema* (2003), and *Experimental Cinema: The Film Reader* (2002), co-edited with Gwendolyn Audrey Foster. In April 2003, he was honored with a retrospective of his films at the Museum of Modern Art in New York, and his films were acquired for the permanent collection of the museum, in both print and original format.

KRISTINE BUTLER KARLSON is an associate professor of French at the University of Wisconsin–River Falls. Her publications include a chapter on the work of Chantal Akerman in *Identity and Memory: The Films of Chantal Akerman* (2002), and "Irma Vep, Vamp in the City: Mapping the Criminal Feminine in Early French Serials" in *A Feminist Reader in Early Cinema* (2002).

SARAH KOZLOFF is a professor of film in the Department of Drama and Film at Vassar College. Her major publications include *Invisible Storytellers: Voice-Over Narration in American Fiction Film* (1988) and *Overhearing Film Dialogue* (2000). She has written a widely taught summary of "Narrative Theory and Television," and is a consulting editor to the forthcoming *Routledge Encyclopedia of Narrative Theory.*

MARCIA LANDY is Distinguished Service Professor of English and Film Studies with a secondary appointment in the French and Italian department at the University of Pittsburgh. Her publications include *Fascism in Film: The*

Italian Commercial Cinema 1930–1943 (1986), *Imitations of Life: A Reader on Film and Television Melodrama* (1991), *British Genres: Cinema and Society 1930–1960* (1992), *Film, Politics, and Gramsci* (1994), *Cinematic Uses of the Past* (1996), *The Folklore of Consensus: Theatricality in the Italian Cinema, 1929–1943* (1998), *Italian Film* (2000), *The Historical Film: History and Memory in Cinema* (2001), *Stars: A Reader* (with Lucy Fischer, 2003), and *Monty Python's Flying Circus* (2005). Her essays have appeared in *Screen, Cinema Journal, boundary 2, Critical Quarterly,* and numerous anthologies.

CATHERINE L. PRESTON is an associate professor of film at the University of Kansas. Her research interests center around reception in the visual culture and the construction of identity, theories of representation, and visual memory. Her book *In Retrospect: FSA Photographs and American Visual Memory* is forthcoming from Smithsonian Institute Press.

JOANNA RAPF is a professor of English and film and video studies at the University of Oklahoma, and a regular visiting professor in the Department of Film and Television Studies at Dartmouth College. Her books include *Buster Keaton: A Bio-Bibliography* (1995), *On the Waterfront: A Handbook* (2003), and *Interviews with Sidney Lumet* (2005). She has published articles on diverse film topics in such journals as *Film Quarterly, The Journal of Popular Culture, Literature/Film Quarterly, Post Script,* and *Quarterly Review of Film and Video.*

STEVEN JAY SCHNEIDER is a Ph.D. candidate in philosophy at Harvard University, and in Cinema Studies at New York University's Tisch School of the Arts. His most recent publications include *Underground U.S.A.: Filmmaking Beyond the Hollywood Canon* (2002), *Designing Fear: An Aesthetics of Cinematic Horror* (2003), *1,001 Films You Must See Before You Die* (2003), and *New Hollywood Violence* (2004).

NICHOLAS SPENCER is an assistant professor in the Department of English at the University of Nebraska–Lincoln. He was educated at Saint John's College, Oxford, and Emory University. He has published articles and reviews in *Contemporary Literature, Arizona Quarterly, Quarterly Review of Film and Video,* and elsewhere. He is currently writing a book on the politics of space in twentieth-century American fiction.

TONY WILLIAMS is a professor and area head of film studies in the Department of English, Southern Illinois University at Carbondale. His major books include *Hearths of Darkness: The Family in the American Horror Film* (1996), *Larry Cohen: Radical Allegories of an American Filmmaker* (1997), and *Structures of Desire: British Cinema 1939–1955* (2000).

INDEX

CPSIA information can be obtained at www.ICGtesting.com
Printed in the USA
269366BV00002B/3/P